PROFESSIONAL TELEPHONE SURVEYS

PROFESSIONAL TELEPHONE SURVEYS

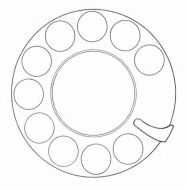

A. B. BLANKENSHIP

Professor of Marketing
Bowling Green State University

McGRAW-HILL BOOK COMPANY

New York   St. Louis   San Francisco   Auckland   Bogotá
Düsseldorf   Johannesburg   London   Madrid   Mexico
Montreal   New Delhi   Panama   Paris   São Paulo
Singapore   Sydney   Tokyo   Toronto

Library of Congress Cataloging in Publication Data

Blankenship, Albert Breneman, 1914–
   Professional telephone surveys.

   Includes index.
   1. Telephone surveys   2. Marketing research.
                  I.   Title.
   HF5415.2.B553   658.8'35   77-7023
            ISBN 0-07-005862-8

The editors for this book were W. Hodson Mogan and Joan Zseleczky,
the designer was Elliot Epstein, and the production supervisor
was Teresa F. Leaden. It was set in Palatino
by University Graphics, Inc.

Printed and bound by The Kingsport Press.

CONTENTS

PREFACE

Basically there are three methods of collecting information in surveys: personal interviews, mail questionnaires, and telephone interviews. Over the years much more has been written about the personal interview than about either of the other two methods. In 1970 Erdos wrote the only—and authoritative—book on mail surveys (Paul L. Erdos, *Professional Mail Surveys*, New York, McGraw-Hill, 1970). Today the telephone survey is more common than either of the other two forms, though little has been written about it.

At one time, the telephone survey lacked respectability; it was regarded as a less expensive method of gathering data, but a method that was based on a poor sample, because so few families had telephones. Today, because of the high incidence of telephone ownership—about 95 percent—it is no longer regarded as a stepchild, and interviewing from a central location, with a supervisor who can listen in on the interviews through use of a monitor, means that telephone interviewing now obtains quality control that is lacking in the personal approach. The telephone interview now offers many advantages over the other two methods. There is some evidence that in terms of contacts, it is now used more than either of the other two.

Thus there is a distinct need for this book. As a modern, professional method, the telephone survey has never received complete, organized attention. There are relatively few articles in professional journals about it. There are no books. There hasn't been a summary of what has been published about the method. Most information about the method, in fact, has not even been published. The author depended in considerable part upon personal meetings and correspondence to collect most of what is reported here.

This book is intended primarily for two types of readers. One is the nonprofessional buyer of marketing research; the book is intentionally written in easy-to-understand language with a minimum of technical vocabulary. The other is the professional marketing researcher, who still sometimes retains an old image of the telephone survey as an inferior fact-gathering method. But the book is aimed at the generalist in marketing research, not the specialist in telephone research, who will know almost all of what is included here anyway, though perhaps without ever having put it into an organized primer. This text is not designed to show the professional researcher how to set up a professional telephone survey center; it intentionally omits too many of the fine technical points to achieve that goal. However, the book might well be a beginning learning device for a research firm or other company that is considering entering this sort of business, though much more knowledge of technical equipment and facilities will be required.

Also, the book should be of some value to the marketing research teacher, who may want to pass on to his or her students more knowledge of telephone surveys than appears in the elementary texts on marketing research. Finally, the book should be of reference value to the marketing research student.

Basically, the eleven chapters of the book fall under three headings:

Introductory Chapters

1. The Development of Telephone Surveys as a Tool in Survey Research

2. The Development of Professional Telephone Surveys

3. Overall Evaluation of Telephone Surveys

Chapters on Technique

4. Sampling

5. Questionnaire Construction and Testing

6. Interviewers and Interviewing

7. Data Processing

8. Reporting

Concluding Chapters

9. Special Uses of the Telephone Survey

10. Final Considerations and the Future

11. Buying a Professional Telephone Survey

The book could not have been put together without considerable help from a number of people, many of whom are executives in research firms offering professional telephone surveys. Here is a partial list of those whose helpful cooperation has been obtained:

James S. Bacharach, Managing Partner, Trendex, Inc.

Hilda N. Barnes, President, Research Information Center, Inc.

Sylvia Barr, Manager, WATS Interviewing Division, Walker Research, Inc.

Michael Cohen, President, Metro Survey Service, Inc.

Sanford L. Cooper, President, Burke Marketing Research, Inc.

Archibald M. Crossley, former President, Crossley, Inc.

Fred Currier, President, Market Opinion Research

Wanda Derden, Sampling Supervisor, MARC

Ann Fenton, Director of WATS Operation, MARC

Ted Fritzler, Vice-President, MARC

Dr. George Gallup, Chairman, The Gallup Poll

Helen Wippich Greene, Valley Forge Information Service

Mark Hanna, Executive Vice-President, National Family Opinion

David K. Hardin, Chairman, Market Facts, Inc.

M. A. Hardin, Manager of Research Design, Marketing Information Service

Lee Hite, Director, Management Science, MARC

Sarah Huneycutt, Vice-President, Opinion Research Corporation

Dean J. Kilpatrick, Group Research Manager, Chilton Research Services

John Kofron, President, Chilton Research Services

John R. Lasley, Senior Vice-President, Opinion Research Corporation

Dr. Darrell B. Lucas, Emeritus Professor of Marketing, New York University

W. Bruce McEwen, retired Executive Vice-President, C. E. Hooper, Inc.

Frank B. McHugh, President, The Data Group Incorporated

Louis Meier, Market Opinion Research, Inc.

Harry O'Neill, Executive Vice-President, Opinion Research Corporation

Samuel C. Reed, Vice-President, Opinion Research Corporation

Dr. Mathilda White Riley, Professor of Sociology, Bowdoin College

James. E. Sammer, Vice-President, Walker Research, Inc.

Eugene Telser, Vice-President, Custom Research Service, A. C. Nielsen Company

John F. Uhles, Vice-President, Research Information Center, Inc.

Suzanne Verdone, Account Executive, Burke Marketing Research, Inc.

Frank Walker, President, Walker Research, Inc.

The author is indebted to all of these.

A. B. Blankenship

Bowling Green, Ohio

PROFESSIONAL TELEPHONE SURVEYS

THE DEVELOPMENT OF TELEPHONE SURVEYS AS A TOOL IN SURVEY RESEARCH

This chapter includes an introduction, a history of marketing research, and a history of telephone surveys prior to those of the professional variety.

INTRODUCTION

Survey research is a form of marketing research (although used by political pollsters, sociologists, psychologists, and other social scientists as well as by marketing researchers). Marketing research is research designed to increase the efficiency with which marketing is done (getting the product from the factory door into the hands of the consumer).

Survey research, sometimes known as the sampling survey, is a study which typically asks questions of a cross-section of particular kinds of people. For instance, people who use soft drinks may be asked their recall of any soft-drink advertising they have recently seen or heard.

Note the emphasis on *people* in this definition of surveys. We are excluding surveys of stores, of products, of advertisements, of cars. All these are surveys, but our surveys are people surveys.

As noted in the introduction, there are three basic methods of obtaining information from those approached in surveys. One of these is the personal interview. In the past, this was most often done in homes, although today much personal interviewing is conducted in areas such as shopping malls, where clusters of people are available. The personal interview was the first form of survey, probably because it requires no unusual "props" or facilities.

The mail survey was the second form of collecting information devised for survey research. Erdos reports that an early mail survey was conducted in 1839 among clergymen in the Church of England.[1] The telephone survey came latest of all. The first telephone survey was probably done around 1927.

Sampling surveys, whatever their form, are the major tool of marketing research. To be sure, there are other methods, such as observation, library research, economic analysis, sales analysis, etc. But the sampling survey is the most often used tool of marketing research.

A HISTORY OF MARKETING RESEARCH

Marketing research has a long history. Its history can be divided into early forerunners, nineteenth-century developments, and the development of marketing research as a specific tool.

Centuries ago, Socrates used the questioning method as a teaching tool. The Children of Israel sent out investigators to sample the products and markets of their neighbors, for trade reasons.

Early in the nineteenth century, Marquis Pierre Simon de LaPlace, famed French statistician, estimated births and marriages through sampling surveys. In England, William Eden estimated the size of the labor force through surveys.

In America, the first known surveys were straw votes. In 1824 the (Harrisburg) *Pennsylvanian* tested the nation's sentiments about presidential candidates. That same year the (Raleigh) *Star* canvassed a political meeting in North Carolina to measure the relative strength of the various presidential candidates.

In 1879 the first real marketing research study was done, though it wasn't a survey, and no one even recognized that a major business tool had just been invented. N. W. Ayer & Son, then and now a leading national advertising agency, was soliciting the account of a major Midwestern threshing machine manufacturer. H. N. McKinney, an agency partner, was soliciting the business. As background, he asked the prospective client for a copy of the advertising media that had been used previously; he was refused it. He was told, probably reasonably enough, that the manufacturer expected the agency to develop its own list of media, along with rationale for the selection of the list.

When McKinney returned to his Philadelphia office, he began to do some checking. He quickly learned that the federal government had no statistics of crop production. So he sent wires to officials in every state, asking for crop production by county. At the same time, he got in touch with publishers of various farm publications to determine their circulation by county. He thus was able to match this circulation with crop production and to recommend a list of the media which most efficiently would reach farmers in the right areas. When he showed this to the amazed manufacturer, the manufacturer wanted to buy it. McKinney refused, saying that it would be given free to the manufacturer if Ayer got the account. Ayer got it. But more significantly, no one realized that the first marketing research study had just been completed.

Little was done in the way of marketing research or surveys until about the turn of the century. Then a few academic psychologists began to do some experimental work using advertisements. Harlow Gale of the University of Minnesota used mail questionnaires as early as 1895 to secure opinions about advertising. Walter Dill Scott, who later became president of Northwestern University, did experimental work in advertising in 1901.

The Development of Marketing
Research as a Specific Tool

Marketing research birth and development can be described under four broad headings: the growth of commercial research departments, the growth of research firms, the development of educational facilities, and the development of technology.

The Growth of Commercial Research Departments. In 1911, Charles C. Parlin was hired by the Curtis Publishing Company (of *Saturday Evening Post* and *Ladies Home Journal* fame) as its first director of commercial research. The advertising director at Curtis suddenly realized that advertising would be easier to solicit if he and his sales force had facts and figures about a particular company or industry. They could then slant their appeals to the needs of the potential buyer. There wasn't anyone around who had done this sort of work, but he thought of one of his former schoolteachers who seemed creative. Parlin himself was creative. He did some landmark studies and is commonly regarded as the father of marketing research. He made such an impact that within five years Dr. Paul Nystrom, later marketing department head at Columbia University, was appointed manager of commercial research at U.S. Rubber (now Uniroyal) on Parlin's recommendation; just two years later Dr. L. D. H. Weld began to handle marketing research at Swift—a move also inspired by Parlin.

There was little expansion in marketing research departments within user companies in the 1920s—business was too easy. But by 1973, according to a study undertaken by Dr. Dik Twedt for the American Marketing Association,[2] over half of the companies in his sample had such departments. Expansion has occurred and is still occurring.

The Growth of Research Firms. In 1908, J. George Frederick established the Business Bourse, the first marketing research firm. Eight years later R. O. Eastman, who formerly conducted surveys as an employee of the Kellogg Company (the cereal manufacturer) and Fuller & Smith (an advertising agency), set up his own research firm, specializing in conducting readership studies for magazines and newspapers. Shortly afterward, in about 1918, Percival White and Pauline Arnold set up the Market Research Company, now operating, though obviously under different management, as the Market Research Corporation of America.

During the 1930s several firms still active today began their operations. Daniel Starch & Staff (now part of Starch/INRA/Hooper) was set up. Opinion Research Corporation was another early firm and is still in operation (part of this operation is described later). C. E. Hooper, Inc., was also set up during this period (another portion of the Starch/INRA/ Hooper firm). Archibald Crossley set up Crossley, Inc., during this period, and the firm still operates as Crossley Surveys. Lloyd Hall was set up during the same period, and it still operates under that name. Cherington & Roper was organized to conduct market research and opinion polls, and today Elmo Roper's son, Burns W. Roper, heads the Roper Organization.

Today, according to the listings of research firms in the 1976 Green Book[3] there are approximately 575 research firms in the United States. These come in several varieties. There are firms that offer subscriptions to all kinds of ongoing data; there are others which take only assignments customer tailored for the buyer. There are firms that take on only pieces of the assignment (such as field work or data processing); there are those that will accept only a complete study, from the design of the questionnaire and sample, through data collection and processing, to an interpretive report. There are general practitioners, who claim to be able to undertake surveys on almost any topic, and those who specialize (in terms of store audits, motivation research, panels of consumers, etc.). There are firms which specialize according to the method of collecting data: personal interview, mail, telephone interviewing. The operating methods of a number of these telephone survey firms will be examined in some detail later.

The Development of Educational Facilities. The Bureau of Business Research of Harvard University was organized in 1911. Here is how it started:

> One afternoon in April 1911 A. W. Shaw and [Dean E. F. Gay] were walking across the Harvard Yard. . . . The conversation turned to the importance of scientific research in the field of distribution. 'What is needed,' [Dean Gay] said, 'is a quantitative measurement for the marketing side of distribution.' 'Why don't you get it?' asked Mr. Shaw.[4]

The first academic course in marketing research was offered by a Professor Griffin in the fall semester of the school year 1927–1928 at the University of Michigan. Said the catalog of that period:

> This course is a continuation of B.A. 251. Attention is largely devoted to sales research, involving specifically the agencies for marketing research; the estimating and analyzing of consumer demand, discovering new sources of demand; determing sales quotas and measuring the effectiveness of distribution. Concrete market surveys will be undertaken by the class.

One of the signs of maturity in a particular field is the offering of graduate degrees in that field. Toward the end of the 1930s, Dr. Paul F. Lazarsfeld first offered a combination of academic course work and dissertation in the specialization of market research. He established the Office of Radio Research at the University of Newark under a three-year grant from the Rockefeller Foundation. At the end of that period he was appointed professor of sociology at Columbia. He transferred the Office of Radio Research to that institution and renamed it the Bureau of Applied Social Research. It operates to this day, under a successor and a large staff.

Almost all the bureau's research studies provide opportunities for training of graduate students, who do library research as well as working on projects as interviewers, editors, and coders, or on any other assignment where they can make a contribution.

In 1938 John G. Jenkins, then professor of psychology at Cornell University, took the chair of psychology at the University of Maryland. One specialized field he offered was a degree in consumer psychology, a distinct marketing application. Unfortunately this program died with Dr. Jenkins in 1948.

The National Opinion Research Center was set up at the University of Denver with a grant from the Field Foundation in 1941. It served as the field arm for the Survey Division of the Office of War Information during World War II. It is currently affiliated with the University of Chicago, where it offers students an opportunity to take courses that replace some of their elective options in the social science departments. Dissertations may be written under the supervision of NORC staff members.

In 1946 Dr. Rensis Likert, a psychologist who had directed the division of program surveys for the Department of Agriculture, and whose division did almost all federal surveys except for those of the Bureau of the Census, ran into congressional budgetary problems because of some studies he had done which certain Southern Senators found distasteful. Likert took his top professional staff to the University of Michigan, and today the Institute for Social Research is an interdisciplinary agency which maintains close relationships with the various social science teaching departments. A graduate student at the university takes research methodological courses within one of the departments within the university, though the instructor is likely to be a member of the institute. The doctoral research may be handled through the institute, and the student may be able to handle dissertation research through the institute as well.

In 1960, Purdue set up a graduate program in consumer psychology, which still operates today.

The Institute for Survey Research was organized at Temple University in 1967. It is one of three institutes in universities in the United States which have full national capabilities in conducting surveys (the others are the Institute for Social Research at Michigan and the National Opinion Research Center at Chicago). It conducts studies by personal interview, mail, or telephone, as required. It has complete facilities for conducting all stages of a survey.

In 1976, the University of Illinois set up an M.B.A. program in marketing research management. It is aimed at training people for business or government positions in survey research and in the administration of research. It offers a combination of course work and practical experience with the Survey Research Laboratory at the school.

Technical Innovations. The progress of marketing research can also be traced through the various major technical innovations that took place over the years. (Those for telephone surveys will be covered in Chapter 2.)

The year 1932, for one reason or another, was a banner year methodwise in marketing research. In that year Dr. Daniel Starch (Daniel Starch and Staff) started the first continuing service measuring both advertising and editorial leadership. The service continues today.

In the same year Dr. Henry C. Link, of the Psychological Corporation, offered the first continuing omnibus survey service. (An omnibus survey is one in which a buyer submits a list of questions which are combined with questions from other buyers. This reduces the cost to the individual buyer, since overhead of the total study is shared.) The Psychological Corporation is no longer in the survey business, but there are many omnibus services, all descendants of this original one.

In 1932, the first panel in marketing research was set up. A panel is a group of people who agree to answer questions over a period of time; these are usually (but not always) conducted by mail. In that year Al Forster, director of market research for Lever Brothers, set up the first panel, mainly for use in consumer product testing (where consumers are given a sample of the product to try, and react to it after the trial).

In 1933, W. B. Murphy, then an executive with the A. C. Nielsen Company (today the world's largest marketing research firm) suggested that Nielsen set up a sample of drug stores to be used to check the flow of retail drug purchases. Today the Nielsen Food and Drug Index is the most respected generator of brand sales data in the industry, and there are few major food or drug manufacturers who have the temerity to be without the service. It plays a vital role in helping marketing management assess the success of its efforts. Murphy, by the way, later turned up as president of the Campbell Soup Company.

In 1935, another technical landmark in marketing research was reached when Professor T. H. Brown, of Harvard, published tables showing the theoretical relationship between sample size and sampling error. Henry C. Link, two years later, published empirical results demonstrating that Brown's estimates really worked. This assessment of the relationship of sample size and accuracy was a major contribution to the still young field of surveys.

In 1936 Nielsen acquired the Audimeter, an invention of Robert F. Elder and Louis Woodruff, professors at the Massachusetts Institute of Technology. This is a small, automatic recording device attached to radio (and now television) sets, automatically turning on when the set is on and recording the station or channel. The Audimeter became the second most important part of the Nielsen business (second only to the Food and Drug Index).

Toward the end of the 1930s, a young psychologist from Vienna entered the American marketing research scene. His name was Dr. Ernest Dichter, and he worked first with the advertising agency of J. Stirling Getchell, where, with depth interviewing, he developed motivation research. His highly interesting and controversial studies soon got him an important research position at Columbia Broadcasting System, but eventually he set up his own firm. It and he operate today.

In late 1939, WOR, the leading radio station in the New York area, wanted to demonstrate its position in every possible way through the use of marketing research. Henry Brenner, then of Burnett & Brenner, conducted the first survey of radio listening afloat. One of his boats cruised the Westchester shoreline of Long Island Sound, the other the north shore. Each time that choppy Sunday a research boat came to a parked yacht, the skipper would be asked if the radio was turned on, and if so, to what station. Imagine the surprise of some of those skippers!

In 1937, scientific sampling (selection of the people to be questioned) was first developed by Morris Hansen of the Census Bureau. But it remained for Dr. Alfred N. Watson, then a statistician with the Curtis Publishing Company, to see the possibilities of scientific sampling in marketing surveys. He developed area sampling, a technique which selected, on a statistically random basis, areas within parts of the country to be sampled, areas within each of these points to be sampled, and households within each of these communities. It was another major technical breakthrough in marketing research, and the more "scientific" personal interview surveys done on a door-to-door basis today still utilize the basic Watsonian principles.

Samuel G. Barton introduced a major innovation in 1944. Through his panel operation, Barton made media audience analyses by heaviness of product usage and by demographics of the user. Today there are two major syndicated services which offer just such analyses: Target Group Index and Simmons.

The next major technical improvement was one not limited to the survey field: the computer. Survey researchers had to learn the computer and what it could do. Since that time, a number of special computer programs have been developed for the use of marketing researchers. (However, these will not be described; we leave that to more technically oriented books on marketing research.)

Other Signs of Maturation. One other sign of the maturity of marketing research is the growth of professional organizations. Perhaps the very first group devoted to marketing research was set up as the Research Group of the Advertising Club of New York. At its first meeting on October 23, 1924, there were 100 people present! But it did not survive.

In 1927 the Market Research Council was formed in New York. This was and is a forum-social kind of organization which holds monthly meetings for 10 months of the year. It is an organization that invites limited membership, and its meetings are highly professional and sophisticated.

The Advertising Research Foundation was set up only a few years later. This group, composed of those interested in marketing research from advertisers, media, and marketing research firms, is interested in increasing the professionalization of marketing research. It has a heavy membership dues allocation, which is necessary for it to continue its own studies and staff. It has made a significant contribution to the field of marketing research. One of its functions is to examine and audit studies by media. For it to do this, the medium must consult with it from the planning stage on. If all is concluded well, the ARF puts together a letter about the study which carries, with advertisers, the equivalent of the Good Housekeeping Seal of Approval.

The Conference Board (formerly the National Industrial Conference Board) in 1946 set up a restricted group, with membership by invitation only, of the Council of Marketing Research Managers (of member companies). This extremely useful group holds off-the-record meetings to let others in the marketing research field know things they are doing but which cannot be publicized.

There are many, many different kinds of professional groups active in the marketing research field. Today the New York area boasts of a Copy Research Council (with membership by invitation and meetings to discuss research about advertising copy) and a Media Research Directors Association (with membership by research directors of various advertising media). Nationally there is the Market Research Association (a group of professionals in the field who provide chiefly data collection services, such as personal and telephone interviewing), the Association for Consumer Research (a group of professionals, mainly academic researchers, interested in consumer surveys), and the American Marketing Association, giant of them all, with some 18,000 members, whose broad interest is in the advancement of marketing as a field, but which has a very substantial interest in the specific field of marketing research.

Another sign of maturation is the field of periodicals. For years, the only major periodical devoting much space to marketing research was the *Journal of Marketing*, published by the American Marketing Association. *Public Opinion Quarterly* and the *Journal of Applied Psychology* have, over the years, devoted some space to articles about the field of marketing research, and so have a few other journals. However, since 1960 the field of marketing research has developed periodicals which it may call its own. The first of these was the *Journal of Advertising Research*, published by the Advertising Research Foundation under the capable editorship of Dr. Charles K. Ramond. This publication tends to stress practical applications of marketing research. The *Journal of Marketing Research*, published by the American Marketing Association, first saw print in 1964. It tends to have a mix of theoretical articles, including many with heavy statistical emphasis, and practical articles. The *Journal of Consumer Research*, first appearing in 1974, is sponsored by a group of associations in the fields of social science and statistics. It tends to stress the theoretical side of marketing research.

THE HISTORY OF TELEPHONE SURVEYS

The history of telephone surveys reported here does not include the *professional* telephone survey, but only its predecessor, the telephone survey. At this point it is necessary to give two definitions: that of the (nonprofessional) telephone survey, and that of the professional telephone survey.

The (nonprofessional) telephone survey is a telephone survey done without personal supervision, without monitoring (where the supervisor can listen in on the dialogue between interviewer and respondent), and where the interviewer typically uses the telephone within the home of the interviewer. The professional telephone survey is the precise opposite: the telephoning is done at a central location, with a supervisor and with monitoring.

Developments Prior to 1940

The use of nonprofessional telephone surveys probably started about 1929. There was no general acceptance of the technique at that time; most of the surveys then being made were by personal interview, or sometimes by mail.

In 1929, Dr. George Gallup, who later gained fame as the developer of the Gallup Poll, was head of the Drake University department of journalism. He conducted a house-to-house coincidental radio study in which he asked whether the radio was on at the time of the call, and if so, to what program and station it was tuned. He also asked for identification of the sponsor. He followed this study with a parallel study conducted by telephone. He got just about the same results. This, today, does not seem too surprising, since it is likely that the relatively small proportion of families with telephones was almost identical to the relatively small proportion of homes with radio sets. Five out of six telephone families had radio sets, but only one in nine of the nontelephone homes had sets. Thus telephone covered 81 percent of all radio homes but only 37 percent of the general population, with telephone ownership probably concentrated in the upper class and the upper middle class.

In 1932, when Dr. Gallup started the copy research department at Young & Rubicam (one of the country's leading advertising agencies), he instituted a national weekly telephone coincidental study of radio listening.

The Market Research Company, mentioned earlier, was also doing telephone radio coincidentals as early as 1929, according to Dr. Mathilda White Riley, daughter of one of its founders.

Crossley, Inc., and the Cooperative Analysis of Broadcasting[5]

In 1927 S. H. Giellerup of the Frank Seaman Advertising Agency asked Archibald M. Crossley, of Crossley, Inc., to determine how well the Davis Baking Powder program was coming through locally. Two years later Giellerup wanted a repeat of that study. Crossley countered with a suggestion that they report how many had heard the program. This was done for Carlton Healy of the Eastman Kodak Company who, as a member, reported the survey results to the Association of National Advertisers. Giellerup followed up with the suggestion to Crossley to offer a continuing service on a subscription basis to interested companies.

Beginning in the early part of 1929, Crossley, Inc., planned and undertook a series of individual studies of the radio audience, totaling some 30,000 telephone interviews in forty-four cities. These determined the potential and actual radio audience by day and hour, how the program could be improved, and whether the right stations were being used for maximum audience at lowest cost. The day-part recall method was used, where people were questioned for a program period of four hours, later cut to two.

All this was occurring in the heyday of radio. Radio had started commercial broadcasting in 1921, and at its peak was offering such memorable programs as Amos 'n' Andy, Eddie Cantor, Jack Benny, Major Bowes and His Amateur Hour, and Charlie McCarthy (Edgar Bergen, now best known as father of Candice).

In November 1929, Crossley, Inc., suggested and prepared an operating plan for a continuing service to be bought by the Association of National Advertisers on a total fee basis, with results to go to any or all of the membership. ANA turned down the proposal but agreed to endorsement if the Crossley firm would offer the service directly to subscribers. The survey was to cover listening during the preceding 24 hours by family members and to include stations as well as programs. (Later on, as a result of numerous comparative tests including mechanical recorders, respondents were queried on a period of four hours, and still later on a period of two hours.)

The Cooperative Analysis of Broadcasting began operations in February 1930, with each 4-month report covering some 17,500 set users in an estimated 30,000 families. At the end of the year it received the Harvard Advertising Award.

In 1934, Crossley was asked to enter into a single contract arrangement with what ultimately became a tripartite committee representing advertisers, agencies, and broadcasters.

C. E. Hooper, Inc. In 1934, Clark-Hooper (later C. E. Hooper, Inc.) first used the telephone coincidental to measure the size of radio audiences. In this method, five questions were typically asked:

1. Were you listening to the radio just now?

2. To what program were you listening, please?

3. Over what station is that program coming?

4. What advertiser sponsors that program?

5. Please tell me how many men, women, and children, including yourself, were listening to the radio when the telephone rang.

The method was based largely on the Gallup procedure, and Gallup cooperated in giving the new service all the background information it needed. Hooper sold the service on a subscription basis; it was never handled as an industry project, as the Crossley service had been for a time. It was sold to both buyers and sellers of radio time.

In 1941, Dr. Matthew N. Chappell was retained by Hooper as a consultant. Chappell examined the results and the methods of Crossley and Hooper. There were many marked differences for specific programs. He came up with a lot of answers.

For one thing, Chappell found seasonal variations in not-at-homes. There are proportionately more people at home during January and February than in July and August. The Crossley ratings were based only on those at home at the time of the call; the Hooperatings (a Walter Winchell term) were based on those at home at the time the program was on.

Another source of difference was the geographical variations in not-at-homes. Chappell found that the Pacific states, the North Central states, the South, and the East have higher not-at-homes than the other regions of the country. This affects program ratings of the two methods.

Third, the not-at-homes for a particular listening period affect the results. In the Crossley method, many of those not at home at the time of the call were part of the audience for an earlier time period.

In the recall (Crossley) method, there is also a tendency to forget that one was not at home during an earlier period.

Memory varies with the age of the program, Chappell found. Programs which were over one year of age obtained scores appreciably lower compared to their coincidental scores (Hooperatings).

There were also inherent memory variables, Chappell found. Recall ratings for high-rating programs were appreciably higher, in comparison with their coincidental ratings, than those for lower-rating programs.

Chappell also found that memory varies with the inherent strength of the network. The average recall ratings for the two (then) stronger networks were appreciably higher in the recall (Crossley) method than in the coincidental (Hooperatings).

Finally, Chappell found, memory varies by program type. In recall ratings, all program types except news and "miscellaneous" obtain ratings higher than in coincidentals.

The Confrontation: Hooper versus Crossley (Cooperative Analysis of Broadcasting). The Chappell analysis stirred up a storm. Darrell B. Lucas, a professor at New York University and a prestigious member of the marketing research field, wrote the Cooperative Analysis of Broadcasting in 1942, outlining the weaknesses of the recall technique. Lucas recalls that his letter reviewed the reactions of his class in marketing research:

I pointed out that my students unanimously supported the coincidental. I had classes of about 60, and we would start discussing the two
methods. I told the students to move to the right or left side of the room
to indicate which of the two methods they believed superior. It would
start out about even, but by the end of the period . . . all of the
students would line up on the Hooper side. Mostly it was a case of
emphasizing the same points that Hoop and his consultant—Matt
Chappell—had listed, with evidence.

Lucas goes on to point out that the fact that the day-part recall always
underrated the coincidental for unpopular shows was a fatal blow to
day-part recall, since the coincidental "average audience," by definition, must be smaller than the recall "total audience," assuming complete recall.

The Cooperative Analysis of Broadcasting decided to go the way of
the coincidental in late 1942. It made this major change, and many,
many other modifications in the next three years. It didn't matter. CAB
was disbanded. Television came along after the war ended in 1945, and
with television, continuing radio audience measurements became a
thing of the past. Nielsen, with its little Audimeter, became supreme in
measurement of electronic audiences.

But it wasn't Nielsen alone that did it. In 1950, the Hooper organization sold its rights to television coincidentals to Nielsen, effectively
barring it from entering that field. Even though television ownership at
the time was still low, two members of Hooper's staff, Ed Hinz and Bob
Rogers, decided that the Hooper firm lacked real long-range growth
possibilities. They created Trendex, a firm to conduct television coincidentals. The first nine years or so went well with the new firm; it
produced network and station ratings. But around 1959, the networks
began to sink most of their rating monies into a new service, one which
never really became established. Trendex, to survive, decided to enter
the general business of telephone consumer surveys, and is now one of
two firms (the other being the Hooper portion of Starch/INRA/Hooper)
still conducting telephone surveys from the homes of its interviewers.
Trendex, however, is also in the business of professional telephone
surveys.

Broader-Scale Acceptance and Application of
Telephone Surveys after 1940

In the years between 1940 and 1960, telephone surveys gradually grew
in their acceptance and importance.

During this period, there was a gradual but consistent application of the telephone method to other subject areas and to other universes. In subject areas the method was expanded to include measurement of consumer attitudes, such as political opinions. It was expanded to consumer product testing, where a person would be called to determine whether he or she qualified as a user of a product class (such as a prepared pudding) and then would be sent one or more samples of products to give reactions to (by another telephone call). It was applied to copy testing. The author recalls a study he conducted for one of the networks in 1950. It involved the use of the telephone and a recording, which was played to the respondent to determine whether he or she had heard a particular radio commercial. The telephone interview was beginning to come into its own.

Until now the telephone survey had been used frequently for special population samples, such as physicians, lawyers, subscribers to a particular publication, and automobile owners. But it still had not gained great user acceptance for surveys of the general population of consumers.

Three studies may have changed all this.

In 1955, Crossley Surveys, Inc., successor to Crossley, Inc., conducted a telephone study for the prestigious *Harvard Business Review*.[6] The study was designed to measure executive readership of various publications, thoroughness of readership, and reaction to editorial content and format. The basic list of companies to be sampled was taken from the Fortune 500 list. For each company falling into the sample, the Directory of Officers and Directors published by Standard & Poors was consulted. On a systematic basis, names of those to be included were selected proportionate to company sales.

Approximately 1000 executives were interviewed. An impressive completion rate of over 75 percent was achieved (this means that over 75 percent of those on the list in the sample were actually interviewed; this is a very impressive total). This was ample demonstration that the telephone survey was an ideal instrument for getting those hard to reach, and relatively inexpensive for getting a dispersed sample within a short time period.

The second, done in 1956 by Hooper, was a study on Maidenform for the Ogilvy and Mather advertising agency. It was a repeat of an earlier New York City study concerning brassiere cup sizes used, and brand awareness and attitudes about various brassiere brands. The earlier study had been done by house-to-house personal interview, at that time considered the most reliable way of collecting responses from consumers. The Hooper telephone study was done at a fraction of the cost of the earlier study, and produced virtually the same findings.

In 1960, Benton & Bowles, a major advertising agency, conducted an experimental study for Allied Chemical Company. The purpose was to determine the relative dependability of the house-to-house personal interview, the mail questionnaire, and the telephone interview in getting information from consumers. The telephone was by far the most reliable.

The telephone survey was really on its way to general acceptance. However, the real breakthrough was yet to come, though it was only 4 years away.

REFERENCES

[1]Paul L. Erdos, *Professional Mail Surveys,* New York, McGraw-Hill, 1970.

[2]*1973 Survey of Marketing Research,* Chicago, American Marketing Association, 1973.

[3]*International Directory of Marketing Research Houses and Services,* New York, New York Chapter of the American Marketing Association, 1976.

[4]Melvin T. Copeland, *And Mark an Era,* Boston, Little, Brown, 1958, p. 209.

[5]This portion of the chapter and the next portion, about C. E. Hooper, are largely dependent on correspondence with Archibald M. Crossley and Darrell B. Lucas.

[6]Reported in personal communication with the author by Frank D. Leonard, president of Crossley Surveys, Inc.

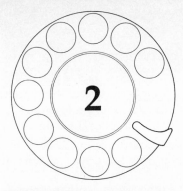

THE DEVELOPMENT OF PROFESSIONAL TELEPHONE SURVEYS

The telephone was invented just over 100 years ago. On March 10, 1876, Alexander Graham Bell tested the first instrument with a message to his assistant: "Come here, Watson, I want you!"

Continuing improvements were made over the years. The year 1914 saw the completion of the first transcontinental line. The first dial service was offered as early as 1919.

The professional telephone survey did not automatically accompany the telephone. It was a lot later—virtually a century—in 1963 that it first appeared with central, supervised, monitored surveys. The implied definition each time the term is used in this book is the use of central location telephoning, with one or more supervisors who have a monitor available for listening in to interviews without the monitor giving any on-line indication of its use. Professional telephone surveys usually are done from a single point to cover most or all localities in the continental United States. Note that the definition does not limit professional telephone surveys to these, however. The calls may be made only within local areas and still constitute a professional telephone survey, so long as the criteria are met.

17

FACTORS CONTRIBUTING TO THE DEVELOPMENT
OF THE PROFESSIONAL TELEPHONE SURVEY

Telephone surveys, as Chapter 1 shows, were first conducted as early as the 1920s. But they didn't become professional telephone surveys for another 40 years. Why? It's simple. The climate had to be right.

The Increase in Telephone Ownership

For many years the proportion of United States families having their own telephones was low, as indicated in Table 2-1. It was only in 1969 that the level approached 90 percent; in 1976, the figure was estimated at about 95 percent.

In sampling surveys one of the problems—to assure accuracy of the results—is to make sure that a high proportion of the total population is interviewed. If surveyors cannot reach a large segment through their sampling methods, there is great risk of a major sampling error which will negatively affect accuracy.

Dr. George Gallup, founder of the Gallup Poll, and the old *Literary Digest* provide an interesting interaction which shows the importance of the nature of the sample. The year was 1936, and *Literary Digest* was a heavy-circulation, highly influential weekly news magazine, not very different from *Time*. Over the years, *Literary Digest* had taken ballots on presidential preferences. It worked from lists of telephone and automobile owners to whom it sent and received ballots by mail. Up to 1936 its forecasts had been remarkably accurate.

TABLE 2-1
The Percentage of Dwelling Units with
Telephones

1940	37%	1967	88%
1950	62	1968	89
1955	70	1969	90
1960	78	1970	92
1965	85	1971	93
1966	87	1972	94

SOURCE: *Statistical Abstracts of the United States*

The race that year was Roosevelt vs. Landon. The country was deep in a depression, and Roosevelt had served his first term.

Gallup was organizing his poll at that time. Unlike the *Literary Digest* ballot, Gallup was conducting his survey by door-to-door questioning. Gallup's first poll preceded that of *Literary Digest,* and his results showed that Roosevelt was strongly in the lead. But Gallup had the temerity also to predict that the *Digest* measure would show a marked lead for Landon. The *Digest* staff was appalled. How could this upstart predict their results! But when their first ballot was complete, Gallup *had* predicted what it would show. But still, Gallup had never predicted a presidential election; the *Digest* had a flawless record.

You know the ending to the story. Gallup was right; the *Digest* was wrong. A year later, with its credibility lost, the *Digest* was interred and Gallup was well established.

Let's backtrack and see what happened. Gallup's foresight was remarkable. He realized that the vote was going to be along economic lines, with the mass of people going for Roosevelt. He also knew that (in those days) owners of telephones and automobiles were higher-income people, and therefore that they would be the segment of the population voting for Landon. Gallup's sample, on the other hand, was from all homes, and he got a cross section. All he had to do to make the magical prediction of what the *Digest* would show was to ask all his families whether they had a car or a telephone. He then summed up separately the replies of those who did: Eureka, the *Digest* prediction!

The point of this story is that the telephone could not become a mass-interviewing device when only a small proportion—the well-to-do—owned it.

The Increasing Resistance to Personal Interviewing

The Gallup success helped to popularize the gathering of survey information by personal interview. For years its popularity grew. It was *the* method of surveying. Telephone interviews did not reach all the population. They had other limitations, which are discussed in Chapter 3. The major problem of the mail survey, whose limitations are outlined in detail in the next chapter, is that so many people do not reply that one wonders whether those who reply are really representative of the total population to whom the mailing was made.

But things are changing. There is a steady increase in resistance to personal interviewing. Mervin Field, West Coast pollster, was quoted in *Time* (November 10, 1975): "Twenty years ago we could count on getting 85% [of a selected sample] with reasonable effort. Now we're hard-pressed to get 60%." Dr. George Gallup, in the same article, shows concern that people simply may not answer the pollster's questions when the doorbell rings. An article in *Business Week* (September 15, 1973) remarks that door-to-door interviewing is becoming increasingly a problem.

The rise in resistance seems to be greatest in ghettos and in affluent areas. The problem is compounded because most personal interviewing must be done during the late afternoon and evening to be sure to get working people into the sample. There are two aspects to this problem. One is the difficulty of getting interviewers—most of whom are women—to go out at night. (Sometimes they will go if sent in pairs, but obviously this doubles the cost of field work.) The other is that many people no longer are willing to open their doors after dark to a stranger, whether man or woman. The increasing crime rate presents very serious problems to personal interviewing.

Local laws may contribute to the problem. Baxter reported, in 1969, that 250 communities in thirty-four states had a version of the Green River Ordinance.[1] This is a statute which requires the obtaining of a license by a firm that wants to do door-to-door soliciting. Its purpose is to prevent families from being bothered by fly-by-night solicitors or high-pressure solictors. The intent is good.

But local police often present problems for the legitimate personal interview survey organization. For one thing, the local police may interpret the law as meaning that survey work is solicitation. For another, there has been so much abuse of the "survey approach" to gain entry for a sales solicitation, that the police may legitimately wonder whether the survey taker isn't really an unlicensed salesperson trying to sell magazines, encyclopedias, vacuum cleaners, or some other product where this sort of misrepresentation has occurred previously.

The Quality Level of Personal Interviewing

There has been an increasing concern about the quality level of personal interviewing. This has been an additional factor which has helped lead to the professional telephone survey.

As background, consider the way that personal interviewing is undertaken.

Usually it is the research firm—the "supplier," as the firm is commonly known today—that has the ultimate responsibility for personal interviewing. The supplier generally sells a whole package of research, on a job basis. This means that the supplier will select the sample of respondents, see that the interviewing (personal field work) is done, and data process the results. Whether the supplier designs the entire study, and whether a report is prepared, depends on the nature of the supplier and the relationships between supplier and client.

These suppliers—with few exceptions—do not have their own field staffs. Instead, they have the names of a number of "supervisors" all over the country. If the supplier finds that 100 personal interviews need to be conducted in Atlanta, he or she simply consults a file to see what supervisor is available there. (In Atlanta, there might be a dozen different supervisors.)

Supervisors are typically men or women (more often women) who operate out of their homes, running an unincorporated business. They maintain a file of interviewers (most often women 30 and older who look to personal interviewing for part-time income). Supervisors usually work on a commission basis, being paid a percentage of total payments for time reported by their interviewers.

The supervisor gets advance notice of an assignment, often by telephone. Then, through the mail, the method of sampling and the method of interviewing are described. Possible difficulties are outlined, along with methods of handling them. By the time these materials have been received, the supervisor may already have lined up the interviewers who will work on this assignment during the time period outlined. Depending on the instructions, the supervisor will either simply hand each interviewer a parcel containing an assignment and the procedures or perhaps hold a personal instruction meeting, going over the procedures in some detail.

These interviewers, once in the field, are on their own. There is no supervision; there cannot be, for to have a supervisor be present during each interviewer's calls would more than double the cost of the field work. Buyers of research are not prepared to pay such costs.

To make matters worse, these field workers are underpaid, usually earning less than $3 per hour!

The supervisor and the interviewers work for many different suppliers (or advertising agencies). There usually is no deep commitment to any source. The supervisor and the staff frequently will receive assignments from firms they have never heard of before.

Then there is the question of timing of payment of the interviewers for their work. The supervisor—who is typically small-scale—is not well capitalized, and usually has to delay paying the interviewers until a check is received from the supplier for the total work done. On some occasions, where the supplier, too, is undercapitalized, this may take three to four months.

Listen to Shirley Colby, a supervisor in Tucson: "I am concerned about the future of the face-to-face, personal form of interviewing. We are plagued with such problems as delayed payment, feast or famine syndrome and poor communication with our market research suppliers and their clients."[2] Assignments seem to come in waves, with too much to do at one time, and too little at another. She also complains, probably rightly, about inept or too lengthy questionnaires.

It is also probable that the level of partially or completely falsified personal interviewing is increasing. If it is, it is probably because of the rapid turnover among interviewers, caused by some of the dissatisfactions that have been outlined.

This problem of falsification must be considered further. In personal interviewing there are many methods of cheating. Worst is the absolute fabrication of the total interview, with the interviewer simply filling in all the forms. Fortunately, this very rarely occurs today, because most personal interviewing studies have a built-in validation procedure, where a proportion of each interviewer's reported respondents are recontacted (usually by telephone) to make sure that the contact was made.

Falsification can be more subtle. The interviewer may ask a few key questions, and make up the rest of the responses, to cut down the actual work time. The interviewer may make contacts by telephone rather than by personal interview.

A sophisticated verification check will catch any and all of these forms of cheating. But that is not the point. Cheating on personal interviews may be on the increase. This increases the cost of the study. Verification costs rise, and these falsified interviews must be replaced.

At least one professional telephone research interviewing service was set up precisely because its two proprietors felt that they were not delivering high-quality work when they turned over personal interviews to their clients. But let Mike Cohen, president of Metro Survey Services in Philadelphia, tell his own story: "We began using centralized, monitored WATS lines in 1965, shortly after the first two research firms had entered the field. We realized that we had too little control over the interviewing we were providing."*

---

*Statements attributed to Mr. Cohen, or others, without further documentation, are a result of a personal interview, telephone interview, or written communication with the person quoted.

Technology

Along with these factors (increasing telephone ownership, increasing resistance to personal interviewing, and the quality level of personal interviewing) there has been a series of technological developments that have encouraged the development of professional telephone surveys.

WATS Lines. The term "WATS" stands for Wide Area Telecommunications Service. It is a system where the bulk user of toll service can purchase telephone time covering various areas of the United States at discount prices. The telephone company need not bill the user for individual calls, thus saving considerable expense on its part. There is no operator involved in the placement of the call (unless it is a changed number, an incorrect number, etc.). A single, direct-circuit connection provides access to the central network of the telephone company.

"Bands" of lines are available. Each band permits access to a specified geographic coverage. The bands available in Michigan are shown in Figure 2.1. Ordinarily Band 1 covers states which are contiguous to the state from which the call is made (but does not include that state). Band 2 includes Band 1 plus other areas wider spread. Each consecutive band includes the previous band plus other, more extensive areas, up through Band 5, the largest area, which covers all 48 contiguous states.

These WATS bands are offered at a flat rate for so many daily hours of usage, and the price rises as the band number rises.

This particular service, on an outgoing basis (there are also incoming bands, for "free calls" by the caller, with an 800 prefix) was introduced nationally in 1961. This was a milestone date for the professional telephone survey. For the first time it was possible to conduct a national study by telephone from a central location. But at that time no one realized the implication of the service from a survey point of view.

The Monitor. The monitor was not a recent technological development, but must be mentioned here, because it is such a vital portion of the professional telephone interview. The supervisor in the central location from which the telephone interviews are conducted is able to listen to any interviewer's conversation with a respondent by means of a simple device attached to each supervisor's telephone. There is no giveaway beep on the telephone line when the supervisor tunes in and out of the conversation. Some firms have installed a one-way speaker telephone to enable the client or project director to listen, or to facilitate the supervisor's recording of respondent replies on an interview form. This latter

FIGURE 2-1.

A map of WATS bands for Michigan.

24

procedure provides a check of the recording accuracy of the interviewer.

The Computer. The computer is not all that late a development, but its development has indeed been a factor in the advancing techniques of professional telephone surveys. One research firm, right now, has such advanced technology that its interviewers can use a keyboard to punch the replies right into the computer memory. This firm is Chilton Research Services. There is more discussion of its capabilities later in this chapter.

The Cathode-Ray Tube. The same firm, following early developments by AT&T, has developed a technology which makes it possible to utilize the CRT to flash the questions to be asked, one at a time, on a screen in front of the interviewer. The technique cuts down on interviewer error

FIGURE 2-2.

A Chilton telephone research interviewer using a cathode-ray tube to read questions and a keyboard to enter data into computer.

in questioning and recording. Again, this development is discussed at greater length later in this chapter.

THE DEVELOPMENT OF THE PROFESSIONAL TELEPHONE SURVEY

Before the mid-1960s, the great majority of telephone surveys were done from the homes of the interviewers. One compassionate firm, for instance, made it a point to try to hire the handicapped and people who could not leave their homes. Telephone interviewing used to be completely a cottage industry.

Not now. Today, the central location in telephone interviewing is a production line: a production line in which breakdowns or slowdowns cannot be tolerated, particularly if the company uses WATS lines, where the heavy telephone charges keep right on accumulating whether the lines are in use or not. Frank McHugh, president of The Data Group Incorporated, says that his operation is "like a production line, with quality control applied at each stage of the process, not when the motor is put into the chassis." The analogy is a good one. Central location interviewing is truly a production-line operation, where supervision and monitoring produce a superior product at a lower cost and where WATS lines can provide the capacity for producing a national study from a single location. Like a true production line, the nature of the equipment is very important. According to McHugh, time and motion studies his firm has conducted show that a push-button dialing system is at least twice as fast as a rotary dialing system. In professional telephone surveys every second saved is important.

Bringing the telephone survey out of the home into a central facility alone was a tremendous production gain. Central location telephone interviewing produces 50 percent more interviews per hour.[3] John H. Kofron, current head of Chilton Research, substantiates this with some later information. He says: "In a study conducted about a year ago via central location and local telephone . . . the central location interviewers completed 54,750 interviews for a completion rate of 10.5 per hour. The local telephone interviewers completed 30,500 interviews for a completion rate of 7 per hour."

Again, a 1975 study, he said, showed a completion rate of .75 calls per hour from a central location, .42 per hour in local interviewing. (This was a study requiring screening calls and a long interview.)

It is very easy for an interviewer working out of the home to slow up between calls, especially since there is no one to discourage doing so. A parent may run and take care of a crying baby, without remembering to deduct that time from the interviewing hours reported. There will be an occasional incoming call that lengthens the period between dialings. A break from the telephone may have to be taken to put dinner on. All these activities slow up production time without equally reducing reported time, and there is simply no pressure on the interviewer to stay steadily and rapidly at it.

Developmentally, there were three steps in arriving at the professional telephone survey of today: central location interviewing with supervision; monitored central location interviewing with supervision; and monitored, supervised central interviewing using WATS lines with on-line computer and CRT.

Bringing the telephone interviewing out of the home into a central location can also change the results obtained. Glasser, Metzger, and Miaoulis[4] report the results of two parallel studies, each using a national probability sample, with one study from a central location with supervision, the other from homes without supervision. Among the supervised interviewers, the proportion of homes reportedly having television sets ranged for 95.3 to 98.5%; the range of ownership among in-home interviewers was 93.0 to 99.2%. Several other questions of fact also showed a similar pattern: a greater range of variation among unsupervised than among supervised investigators.

Central Location Interviewing with Supervision

This type of telephone survey was probably being done sporadically in the 1930s, according to Sanford L. Cooper, president of Burke Marketing Research, Inc. But there are no records of who did it, or how frequently it was done, so we can merely surmise, as we have. Burke itself used the method during this period. But the Burke approach was not unique to its philosophy. At that time Burke was primarily an interviewing service, and a personal interviewing service. It was completely dedicated to quality and emphasized the use of personal interviewers who were employees, subject to thorough training by a supervisor. It was—and still is—doing some of the highest quality fieldwork in the country. So when asked to conduct a telephone study during those early days, it was completely in character for Burke to insist on the same high-quality standards of fieldwork. Supervision and control became the order of the day. As Mr. Cooper says: "If . . . a study called for the use of 15 telephones and we had only 12 in the office, we would probably let three of our most trusted people work from their homes to complete the quota. It was not until the fifties when the hard and fast centralized, supervised *only* was put into effect."

The Burke firm did more than any other research firm to establish the idea of centralized, supervised telephone surveys. In the early 1950s Burke developed the Day-after-Recall method (DAR) to test the effectiveness of television commercials. Briefly, this technique, more fully described in Chapter 10, consists of a telephone interview, during the day after a television commercial has been on the air, to check the degree to which viewers of the particular show can identify the brand advertised, and details of what was said or shown. Says Mr. Cooper: "The demand for this service . . . plus the quite unusual necessity for extreme control over it, caused us, starting in the very early 1950s, to proliferate our central location offices around the country and insist that all work be done in them, and with a supervisor present throughout the interviewing. . . . it was the service that gave rise to how it was to be done. . . ."

By the middle 1950s, ownership of telephones and television sets was running so parallel that it can be assumed that the DAR method did, in fact, give valid results for television homes. Table 2-2 shows the parallel relationship beginning during that period.

Monitored Central Location Interviewing with Supervision

Coincidentally with the availability of WATS lines came monitored central location interviewing. One firm pioneered: it was Sindlinger & Co., introducing monitored, supervised calling in 1959. Two others almost simultaneously pioneered this effort with WATS lines: Chilton Research and Dupont. The years were 1963 and 1964.

TABLE 2-2
Percentage of United States Homes with Telephones and with Television Sets

	Telephones	Television
1950	62%	12%
1955	70	67
1960	78	88
1965	85	92
1970	92	96

SOURCE: *Statistical Abstracts of the United States*

Sindlinger & Company, 1959. In 1958, Albert Sindlinger first set up a central location, supervised telephone service in suburban Philadelphia, establishing a service measuring consumer economic confidence, a service still being offered today (described in Chapter 11). One year later monitoring was begun, and so this was the first offering of a professional telephone survey. Sindlinger has never gone to WATS lines, because all the company's calls are made during "prime time" (after 5 P.M.), to assure inclusion of working men and women. WATS lines are too expensive to lease with that much down time.

Chilton Research, 1963. Chilton terms its centralized telephone facility, located in Radnor, Pennsylvania, "Marketing Telecentral." Its use began in the fall of 1963, with the use of one WATS line to complete a portion of a survey of households. In January 1964, three additional lines were installed to handle another study, and before the end of that study, some six lines had been set up.[5]

DuPont, 1964. There's a real question as to whether this part of the history should be credited primarily to DuPont or to National Certified Interviews, then in existence as a research firm operating out of Chicago but today no longer active in general consumer surveys.

Let's hear from Dr. Malcom McNiven, then manager of advertising research at DuPont (now a vice-president at Pillsbury):

> During 1964 we were doing a great deal of research . . . on public opinion and measurement of the effects of advertising for Teflon Cookware, Lucite Paint, and Dacron Fibers. We measured the effects of advertising through extensive telephone interviewing and we were working with Rome Arnold and Nancy Cooley of National Certified Interviews. Rome Arnold was trying to institute new types of control in interviewing by locating interviewers in certain locations around the country, and then calling long distance into primary sampling units.
>
> Rome and I conceived the idea of doing the entire survey from Chicago, using a combination of DuPont's tie lines, rented WATS lines, [out of Chicago], and long distance calls to fill in the gaps. We built a centralized telephoning center in Chicago . . . and proceeded to conduct thousands of telephone calls a year from that location. As I recall, we started out with six survey stations [interviewer stations] but quickly expanded that to ten or twelve.[6]

This was an important step. McNiven and Arnold knew what they had done. The DuPont ad checks ran close to a quarter of a million telephone calls a year, with the length of the interview anywhere from 2 to 45 minutes. McNiven was increasingly concerned about the quality of normal field work—over which there was inadequate control, the completion rate (the proportion of potential respondents with whom interviews were obtained), and long-distance toll charges. The relationship with National Certified Interviews solved these problems.

The Spread of Such Services. It took five years before considerable interest arose in such services, at least in terms of when new services of the same sort were established. While our list is not complete, we have learned, for instance, that the Data Group Incorporated and Market Facts were both set up in 1969, Walker Research and Trendex Central in 1971, and Market Opinion Research in 1972.

Professional Telephone Interviewing with On-line Computer and CRT

The on-line computer and CRT require explanation. An on-line computer means that there is a computer terminal available to the interviewer. As the respondent is giving an answer over the telephone, the interviewer—having been trained for the specific project—is able to punch the right key to enter the answer into the computer memory bank. Let's take an example. Suppose the question is, "Did you have any soup yesterday?" A *yes* reply might carry the code of 1 (which would therefore be punched on the keyboard), while a *no* reply might carry a code of 2.

But this is only a part of the picture, and picture is the right term. For the CRT (cathode-ray tube) is also an on-line computer asset which looks much like the tube on a television set and functions in much the same manner, though with words and numbers rather than pictures. Each question is displayed on the screen. The CRT can also show the appropriate answer categories, with the code designation (the number to be punched on the keyboard).

The Role of American Telephone & Telegraph. People at AT&T, backed by the technical personnel of the company, were basically responsible for the development of this system.[7]

AT&T has been conducting studies of customer attitude for its member companies for many years, at least since 1925. The method used to be one of mailing questionnaires to homes of customers, with a request that the filled-in questionnaire be sent in a postage paid, addressed envelope. Return rates averaged some 50 percent.

Robert Gryb, director of customer service measurements, began to worry about the accuracy and timeliness of these surveys. His first concern was about the 50 percent who did not reply. Were these people so annoyed at their telephone company that they would not even take the time to send in their reply? Or were they so favorable that they saw no need to reply because there was no problem? (Studies of nonrespondents to mail surveys have typically shown that these two kinds of groups, the very favorable and the very unfavorable, are those who do *not* reply.)

Also, the method required a large amount of human labor and cost, that was increasing each year. All returned questionnaires had to be edited (examined for completeness, consistency, and so on). All answers to questions had to be coded (designated numbers entered onto the questionnaire against each answer to specific questions for purposes of card punching or data entry into the data-processing system), and cards had to be punched (by a process similar to typing, in which each numerical code entered on the questionnaire is punched into the appropriate card column on an IBM card in preparation for data processing).

Gryb first began his changes by telephoning nonrespondents. He found that those approached were very appreciative that they had been called.

Further investigation showed an even greater concern affecting accuracy: the mail questionnaire was frequently returned by a respondent in the household who did not actually have firsthand knowledge of the past event to be evaluated. (The person selected for the respondent was from a sample of people who had, for instance, recently made an operator-assisted telephone call, called repair, had a telephone installed, or made a telephone call to the business office of the telephone company.) Sometimes the person sending in the mail questionnaire would be talking about a telephone experience that had occurred several years before, rather than the more recent one that the telephone company had in mind. So the telephone method had the advantage of screening to get the right respondent, focusing on recent events, and getting prompt replies. (With the mail questionnaire some people sent in questionnaires after many months or years.)

Gryb then got the idea of developing the cathode-ray tube to help automate the interviewing process. The effort required the intense participation of many people in the data processing organization of AT&T. Briefly, the way that this works is this: the logic of the interview is programmed into the computer, as well as appropriate identification limits. If the interviewer makes an error in recording on the keyboard, an error message such as this appears: "Only one response permitted— make correction."

But let's get back to the development process. What we've been talking about took place mainly in 1970. For the first time, AT&T had computerized management of its questionnaires (where the interviewer had no control over what questions to ask or when to ask them) and instantaneous computer input of the replies as the interviewer heard the replies of the respondent.

In cooperation with the operating telephone companies, AT&T selected three firms to conduct these studies at Telsam centers specifically designed for this purpose: Chilton Research, MARC, and Walker Research.

The Role of Chilton Research. Before describing the role that Chilton Research played in the advancement of professional telephone surveys, it is pertinent to talk a bit about the organization. Chilton Research is a part of Chilton Publications and one of its major profit centers. It formerly was the research arm for the company, but has now expanded to conduct surveys for firms without any other connection with the parent company. The parent company publishes chiefly trade publications. In connection with its publishing business, the company uses a computer with a large capacity. This is a part of the secret of success of Chilton Research.

Chilton Research had gained experience with the AT&T development, since it was a participant and since it operated one of the centers for AT&T. Chilton decided to expand on the concept, using its own larger-capacity computer, and, when successful, to offer the service commercially. The Chilton computer is an IBM 340/145. Rather than delving into technology, let's see what Chilton has developed in a practical sense. Here is the way it works.

Each WATS line interviewer, seated in a private litte roomette, faces a TV screen (cathode-ray tube) on which the questions automatically appear. This is shown in Figure 2-2. When the interviewer enters the reply into the console the computer determines what question should be asked next. This is based on a so-called skip-to logic. What this means is that in the typical marketing or opinion research survey, what question is asked after a preceding question often depends on the reply to the preceding question. For instance, if I ask you, "Have you seen or heard any advertising for bread within the past seven days?" and you say no, then I go on to another rather different question, such as how often you eat bread. On the other hand, if your reply is yes, then I may ask you several other questions, such as the brand or brands you have seen or heard advertised, the media (TV, radio, magazines, newspapers, etc.) that each one used, and the message that each one had.

In normal interview questioning, many errors are made. The interviewer may forget to ask the appropriate question or questions dependent on earlier replies. With the computer programming of the sort described here, this cannot occur. The questions are programmed properly according to preceding replies.

If a response is entered into the wrong place on the keyboard, or a reply is not entered, the question "freezes" on the tube. The interviewer cannot ask the wrong question and must punch in all the answers to the correct questions. The entry must be consistent with the answer possibilities. At the end of the interview, all respondent replies are automatically and instantly entered into the computer's memory.[8]

The total story is impressive, and perhaps an example will demonstrate this.

Chilton was conducting a 20,000-interview study, for the Department of Health, Education, and Welfare, on teenage smoking habits. Question 1 flashed on the screen: "What brand of cigarettes do you usually smoke?"

The respondent named more than one brand; the interviewer pushed the proper key, and Question 2 automatically appeared: "What brand do you smoke most?" A list of 60 different brands appeared. (It was also possible for the investigator to add brands not previously listed.) The answer "Winston" happened to be given. When the interviewer pushed the proper digit to record this information, automatically on the screen appeared the appropriate question, "What types of cigarettes?", and the appropriate answers for Winston, namely, the four types of Winston then on the market. The respondent then named the appropriate type, and the interviewer punched the appropriate key. Had a different brand been given, its appropriate types would have appeared accompanying the type question.

The next question was, "What brand do you smoke next most often?" The brand was Doral, and the types of Doral were then flashed on in connection with the type question.

And so the program goes. The sequence is completely keyed, and the proper question to be asked next comes on automatically as a response is punched into the keyboard. Any special listings appropriate to only a single reply are part of the program.

This is the professional telephone survey in its most advanced form today.

REFERENCES

[1]Richard Baxter. "The Harrassed Respondent," in Leo Bogart (ed.), *Current Controversies in Marketing Research,* Chicago, Markham, 1969, chap. 3.

[2]Shirley Colby, "The Lonely Field Interviewer: Why and How Your Research with Her is Going Wrong," *Advertising Age,* June 30, 1975.

[3]R. K. McMillan, *Telecentral Communication: An Innovation in Survey Research,* 11th Annual Conference, Advertising Research Foundation, Oct. 5, 1965.

[4]Gerald J. Glasser, Gale A. Metzger, and George Miaoulis, "Measurement and Control of Interviewer Variability," *Proceedings of the American Statistical Association,* Business and Economic Statistics Section, 1970, pp. 314–319.

[5]McMillan, op. cit.

[6]M. A. McNiven and R. K. McMillan, *Telecentral Communication—An Innovation in Survey Research,* 11th Annual Conference, Advertising Research Foundation, Oct. 5, 1965.

[7]This AT&T story is partly reconstructed by conversation and correspondence with Robert Gryb, of AT&T, and partly from Boyd L. Peyton, *The Telsam Story: Research Innovation Views a Measure of Quality Control in Telephone Service,* 18th Annual Conference, Advertising Research Foundation, Nov. 14, 1972.

[8]Most of this Chilton material is from J. H. Kofron, D. J. Kilpatrick, and A. J. Brown, *Cathode Ray Tube WATS Line Interviewing,* 20th Annual Conference, Advertising Research Foundation, Nov. 19, 1974.

OVERALL
EVALUATION
OF TELEPHONE
SURVEYS

How do telephone surveys stack up against personal interview surveys and mail surveys as a fact-gathering method? This chapter considers the major limitations of personal interview surveys and mail surveys, then shows how the professional telephone survey overcomes most of these. The advantages of the other two methods are not discussed. This is an intentionally biased presentation! However, no effort is made to hide the limitations of the professional telephone survey.

THE PROBLEMS OF PERSONAL
INTERVIEW SURVEYS

In the typical personal interview survey there is a face-to-face meeting between the interviewer and the respondent. The interview may take place in a central location (such as a shopping mall) or in the home. Wherever located, the chief characteristic of the method is the face-to-face meeting. The method has several major limitations.

Sampling

One sampling limitation is that the sampling must be concentrated, rather than dispersed. To illustrate: A personal interviewer cannot economically interview one person at one location, then travel ten or twenty miles to complete the next call, whether the survey is a house-to-house study or a central location study. Even in a well-done national door-to-door study, there must be some clustering of calls, for economy reasons, although a widely dispersed series of cluster points may be included in the design.

Why is clustering of calls undesirable? Simply because it increases the probability of getting a biased sample. A much purer sample can be obtained with a dispersal of calls.

Another sampling problem in the personal interview survey is the usual low level of completion rates (the proportion of people originally designated for interview with whom interviews are actually completed). This is not a problem in the central location study, which does not meet the high requirements of probability sampling so often found in the house-to-house interview survey.

Chapter 10 discusses in some detail the declining completion rates in the personal interview survey, and the probable reasons. In the typical house-to-house survey only about 33 percent are completed on the first attempt, and to get the completion rate up to around 70 percent is likely to take two call-backs (that is, repeated attempts to reach the desired person at home). For some surveys, even this may be a low proportion of completions; sampling purists rightly argue that anything less than 100 percent completion is not a completely random sample.

A complicating factor may be the Green River Ordinance, discussed in Chapter 2, now law in many communities throughout the United States. This law generally prohibits personal solicitation on a door-to-door basis without the solicitor's obtaining a license to do so. The law does not usually apply to personal interviewing, but a misguided local police department may interpret the law differently.

Subject Matter of the Questionnaire

The nature of the content of the questionnaire in personal interview surveys may be limited, especially for those conducted in a public place such as the shopping mall. In that location, with a limited amount of time in which to conduct the questioning, it is particularly difficult to ask personal or embarrassing questions. The face-to-face contact, even in the house-to-house study, may make this sort of question difficult to ask. A face-to-face conversation with a stranger often inhibits the answering of questions about the use of birth control methods or personal hygiene products, or even questions about personal care.

Interviewing

Interviewer Bias. The interviewer may bias the reply. One early study[1] showed that the political leanings of the interviewer were related to the response obtained in a public opinion poll.

How does this occur?

The interviewer may not intend to bias results. But it is often easy for the interviewer to convey personal feelings or unconsciously react to a reply through facial or other body responses (gestures, frowns or smiles, raised eyebrows, etc.). Most people do not enjoy showing open conflict with others, so the respondent who spots a pattern of disapproval on part of the interviewer often modifies the direction his or her responses take.

Clothes or general appearance of the investigator may also cause bias. An investigator dressed according to normal business style may have some difficulty in interviewing people who as a rule dress more informally (such as students or blue-collar workers).

Finally there is the matter of asking the questions incorrectly. While there is little experimental evidence on this point (since the typical personal interview is done without direct personal supervision), there is a great chance that a question will be asked incorrectly, despite training efforts to preclude this. The problem is that if the interviewer paraphases the question, the measuring device is no longer a standard one from one respondent to another, and it is impossible to report accurate replies to these questions.

Cheating. Another limitation of the personal interview—particularly the houes-to-house interview—is the opportunity it provides for cheating, as discussed in Chapter 2. It is much easier and more pleasant for the interviewer to fill out the forms in a lounge, while sipping beer and being paid for it. There are more subtle forms of cheating, too, such as asking the respondent a few key questions, and then filling in the rest.

True, little cheating occurs in the personal interview. But this is true only because the interviewers are told—in advance of the work—that a portion of their completed interviews will be "validated"—that is, callbacks made on a sample of the work to determine that the respondent was really interviewed, that the questions were all asked, and asked in the right way. Typically from 10 to 20 percent of the personal inter-

viewer's work is validated, and there are special questioning techniques to check that all questions were asked. Today, virtually all
personal house-to-house interviewers are checked on each assignment,
so while there is occasional cheating, it is almost always discovered.

Possibility of Third-Party Influence. Another interviewing error may
occur when there is a bystander to the face-to-face contact. In almost
any kind of personal interview situation (central location or house-to-
house) there may be another person (the spouse or a friend) present
when the respondent is interviewed. If the second person is the domi-
nant person of the pair, there may be a tendency for the respondent to
defer to that person, suggesting that he or she is better qualified to reply
to the series of questions. In other cases it doesn't require an invitation
for the third person to intervene; he or she will often do so voluntarily
and spontaneously. Even if the additional person does no talking, there
is a good chance that the respondent may modify replies simply
because of knowledge or a hunch that another answer may be more
acceptable to that person.

The interviewer is usually instructed how to handle the cases where
the additional person begins to reply. But there is no way in any
personal interview situation to eliminate the presence of that person.
This, in itself, becomes a problem. If the interviewer avoids such
situations entirely, then there is the risk that the nature of the sample
has been affected.

Efficiency

By efficiency, we mean costs and timing. An efficient survey offers
reasonable costs per completed interview and is done within a reasonable span of time.

Cost. The cost of personal interviewing surveys conducted in malls or
other central locations is reasonably modest. The cost of house-to-house
personal interview surveys is not.

One reason is the need for as much dispersion of calls as possible, to
obtain a good sample. While it is true—as mentioned in the preceding
discussion of sampling limitations—that some concentration of calls is
followed, it is also true that as much dispersion as possible (within
economy limits) should be introduced. This raises the costs of field
work in two ways.

One is that there is a large proportion of travel time. Personal interviewers, unlike most other employees, are paid an hourly rate for

travel, only because so much travel time is required. Getting from one sampling area in a city to another requires travel time. In nonurbanized interviewing the travel time may be even greater.

The other is the high cost of call-backs. Visualize what may typically occur when a particular investigator has been assigned five cluster points. Each cluster may include an assignment of ten interviews to be completed, each in a designated household. The first visit to that cluster may produce three of the ten calls; the respondents are not at home in the other seven. So the investigator moves on to another cluster. Sooner or later, with the call-back system, the interviewer must return to the original cluster. This time, with some luck, two additional calls may be completed. More call-backs may be required; each visit becomes increasingly less productive, for the not-at-homes are frequently not at home. The proportion of travel time (unproductive) to interviewing time (productive) rises on each visit to the cluster.

Time. The central location personal interview study can be completed relatively quickly, although there is inevitably some wasted interviewer time between the completion of each call. In the house-to-house study, the survey cannot typically be done rapidly. It takes time for the interviewer to get to all the designated areas and homes. With a well-designed sample, including call-backs for the not-at-homes, there is no way in which the study can be completed—including data processing—in much less than one month.

THE PROBLEMS OF MAIL SURVEYS

The problems of mail surveys can be divided into three major areas: sampling, subject matter, and responses.

Sampling

Problems with the List. Erdos, in his authoritative book on the professional mail survey,[2] puts list problems at the top of his array of limitations of the mail survey. In the mail survey it is essential to begin with a list from which to select names and addresses of people to whom the questionnaire will be mailed.

Perhaps the major list problem is the *absence* of a list. There is no list in the United States which includes the total population.

Another major list problem often is inadequacy of the list. It may be outdated. Some of the entries will no longer be current, and newer entries may have been missed. If the purpose of the survey is to measure reactions of current subscribers to a particular magazine, the current list must be used, not a list several years old. In subscription lists this is no problem, but it is often a problem when the list has originated with a mailing list company, which may provide the names of people owning dogs, for instance.

Mailing lists provided by mailing list companies may be incomplete. Even lists provided by a national advertiser supposedly containing the names and addresses of those who have sent in for a special offer may be incomplete. The full name of the person may have been omitted. The address may be incomplete.

Completion Rate. The completion rate of mail surveys often is low. Most research textbooks report that about 15 percent completion is all that can be expected in a general population survey, but this figure is woefully underestimated. As Erdos points out, "No mail survey can be considered reliable unless it has a minimum of 50 per cent response. . . ."[3] Obtaining a 50 percent completion rate in mail surveys is not difficult, but even that level provides no assurance that the sample is adequate. As Erdos further points out, the Advertising Research Foundation—the one industry group that constantly sets standards for adequate research—recommends an 80 percent or better response on mail surveys.

Mail Surveys Are Also Hampered by the Increasing Unreliability of the Mail. While there are no hard data, nondelivery seems to be increasing, and delivery time seems to be getting longer. Both have had a bad impact on mail surveys.

Subject Matter

There are distinct limitations in the nature of subject matter that can be obtained by the mail survey. One of these concerns personal and confidential information. It is easier for the potential respondent to avoid answering at all, since there is no confrontation with an interviewer. Questions concerning topics such as income will typically be avoided.

Difficult questionnaires cannot be asked by mail. The questionnaire that is too long or involved cannot be successfully handled in the mail survey situation.

Motivation research studies can rarely be handled by mail; these sorts of techniques require the presence of an interviewer to administer the detailed procedures that are required.

Questions designed to check memory cannot be asked by mail. Because of the respondent's desire to please, he or she may "look up" the proper reply. If you wanted to check the proportion of the public who could identify the sponsor using a particular advertising slogan, the mail questionnaire would be no way to conduct the study. Sometimes later questions give away answers to earlier ones. If the respondent has a chance to examine the entire questionnaire before replying, or to make changes in the responses simply with eraser and pencil, bias is introduced.

The mail survey provides no chance for the respondent or the situation to be observed; sometimes this is so important that the mail survey cannot be used. A description of a home or neighborhood may be important. Observation of respondent behavior may be crucial.

In one study a coffee company wanted to know whether people in a particular geographic region preferred stronger or weaker coffee than the rest of the country. Interviewers across the nation, in a house-to-house survey, had respondents put the appropriate amount of water in the coffee pot, and the appropriate amount of ground coffee. Each was measured to obtain an accurate ratio of water to coffee for the measurement.

Response Problems

Erdos[4] mentions the problem of the wrong respondent making the reply to a mail questionnaire. The husband may fill in a questionnaire for the wife, or the secretary for the boss. While there are techniques to minimize this sort of substitution, there is no method of eliminating it.

Another response problem is the answer to open-end questions, where the respondent is asked to write out his or her response (rather than merely checking a prelisted possibility from a series of replies). If asked for his or her reasons for buying a Dodge car, the respondent tends to give a reply that is short, and perhaps not even pertinent or fully explained. In the case of the personal interview survey, the investigator can handle such problems.

Finally, there will almost always be unanswered questions in the mail survey. The respondent may avoid some by choice, others by accident.

HOW PROFESSIONAL TELEPHONE SURVEYS OVERCOME MOST OF THESE PROBLEMS

Professional telephone surveys overcome most, though not all, of these problems.

Sampling

Professional telephone surveys offer numerous sampling advantages.

Higher Completion Rates. A major sampling advantage is that completion rates—within limits—can be almost whatever you want them to be. McMillan[5] points out that the opportunity for call-backs is virtually unlimited. It takes only a few seconds for another dialing attempt. Response rates of 80 percent and better are typical.

Complete Avoidance of the Green River Ordinance. With centralized, monitored telephone interviewing, there is no way that the Green River Ordinance can be a problem, particularly if WATS lines are involved, where the local police can in no way make trouble for the central location of telephoning. Even with the telephone facility working within a single area, the study is typically completed so rapidly that there is no police problem.

Usefulness in Approaching Special Universes. Hard-to-interview populations tend to be relatively easy to reach via telephone. In one study conducted in New York City it was relatively easy to reach those in the Social Register by telephone (the study was done for a charity that wanted to determine interest of this group in a potential fund-raising ball designed to appeal to them). These people would have been virtually impossible to interview personally, since most lived in doorman-guarded apartment buildings.

Other people who are difficult to interview personally, such as physicians, lawyers, and executives, can often readily be approached by the telephone survey. People who are widely dispersed, too, can be easily reached, such as hospital administrators, motel managers, movers, electrical contractors, etc.

Hard-to-find people can also be located within reasonable cost. Examples are people who wear false teeth or toupees, people who are visually handicapped, people who own high-priced stereo equipment.

Greater Level of Cooperation. The telephone is an imperative device. There is a compulsion to answer it, regardless of what we may happen to be doing. McLuhan provides striking evidence in his quotation from a *New York Times* news item of September 7, 1949.

> On September 6, 1949, a psychotic veteran, Howard B. Unruh, in a mad rampage on the streets of Camden, N.J., killed thirteen people

and then returned home. Emergency crews, bringing up machine guns, shotguns and tear gas bombs, opened fire. At this point an editor on the *Camden Evening Courier* looked up Unruh's name in the telephone directory and called him. Unruh stopped firing and answered.

"Hello."

"This Howard?"

"Yes . . ."

"Why are you killing people?"

"I don't know. I can't answer that yet. I'll have to talk to you later. I'm too busy now."[6]

The imperative nature of the telephone is both an advantage and a disadvantage. Its potential for cooperation is clouded by the possibility of poor use of the telephone technique, resulting in annoyance to the respondent.

Dispersed Samples. Unlike the personal interview survey, the sample can be dispersed just as much as desired, with little increase in cost of interviewing. Whether a local or a national survey, the sampling method need not generate telephone numbers of people who live close to each other, though concentration is feasible if desired.

Possibility of Random-Digit Dialing. Through techniques described in Chapter 4, it is possible to use random-digit dialing. The major advantage of this technique, used in consumer surveys, is that unlisted telephone numbers come into the sample. All telephone homes have a possibility of coming into the sample.

Subject Matter

The professional telephone survey offers several advantages in the way of subject matter over one or both of the other two major methods of data collection.

Embarrassing Topics Can Be Covered. Frankness in response is one of the characteristics of the telephone interview, probably because there is only a voice at the other end of the telephone; the respondent does not see the interviewer or the interviewer's reactions. It is less personalized than the face-to-face situation, but still difficult not to reply to (remember that low response rate is one of the disadvantages of the mail survey).

Sylvia Barr, manager of the WATS interviewing division of Walker Research, reports that "people are willing to talk about sensitive topics because they never see you. We have covered successfully such areas as prophylactics and feminine sanitary protection." Kofron, Bayton, and Bortner[7] report conducting a telephone survey on birth control. Hochstim[8] reports that when women were asked their frequency of drinking alcoholic beverages, the proportion replying that they never drink was distinctly greater with the personal interview approach than with either the telephone or mail survey technique.

The author can attest to the difficulty of handling an embarrassing topic with the personal approach. The situation was a group interview where the respondents were women 35 years old and under and the topic was birth control, with the emphasis on their own behavior. For the first fifteen minutes the women were reluctant to discuss the topic in front of an unknown male, even though he had been introduced as "Doctor" for the purpose. Finally one woman responded, encouraging the others to talk openly. In a one-to-one situation, the interview would have been lost.

Controversial Topics Can Be Covered. Such topics can be handled fairly easily for much the same reason that embarrassing topics can: the respondent does not see the reactions of the investigator. If a survey toward the employer and the union is to be made among union members, franker and more honest reactions will be obtained by telephone interview than by personal interview or mail survey, because of the more obvious appearance—though unreal—of anonymity. If the more realistic results are wanted on topics such as women's liberation or civil rights, these too will probably be most accurately measured by the telephone survey.

Immediate Topics Can Be Covered. Reactions to events as they are occurring or immediately after they have occurred can be obtained by the telephone interview, an impossibility with either the personal interview or mail survey. Suppose it is desirable to measure reaction to a television program in depth, with a minimal memory loss. The method is the telephone. All that is required is to invite selected people to watch the particular show over their home sets, and to telephone them immediately afterward for reactions to plot, acting, characters, and all other aspects of interest.

Suppose it is desired to measure the reaction of guests of the Holiday

Inn, at various points throughout the country, to various details of their experience and treatment during their stay. A telephone survey of registered guests would do it. They are still in the stage of experiencing: there is no memory loss, and the impressions are still vivid.

Interviewing

There are several main groups of advantages in the interviewing situation of the professional telephone survey. Many occur because the interviewers receive personal training, and are supervised and monitored. In addition, most organizations offering this type of work have continuing employees handling it, and this continuity also contributes to many of the advantages outlined.

Interviewing Quality Is High. Under the rigorous standards of interviewing maintained by the professional telephone survey firm, there is almost no possibility that poor interviewers will remain on the job very long, if, in fact, they ever reach the production line.

There Is a Decrease in Interviewer Bias. There are several reasons. One is monitoring. There is no chance that an interviewer can ask the question the wrong way—at least for very long—and there is no way that any inflection in the question phrasing can suggest a reply.

Neither can the voice itself bias; the individual who does not have an attractive telephone voice or who speaks with an unusual accent is typically excluded in selecting interviewers.

All personal elements are eliminated. Appearance doesn't matter, because the interviewer isn't seen by the respondent. The interviewer's facial or other bodily reactions don't matter either, since the respondent can't see these reactions.

Interviewer Morale Is Increased. In the professional telephone survey there are always other interviewers in the same physical location working on the same survey, encountering similar experiences and problems. On their breaks, these interviewers typically compare notes. They share their experiences and problems. There is a feeling of togetherness which is not present in the case of the house-to-house personal interview.

The Possibility of Cheating Is Virtually Eliminated. First, the motivation for cheating is eliminated. The interviewer is typically paid on a time basis, and his or her production is observed. If production is unusually high, it is noticeable. Second, the individual is carefully supervised. In most professional telephone survey situations, each interviewer is in sight of the supervisor, so it is obvious if a particular interviewer is spending time writing only, rather than being on the telephone. In addition, monitoring—where the supervisor can break in on the interviewing line without any noise—means that the interviewer cannot possibly take shortcuts in the questioning procedure.

The Respondent Can Be Properly Selected. One of the above-mentioned limitations of the mail survey is that there can be only limited control over making sure that the right person is really replying: the secretary might answer for the boss; the wrong family member might think it is possible to properly fill in the questionnnaire. With the telephone method (as with the personal interview) this problem can easily be overcome, by making sure that the person on the other end of the line is really the individual qualified to reply.

There Is No Third-Party Influence. In the personal interview situation, as was pointed out, a domineering person also present during the interview can bias results. Even the presence of a third person—domineering or not—can bias the replies.

In the case of the telephone survey, this is no problem. The third party may be present at the respondent end of the line, but a person who cannot hear the questions is most unlikely to try to share in the response.

LIMITATIONS OF PROFESSIONAL TELEPHONE SURVEYS

The professional telephone survey, with all its advantages, is not always the perfect data-gathering method, though its limitations seem to be fewer than those of either of the other two basic methods.

Sampling

One sampling limitation of consumer telephone surveys concerns the nature of nonowners of telephones. While in the United States today 95 percent of the households have telephones, there is a bias, demographically, among those who do not. Most of these are farm and ghetto households. Even random-digit dialing will not reach these people. Any time that either group is likely to have reactions different from the rest of the population, bias is introduced. It probably is not a serious distortion, because of the small percentage involved, but it is still distortion.

A second potential bias is that of numbers unlisted in directories. Random-digit dialing will minimize or eliminate such bias. However, because random-digit dialing seems to be used only in a minority of professional telephone surveys, this bias has to be listed—at least currently—as one of the limitations of the method.

Subject Matter

The amount and nature of subject matter of the survey are somewhat restricted in the professional telephone survey.

Amount of Subject Matter May Be Limited. It is often argued that there is a time limit to the telephone interview. Sylvia Barr, of Walker Research, says that the typical telephone interview cannot run for more than 20 minutes. Jay Schmiedeskamp,[9] former director of the University of Michigan's survey research center, says that his group restricts its telephone calls (and these are with people previously personally interviewed) to 11 minutes.

Illinois Bell, in conducting its telephone surveys, runs interviews an average length of 7 minutes, though on occasion an interview will go as long as 35 minutes. Frank McHugh, president of The Data Group Incorporated, says that a length of 20 to 30 minutes is now quite common, though a decade ago it was felt that 10 to 15 minutes was the maximum. Ann Fenton, of MARC, reports that the maximum should be 30 to 35 minutes, though that is longer than her organization really likes.

The author once conducted a telephone survey with women on home hair grooming which ran an average of 45 minutes, without trouble. Frank McHugh, president of The Data Group Incorporated, says that there is no difficulty with longer interviews, so long as they are *really* interesting. The real answer, as Kildegaard[10] points out, is that maximum interview length depends on the nature of the universe and the topic of questioning. She rightly says that only pretesting (trying out the questionnaire with a small number of typical respondents) will provide the answer.

Questions Requiring Looking Up Information Cannot Be Asked. For instance, occasionally on a survey it is desirable to have a respondent check to determine brand and package size of items in the pantry or bathroom. In a telephone survey it is unfeasible to ask a question of this sort. Again, in one study the serial number on refrigerators had to be checked so as to get not only the make—which was easy—but the age as well.

Often in readership studies, it is not enough to take the respondent's word for the publications that are on hand. They should be gathered by the respondent, and then the names reported. But it is not usually feasible to have the respondent take any action that is away from the telephone. There is too much risk that the respondent will not return. If the calls are made from a WATS facility, or if the local service is being charged by time units, such questioning will run up telephone charges.

Questions Requiring Behavior Cannot Be Asked. One of the most repetitious forms of questioning, too often occurring in market research, is the use of a semantic-differential series of questions covering various products or companies. In the semantic-differential there is a 7-point scale, varying between two word extremes at either end. To use a simple illustration, the scale might have "very favorable" at one end and "very unfavorable" on the other. This scale might be used for twenty-two product attributes, such as flavor, consistency, amount of salt, sweetness, etc. It gets boring enough if the respondent is asked only about one product; suppose that there are three products in the list! This is a serious challenge to get through even with a personal interview; it becomes absolutely impossible in a telephone interview, without the physical presence of the investigator to keep the interview going.

Observational Data Cannot Be Obtained. Since there are no visual cues in the telephone situation, no observations can be made. Payne[11] mentions two kinds of data, one of which may be termed "demographic" and include points such as race, ethnic origin, age, type of dwelling, and socioeconomic status. Some of these may successfully be asked directly.

The other kind of observation data which cannot be observed consists of behavioral cues such as grins, winks, or even puzzlement. However, this sort of information, even when observed in a personal interview situation, is rarely reported by the investigator anyway. This disadvantage is more apparent than real.

Visual Aids Cannot Be Used in Questioning. Just as the interviewer cannot make visual observations, neither can the respondent. Visual aids cannot be used in questioning. No photographs or drawings can be displayed; this eliminates concept testing in which a prototype, a photograph, or drawing of the proposed product is commonly used in the interview situation.

Copy testing—except for radio—is eliminated as a telephone interview procedure because no print ads, no TV commercials, no storyboards can be demonstrated. The typical publication readership or audience study requiring that the respondent go through one or more issues to determine internal readership is *almost* eliminated because the publication cannot be shown. However, at least one research firm has been ingenious enough to come up with a procedure (mailing the issue ahead of time with instructions not to open until time of the telephone survey) to overcome the problem.

No package testing of the usual types can be done, because it is impossible to show packages.

Only a limited amount of reading material is possible in the telephone interview. In a mail or personal interview survey it is possible to have the respondent read material. In the telephone interview the material has to be read to the respondent, and as Sylvia Barr, of Walker Research, says, "A lengthy statement of an idea, without eye-to-eye contact, fails to keep the attention of the respondent."

Interviewing

A third limitation of the professional telephone survey falls under interviewing. The interviewer has little time to jot down replies, particularly to open-ended questions, which have to be written out in detail instead of merely checking an answer box. In personal interviewing the respondent can see that the interviewer is taking the time to write down the reply. But the respondent cannot observe this in the telephone interview; so far as the respondent is concerned there is simply a blank spot in the conversation, without any apparent reason. The exception occurs where the interviewer has been trained to classify the response into a preset code, or punched directly into a consumer terminal.

Some professional telephone research firms make an effort to minimize this by training the investigator to explain that he or she is taking the time to write down the comment. Sometimes the respondent talks too rapidly for the interviewer to record. In this case Burke Marketing Research instructs the interviewer to say "Just a moment, please. I am writing this down."

Response

There are certain response limitations which are inherent in the telephone survey.

Replies Are Shorter. Did you ever notice that when you talk with the neighbor over the back fence, the discussion may run half an hour or an hour, without your being aware of it? But when you talk to that same neighbor over the telephone, unless you are not typical, your conversation will be much shorter, and more likely to be limited to the topic or topics for which the telephone call was started. The personal interview situation is a more normal situation and encourages discussion. Oakes[12] reports, in one study, that the average number of responses per respondent was double in the personal interview than over the telephone.

It Is More Difficult to Probe. The lack of full answers in the telephone situation cannot be easily corrected. It might be thought that all that is necessary is to instruct the investigator to use the usual probing techniques of the personal interview, to get more detailed or more understandable replies to an open-end question by asking a nondirective question, such as:

Do you have anything else to add to that?

What do you mean by that?

In the telephone survey the follow-up probe question can be a real source of annoyance to the respondent. If there is too much of such probing, the chances for a terminated interview are great.

There May Be Reluctance to Give Committed Answers. Schmiedeskamp[13] shows evidence that typically people are more willing to take a definite position when interviewed personally, rather than by telephone. The frequency of neutral replies, he reports, is greater in telephone studies.

This probably means that those who have mild feelings about the issue are likely to report neutrality over the more impersonal telephone medium.

There May Be a Greater Proportion of No-Answers. One annoyance to the market or opinion researcher is the person who does not answer a question. Tigert, Barnes, and Bourgeois[14] report a greater tendency for telephone interviewers to hurry when the respondent delays, thus forcing a reply of a "no-answer." One might first suspect that these were untrained interviewers, but the authors report that the interviewing was done from a centralized location, using trained, supervised interviewers, so it would appear that this was, indeed, a professional telephone survey.

COMPARISONS OF RESULTS OF TELEPHONE SURVEYS WITH MAIL, PERSONAL INTERVIEW SURVEYS

With all these criticisms of the telephone method, does it actually provide results that are similar to those of the personal interview survey, heretofore considered *the* method of collecting data from individuals?

The evidence suggests strongly that it does. The first of this evidence was the early Hooper Maidenform study, reported in Chapter 1. But there is more.

Cahalan[15] did a yesterday readership study of a New York City newspaper among owners of new cars. He used the telephone method. Then, personal interviews were made with the respondents, who, page by page, were taken through a recognition procedure. There was a high correlation between results of the two approaches.

Kofron, Bayton, and Bortner[16] report a Chilton Research study done for *The New York Times* in which 3251 WATS interviews and 517 personal interviews were completed. The results were highly comparable in terms of:

the amount of time spent watching television yesterday

amount spent per week on foods and groceries

family income

number and type of organizations in which the person was active (church, social, civic, etc.)

involvement in activities (concerts, plays and shows, visiting or entertaining, clubs and groups, etc.)

Perhaps even more important than the comparability was the finding that the telephone approach produced a greater proportion of interviews with individuals in elevator apartments. This suggests that the personal interviewer has difficulty gaining access to such apartments, often guarded by doormen.

The significance of this finding is that the telephone survey, when well done, is probably even more dependable than the personal interview survey, because it includes these kinds of people in their proper proportion. Therefore any time a study is run where results might differ by apartment- and non-apartment-dwellers, the telephone method will produce more valid results. The point is that in advance of a study, one cannot predict when these two groups will be different.

EVALUATION OF DEGREES OF PROFESSIONAL TELEPHONE SURVEYS

For purposes of this discussion, there are three degrees of professional telephone surveys. One is central location with monitored supervision. A second is central location with monitored supervision and WATS lines. The third is central location with monitored supervision, WATS lines, and computer terminal tie-in with CRT (cathode-ray tube). Each successive stage adds advantages. Some present disadvantages.

Advantages

Central Location with Monitored Supervision. The advantages of this system fall under four headings: interviewing, efficiency, exchange of information between interviewers and coders, and client monitoring.

With central, monitored supervision, there is usually considerable attention paid to selection, training, and supervision of the field staff. Most research firms in this field keep busy enough with the work to maintain a permanent, continuing relationship with interviewers, who usually do not work on a full-time basis but nevertheless are dealt with as continuing employees. (Some firms keep the interviewers at work on a full-time basis.)

Training (much more of which is spelled out in Chapter 6) is usually both general and specific. It is done in-house, with broad-stroke painting of the field of marketing research and telephone interviewing; and specific training for individual studies, usually with practice interviewing done by the investigator in advance of the actual start on the interviewing assignment.

Close supervision and monitoring—practiced by all these firms—results in a number of specific advantages. There is better questioning control, better voice control. Most of these research firms have an immediate editing/review of completed questionnaires, so that errors are caught early. Frank Walker, president of Walker Research, refers to this as "an early warning system." It permits discovery of problems and isolates interviewer interpretation errors early, thus helping to assure the quality of the field work.

The close supervision and monitoring also virtually eliminates the need for validation. Almost no firms offering this kind of service include validation, since there is so little opportunity or motive for workers to cheat.

Efficiency is also increased under this system. It has already been reported that central location interviewers produce 50 percent more interviews per hour than interviewers making telephone calls from their homes. McMillan[17] stresses the efficiency advantage of a high rate of completion.

Another efficiency advantage is that typically this sort of telephone survey costs significantly less than the same survey done by personal interview. This tends to be true whether the sample is physicians, executives, or consumers; or whether the sample is local, regional, or national.

A highly important aspect of efficiency is speed, and this sort of study can be done amazingly fast. A recent Burke ad says:

> Overnight, Burke can give you the findings of a telephone survey in more than 30 different markets. As many as 1500 consumer interviews, coast to coast, in five major geographical areas. Notify Burke of your needs before noon on a given day; you'll have results by 9:00 A.M. the next morning.

Or listen to the way Harry O'Neill, executive vice-president of Opinion Research Corporation puts it:

> From Friday afternoon through Sunday evening we can do a national sample of 1000 cases. In political polling, this means that studies can be completed quickly before a major, unanticipated event takes place which might influence the results.

Speed may be important, too, in marketing studies. The marketing manager always seems to be faced with emergency situations which require amazingly rapid research results.

Client monitoring, where it occurs, is also a major advantage of the system. If the client can be persuaded to monitor, it is a big plus. Most research firms in the business invite their clients to come and monitor—particularly in the early stages—in order to distinguish subtle errors in planning the procedure or in interviewing. However, it is also possible for the client (assuming the client is sufficiently large and does sufficient research) to arrange remote monitoring, so that the monitoring can be handled at the client's location regardless of the location of the research firm.

The other important thing about client monitoring is that it assures the research user that all is well with the handling of the study. The research director of the client firm is thus in a position to *know* that the results of the particular survey are dependable—that there were no major interviewing errors.

The exchange of information between interviewers and coders is another *potential* advantage (not always realized) of central location, supervised monitoring. At this point let's explain what the coder does. The coder converts the particular reply on a questionnaire to a digital form that can be entered into a computer. Frequently the coder must interpret the meaning of the reply before one or more digits can be assigned to it. In those research firms offering central supervision, some make it a point to see that interviewers and coders have contact. The classification of open-end replies is thereby facilitated. Editing (see Chapter 7) can be discussed with the coders.

McMillan[18] mentions still another advantage: the possibility of assigning each investigator equivalent samples. When one is dealing with a directory list, a mailing list, or banks of random-digit numbers, such assignments are simple to make, but they cannot easily be made with house-to-house personal calls, since neighborhoods (Primary Sampling Units, or PSUs) assigned are likely to vary so radically.

Giving each interviewer an equivalent sample makes it possible to compare interviewer variability and hence to spot possible interviewer bias or cheating, though the chance of each seems low because of the controls imposed. However, at least one research firm, MARC, considers this important enough so that results by interviewer are provided to the client on each study the firm handles.

Central Location, Monitored Supervision, with WATS Lines. This somewhat more sophisticated method offers not only the preceding advantages, but also some of its own, having to do with sampling.

The WATS lines mean that a national or regional probability sample is possible. In addition, sample dispersion is feasible at no increase in cost.

Central Location, Monitored Supervision, with WATS Lines, and Computer Terminal Tie-In, with CRT. The computer terminal tie-in creates greater efficiency of operation. Many processing steps are eliminated. Coding, card punching, and verifying procedures (discussed in Chapter 7) are all eliminated by the interviewer's pushing the proper digital button to record the reply directly into the computer data bank.

There is immediate data processing upon completion of the interviewing; this method of professional telephone interviewing certainly offers the greatest speed of any in completion of the entire study. The ability to process the data instantaneously on completion of interviewing makes it possible, if interviewing by area is carefully equated for each day of work, to check results on a daily basis. Variability of each day's results can be compared, and when sufficient stabilization has been achieved, interviewing can be terminated. This sometimes makes it possible to use fewer interviews than had been anticipated, thus saving money.

If the computer terminal tie-in also means that there is a CRT in use (and presently it does, with the two facilities making use of it), there are additional advantages. There is more accurate question phrasing, for one thing. Here's an example, from Kofron, Kilpatrick and Brown:[19]

Chilton Research conducted a 6000-interview study for the U.S. Coast Guard. After boat ownership was established, the person was asked: "What type of boat is your primary boat?" A total of 20 types of boats were precoded into the CRT system. In one case a respondent reported that the boat was a single-engine outboard, and this response was entered into the system.

Then came a question about the total horsepower of the motor. The particular answer, "250," triggered a verification question: "Let me just verify that. The horsepower on your *outboard* is 250?"

Through precoding, an answer outside normal limits (as in the example) can be automatically spotted and checked. In the particular case the type of boat was wrong, and the interviewer returned to the question on boat type. The system, by the way, does not finalize entries into the data bank until entry of the answer to the final question.

The next question was about the material that the *inboard's* hull was made of. The investigators probed for any other materials to give the boat owner a chance to mention all the materials. All multiple replies were entered until the code for "no more" was used by the interviewer, and then the questioning went on to other areas.

The people in the household who operated the boat were then identified by age and sex. Then the respondent was asked the proportion of time each person operated the boat. If the figure for all family members did not total 100 percent, the computer flashed the message: "Does not add to 100%."

The example shows that another advantage of the CRT is that it makes for more accurate recording. If the interviewer pushes a button inconsistent with the pattern, the CRT takes care of this. If the interviewer pushes a button outside of the acceptable array of digital entries for the response to the question, the CRT flashes a message to that effect. It is almost impossible for the investigator to make an error in recording.

Still another advantage is offered by the CRT setup. As experienced market and opinion researchers know, the sequence of items in questions or alternative responses can affect replies. If you are going to ask a series of perhaps five or six questions on each of a number of brands, for instance, then rotation of the order in which brands are asked is vitally important. The CRT can be programmed to provide this rotation automatically. Again, if you need a ranking of brands, companies, personalities, or whatever, a rotated order of presentation is vital, and the CRT can handle this as well.

Disadvantages

With WATS Lines. For the buyer of research, there seem to be no particular disadvantages associated with the use of WATS lines, over and above the limitations of the telephone method in general. However, to the firm that owns WATS lines for research use, there is a major risk: those lines can be disastrously expensive unless they are kept in use constantly for 12 hours a day or more. It is significant that two research firms who use their centralized, monitored facilities only for consumer calls do not use WATS lines, but instead make long-distance calls. Most consumer surveys—whether done by telephone or by house-to-house calls—do not begin until 4 or 5 P.M., and then run until 9:30 or 10 P.M., local time, to include people who work. Thus, the WATS bands would be idle the better part of the day. The research firms using WATS lines either also use them for calling specialized professional or executive groups during the day (physicians, engineers, architects, etc.), or else are subsidiaries of firms with WATS lines available for parent-company use during the day, and becoming available for consumer telephoning during after-hours.

With Computer Tie-In. One researcher whose facility does not include a computer tie-in expressed the reservation that with a tie-in system there is no permanent record of the interview. What the researcher is saying is that there is nothing visible; it is rather like a checkless society in which your deposits and withdrawals are all handled by computer, and you never have any visible evidence to examine each transaction.

Is this a valid criticism? It is difficult to know. But it is true that there is no tangible evidence of each interview. It would be difficult and expensive to reproduce the results of any individual interview. With the on-line computer it is difficult to handle replies to open-end questions. The only way that open-end questions can be accommodated is to provide a list of response categories, and have the investigator interpret and punch in the answer in the appropriate category. Anyone who has gone through the routine of learning to code open-end replies knows the dangers of this sort of procedure. Different coders (in this case investigators) interpret replies differently, and enter codes differently for similar replies. The only real way that this problem can be overcome is with close supervision of the coding process, but with the central location CRT setup, there is simply no way that *this* sort of close supervision can be applied.

FINAL COMMENTS

This chapter has—with only minor reservations—strongly proclaimed the virtues of professional telephone surveys. But how do major manufacturers who are ultrasophisticated in marketing feel about it?

Consider General Foods Corporation. They are producers of such name brands as Maxwell House, Sanka, and other coffee brands; Jell-O; Tang; Post Toasties and other cereal brands; Kool-Aid; Shake 'n Bake. J. L. Buiede, their survey operations manager, says:

> General Foods makes extensive use of telephone interviewing, most of which is done from central locations with monitoring by supervisors. This type of interviewing is done either internally through our Telephone Interviewing Center or through outside suppliers who have WATS centers.

Procter & Gamble is the most sophisticated marketer in the world. In any case the corporation is commonly believed to have the largest total marketing budget in the world, and produces consumer products such as Ivory soap, Folger coffee, Sure and Secret deodorants, Charmin toilet paper, Dash detergent, Crisco cooking oil, Pringle's Newfangled potato chips, and Duncan Hines cake mixes. Richard Shepherd, manager of field operations of the market research department, reports:

> We use telephone interviewing, via our WATS lines, for every study we possibly can. It offers the flexibility of a personal encounter without the expense.

That's what two of the major marketers in the United States say about the professional telephone survey.

REFERENCES

[1]A. B. Blankenship, The Effect of the Interviewer upon the Response in a Public Opinion Poll, *Journal of Consulting Psychology*, vol. 4, 1940, pp. 134–136.

[2]Paul L. Erdos, *Professional Mail Surveys*, New York, McGraw-Hill, 1970. (See page 10.)

[3]Erdos, op. cit., p. 144.

[4]Erdos, op. cit., p. 13.

[5]Robert K. McMillan, *Telecentral Communication: An Innovation in Survey Research*, 11th Annual Conference, Advertising Research Foundation, Oct. 5, 1965.

[6]Marshall McLuhan, *Understanding Media: The Extensions of Man*, New York, McGraw-Hill, 1964, p. 273.

[7]John H. Kofron, James A. Bayton, and Bruce Z. Bortner, *Guidelines for Choosing between Long-Distance Telephone and Personal Interviewing*, 15th Annual Conference, Advertising Research Foundation, Oct. 15, 1969.

[8]Joseph R. Hochstim, "A Critical Comparison of the Strategies of Collecting Data from Households," *Journal of the American Statistical Association*, vol. 62, Sept. 1967, pp. 976–989.

[9]Jay W. Schmiedeskamp, "Reinterview by Telephone," *Journal of Marketing*, Jan. 1962, pp. 28–34.

[10]Ingrid C. Kildegaard, "Rejoinder," *Journal of Advertising Research*, vol. 6, no. 3, 1966, pp. 40–41.

[11]S. L. Payne, "Data Collection Methods: Telephone Surveys," in Robert Ferber, *Handbook of Marketing Research*, New York, McGraw-Hill, 1974.

[12]R. H. Oakes, "Differences in Responsiveness in Telephone Versus Personal Interviews," *Journal of Marketing*, vol. 19, Oct. 1954, p. 169.

[13]Schmiedeskamp, op. cit.

[14]Douglas J. Tigert, James G. Barnes, and Jacques C. Bourgeois, "Research on Research: Mail Panel versus Telephone Survey in Retail Image Analysis," *The Canadian Marketer*, Spring 1975, pp. 22–27.

[15]Don Cahalan, "Measuring Newspaper Readership by Telephone," *Journal of Advertising Research*, vol. 1, no. 2, December 1960, pp. 1–6.

[16]Kofron, Bayton, and Bortner, op. cit.

[17]McMillan, op. cit.

[18]McMillan, op. cit.

[19]J. H. Kofron, D. J. Kilpatrick, and A. J. Brown, *Cathode Ray Tube WATS Line Interviewing,* 20th Annual Conference, Advertising Research Foundation, Nov. 19, 1974.

SAMPLING

Sampling is the process of selecting a small proportion of the total population (here used in a statistical sense as meaning the total group of homes or people the survey is to be done among) to approach in the survey. The main reason for sampling is economy. It would be too costly and too time-consuming to attempt to question the total population. Anyway, why question all 83 million people who are 16 years or older when a survey of 100 of them might provide sufficiently dependable results?

Dr. Raymond Barker, professor of marketing at Bowling Green State University, cites the example of a physician who draws blood from a patient for a blood test. All the blood in the body is not needed for a test (imagine the poor patient if all of it were!), and neither does the surveyor need to question the total population to obtain reasonably dependable results.

In survey work there are two major types of samples. One is the probability sample, in which each household or individual in the population (or universe) has an equal or known chance of being included in the sample. The other is the nonprobability sample, which includes all other forms of drawing the sample. The probability methods are by far the more dependable methods. Fortunately for telephone surveys probability samples are by far the simplest to use, and one just doesn't hear of nonprobability methods ever being used.

There is a need for a *frame* (a list of households or individuals in the universe) in sampling. There are three types of listings used in telephone surveys. One is a list of individuals put together from some common characteristic other than telephone ownership, referred to as a nontelephone list. The second is a list of telephone owners (most often, but not exclusively, published by the telephone company). The third is randomly generated telephone numbers.

The frame is crucial to sampling in market and opinion research. It is the only sound basis for sampling. Only a complete list of those in the frame permits the sound selection of a sampling of telephone homes.

There is one problem inherent in dealing with most lists based on telephone ownership. Telephone exchanges and telephone books do not follow political boundaries. In most personal interview surveys—at least those done on a house-to-house basis—political boundaries can and are followed, not only because so many other marketing data are reported that way, but also because the basic census material on which house-to-house samples are based is reported that way. This is not an easy problem to overcome in telephone surveys, where neither telephone books nor exchanges follow political boundaries. Jim Sammer, vice-president of Walker Research, says: "You can ask the respondent what county he lives in, but many won't know, so this is not a generally satisfactory solution." Fortunately, most marketing research studies can be reported with only larger areas being reported. The problem is a greater one when political surveys are being conducted, in which case it is often crucial to know results by small political areas. If this becomes important, then, as the chapter will show, there sometimes are techniques feasible for meeting the need.

SAMPLING FROM THE NON-TELEPHONE LIST

The list may be provided by the sponsor of the study, and may consist of charge account customers, subscribers to a publication, those who have donated to a particular charity, coupon redeemers, warranty holders, dog owners, etc. It may be purchased from a company that maintains specialized mailing lists, and include such possibilities as newlyweds, owners of hi-fi equipment, people earning an estimated $20,000 or more per year, company presidents, and the like. The list may come from a directory (other than a telephone directory), and may include physicians (the American Medical Association directory), psychologists (the American Psychological Association), architects, chemical engineers, or the graduates of a particular college or university, to name a few.

Sampling Methods

There are three somewhat different methods of sampling from these lists: the straight random, the systematic, and the stratified random.

Straight Random. The "pure" method of random sampling is the use of random numbers (which can be computer generated or drawn from existing tables of random numbers). It is time-consuming to apply this system, for it requires the counting of names.

Systematic. The systematic method of sampling is far more common, and unless there is some bias in the way the list was put together, it is usually just as good. In the systematic sample, if there are 1000 names in the list and 100 are to be drawn, then every tenth name is drawn, after a random starting point of between 1 and 9 is selected.

Stratified Random. In a stratified random sample, the list is classified in some manner before the sampling occurs. Then the random or system-

FIGURE 4-1.
Alphabetic telephone directories: the lifeblood of up-to-date directory sampling. *(Walker Research Inc.)*

atic process of pulling the sample occurs within each of the selected strata. The AMA directory provides a classification by specialty of the physician, so that it becomes possible to use each classification in drawing the sample.

Let's take another example—one that is virtually self-stratifying. A particular publication has its lists of subscribers arranged alphabetically within each state. By taking every tenth name in the list, there is automatic stratification by state. The advantage of stratification, where feasible, is that it guarantees proper assignment of interview numbers within each stratum used, without in any way negatively affecting the random selection process.

Problems

These lists are not always easy to work with. There are several major problems.

Some Lists Are "Dirty." The client-provided list (and sometimes the other two types, as well) often provides partial and sometimes even incorrect information. The name of the person may be misspelled. People who do not qualify may be included. (The name of a retired physician may be included among those believed to be still practicing.) If a telephone number is included, there may be an error (in the area code, in the exchange, in the last four digits).

Getting Numbers from Directory Assistance Can Be Slow. Many lists include no telephone number. Then there are two alternatives. One is to go to Directory Assistance. The other is to go to an alphabetical telephone directory. Each presents problems.

Obtaining numbers through Directory Assistance can be a time-consuming affair if there are many numbers to be looked up. As a general policy, Directory Assistance will report only three requests in one call (and this decreases to only two or one when the demand is heavy). One research firm averages a minimum of 40 completed checks per hour when checking names in rural areas or with incomplete addresses. The rate rises to a maximum of 65 per hour for lists in alphabetical order, containing first and last names with complete addresses.

Sometimes it is difficult to track down a telephone number by using Directory Assistance. The information operator does not have time to scan for a listing. If a listing for Mrs. Amanda Walker at 1212 Main Street is requested and there is no such listing, the telephone number for Mr. William Walker at the same address may not be reported. However, this problem can usually be overcome if the request is made for the "(*last name*) family" at the specific address. The full name can be requested only when more than one listing for that family name exists at the desired address.

In general, alphabetical directories can be used only if the original listing is a male name. This is true because most residential listings are in a male family name. However, because many men and women today are listed only by their initials, sometimes a full name without a correct address may be insufficient information for obtaining a telephone number.

SAMPLING FROM ALPHABETICAL DIRECTORY LISTS

There are two kinds of telephone directories useful as lists of telephone homes. Most commonly known is the alphabetical list. The other is the crisscross list. The use of the alphabetical list will be considered first.

As a starting point, it should be mentioned that AT&T publishes a Directory of Directories. The truly competent telephone survey firm knows this already, and has hundreds of current alphabetic telephone directories on its premises.

Bell & Howell offers an annual subscription service which makes current telephone directories available on microfiche, a product similar to microfilm. The service covers 245 metropolitan areas (yellow pages as well as alphabetical). This has the advantage of requiring less storage space than conventional books, as well as considerably less susceptibility to damage. One major advantage is a community cross-reference guide, which lists thousands of communities in the United States and denotes the specific telephone directory in which each can be found.[1]

Methods of Using Alphabetical Directories

Basically, the same three methods apply here as was true with sampling from lists of other than telephone homes: pure random, systematic, or stratified.

The pure random method is rarely used. It is unnecessary, and it is too costly.

The systematic method (or a variation thereof) is the one most often used for local telephone surveys. One method is to divide the number of pages in the directory by the number of interviews required. The figure resulting tells how many pages from which it is necessary to sample. Then a random starting page can be selected. However, the first and last pages typically are avoided, since it is argued that these are overused in telephone solicitations. Then every nth listing on the designated pages is selected.

In practice, this process can be sped up by making a template, perhaps simply in the form of a shortened piece of cardboard, which, when aligned vertically from the top of the page, will indicate precisely where the listing is to be read.

There is a problem. The listing selected may not be a residence. Commercial and government listings are to be avoided; one way is to take the first residence listing above or below that of the one originally selected.

There is still one other consideration which has not yet been raised. That is the question of call-backs. It will be necessary to provide additional names and numbers which are permissible in case the originally listed household or individual within it cannot be reached.

There are many ways of handling these additional listings. One of the simplest is to take the next successive or preceding listing. If it is a study where up to four call-backs will be made, then a total list of five times the required number of completed calls will be required.

Use of a stratified sample from alphabetical listings is possible only when the study is conducted in more than a single area, working from more than one telephone directory. In that case stratification by location is generally followed. The most practical system is to use the total number of listings in the particular book as indicative of its residential listings, and allocating calls proportionately to this by book. However, in some areas this will not work, and so census data are used instead for allocation.

The strata most commonly used are geographic area and county. The number of families within each geographic area is first checked from census data. Then a unit such as counties is listed, with its number of families. A selection of counties is made on some sort of random basis. Then, from the appropriate alphabetical directories, the selection of residential listings is made.

Louis Meier, of Market Opinion Research, points out that stratification from alphabetical books is possible only when the book contains subsections for political units. If it is a conglomerate book, he says, then there is simply no chance to stratify. However, he goes on, you can ask whether the respondent lives east or west of a certain waterway, street, or highway. While this is an improvement over asking what county the person lives in, it still is risky—some proportion (unknown) of the population won't even know this. Also, the procedure adds to costs, which must be so tightly controlled in the professional telephone survey.

Example of Use of Alphabetical
Lists for National Samples

Mrs. Helen Wippich Greene, of Valley Forge Information Service, talks about her firm's national probability sample. "It is a sample of 400 points, stratified by area, and by community size. Communities are the basic PSUs [Primary Sampling Units]." There are four replications of 100 points each.

For any particular survey, Mrs. Greene explains, alphabetical telephone directories are used as the source, with a systematic selection of numbers.*

Problems in Using an Alphabetical List

There are several problems in the use of an alphabetical list. (One of these—the fact that the boundaries of the listing are rarely political—has already been discussed, so will not be reconsidered here.)

The Family May Be Listed in More Than One Book. In many areas of the United States, a family may be listed in more than one alphabetical directory. This naturally causes problems for the survey researcher who is trying to select a sample from such books; it means that the sample frame as drawn is not pure, and it becomes expensive to select a really fine probability sample.

There Are Many Errors and Omissions in Alphabetical Directories. The downright errors are relatively rare, according to a study by MARC using a technique of random-digit dialing, which basically avoids use of the alphabetical directory, depending instead on the selection of random numbers to be dialed. However, the same study showed that almost 15 percent of the total numbers telephoned were unlisted by request, and close to 5 percent were connections too new to be listed.[2]

---

*Mrs. Greene also reports that the method is easily converted to random-digit-dialing studies described later in this chapter, by adding random digits or a constant digit. Naturally this adds to costs, both clerical and dialing.

TABLE 4-1
The Forms of Nonlisting in a National
MARC Random-Digit-Dialing
Telephone Survey, 1973

Unlisted by request	13.3%
Too new to be listed	3.7
Listed incorrectly	.8
	17.8%

Glasser and Metzger[3] reporting a study by Statistical Research, Inc., found an even greater proportion of unlisted homes (19.2 percent).[3]

When using alphabetical lists nonlistings are not important unless (a) there are demographic or psychological differences between those listed and unlisted, and (b) it can be demonstrated that these differences cause a difference in response to questions. Unfortunately, both hypotheses, as stated, happen to be correct.

Table 4-2 summarizes the results of the MARC study, previously mentioned.[4] It shows that the proportion of unlisteds in total is highest in the Pacific and the Middle Atlantic regions. This is reasonably consistent with the Glasser and Metzger analysis[5] though the regions analyzed were somewhat different.

In the MARC study, as in the Statistical Research study, the unlisteds are proportionately higher in the more populated areas, lower in the less populated. The MARC study shows that unlisteds are proportionately higher in the $10,000–$14,999 income group than in others. The Statistical Research study found a higher proportion in lower-income homes.

The MARC study found that the proportion of unlisteds rise as county population increases. In the Statistical Research study, reported somewhat differently, unlisteds were higher in the larger metropolitan areas. Both the MARC and the Statistical Research studies show that unlisted numbers are proportionately more frequent among families whose head is younger.

The MARC study also shows that the proportion of unlisteds is higher in homes where there are children than in homes without children. The Statistical Research study also showed a higher proportion of unlisted homes among blacks and among those with less education.

These two sets of national data show conclusively that there are demographic differences between listed and unlisted homes. There is also evidence in studies reported by Leuthold and Scheele,[6] by Brunner and Brunner,[7] and by Trendex[8] that there are demographic differences between the listeds and unlisteds in a number of local areas (as opposed to nationally).

These differences—or others unmeasured—are related to differences in response. The Brunner and Brunner study, although limited to the Toledo, Ohio, area, showed that multiple ownership of such items as air conditioning and color television was higher among listed than unlisted subscribers. The Trendex study shows unlisted proportionately greater among the younger, among nonwhites, and among the less educated. A Nielsen study[9] in two metropolitan areas confirms the finding that unlisteds are proportionately greater among dwellings in which the head of the household is black.

One exception is a Trendex study among over 50,000 listed and unlisted telephone homes, which showed that exclusion of unlisted homes from a sample had little impact on the results of questions about the purchase of consumer goods and media exposure.[10] But this single exception proves nothing. It means only that in the kinds of question covered, there was no difference between listed and unlisted homes. The lack of difference must—for any inquiry—be demonstrated as a fact. There is simply too much evidence of the likelihood of differences in response to questions among the two types of home. The burden of proof is on the person or firm who claims it makes no difference.

The Solution to Unlisted Numbers

The solution to the problem of unlisted numbers is the use of random-digit dialing. The idea of using random-digit dialing was first conceived of and used by Sanford Cooper,[11] now president of Burke Marketing Research. Cooper created these numbers by working with a crisscross directory—a directory which, among other things, lists numbers by exchange. This kept down the cost of using completely randomly selected digits for the last four digits of the number. Since, as will be shown, there are more unused than used exchange numbers, the use of completely random numbers would result in many, many wasted calls, and therefore increase costs. The various specific means of selecting random digits currently in continuing use all include some method to cut down on such waste. As of now no commercial firm utilizes crisscross directories for this purpose, for reasons shown a little later in this chapter.

SAMPLING FROM CRISSCROSS DIRECTORY LISTS

A crisscross directory, also known as a cross-reference or cross-index list, is a privately published directory showing listings by street name and number along the street, and by number listing within each exchange. These are published by twelve different firms across the United States, all members of the International Association of Cross-Reference Directories. A few are duplicated, with more than one company providing service for the area. These are generally published

TABLE 4-2
National Percentage of Unlisted Homes
for Selected Demographic Groups, 1973

	Listed Incorrectly	Unlisted By Request	Too New To Be Listed	Unlisted Total
TOTAL	.8%	13.3%	3.7%	17.8%
Region				
New England	.7	11.7	2.3	14.7
Middle Atlantic	.6	15.5	4.9	21.0
East Central	.5	12.1	2.2	14.8
West Central	.6	7.2	5.7	13.5
Southeast	.8	10.8	2.9	14.5
Southwest	1.1	8.0	6.4	15.5
Pacific	1.5	17.3	4.5	23.3
County Size*				
A	.7	20.1	3.3	24.1
B	.7	13.4	4.0	18.1
C	.8	6.1	3.8	10.7
D	.8	4.5	4.5	9.8
Annual Income				
Under $5,000	.9	9.7	3.6	14.2
$5,000–$9,999	.6	14.8	5.0	20.5
$10,000–$14,999	.6	15.0	4.4	20.0
$15,000 and over	1.0	12.7	2.9	16.6
Age of Children				
No children	.8	9.5	3.6	13.9
Children under 2	1.1	17.7	7.5	26.3
Children 2–5	1.1	17.9	5.6	24.6
Children 6–12	.7	17.9	2.9	21.5
Children 13–18	.5	16.0	1.5	18.0

TABLE 4-2
National Percentage of Unlisted Homes
for Selected Demographic Groups, 1973 (cont'd.)

	Listed Incorrectly	Unlisted By Request	Too New To Be Listed	Unlisted Total
Age of Male Head				
None	—	13.0	2.2	15.2
Under 25	2.5	13.7	12.6	28.8
25–34	.8	17.6	7.3	25.7
35–49	1.2	16.0	3.3	20.5
50 and over	.2	8.5	1.0	9.7
Age of Female Head				
None	1.8	10.9	7.3	20.1
Under 25	1.5	18.0	11.9	31.4
25–34	.7	19.0	6.5	26.2
35–49	1.1	15.2	1.9	18.2
50 and over	.2	6.5	.8	7.5

*These are Nielsen county sizes as follows:
A = 1,100,000 and over   C = 35,000 to 149,999
B = 150,000 to 1,099,999   D = Under 35,000

SOURCE: Marketing and Research Counselors national random-digit dialing study, with 3,004 respondents. Refusals to the question, totaling 183 respondents, were subtracted before calculating percents.

annually, covering complete city and suburban areas. There are about 375 of them throughout the United States. Some cities, such as Chicago, are broken into smaller areas.

Methods of Using Crisscross Directories

There are three methods of selecting a sample from these directories: the straight random method, the systematic method, and the stratified method.

Pure Random Method. In this method, all the community's streets, working from an official municipal map available at the office of the city engineer (or other appropriate official) are entered, on a deck of cards, one name to a card. The number of residential listings per street is recorded. These can be thoroughly shuffled, or more systematically, arranged alphabetically. Each card is numbered. Random numbers are selected, and the appropriate card containing the street name is selected. The number of residential listings on each card is accumulated, so that the researcher knows when enough streets have been selected to provide the total listings required. The appropriate numbers are then entered from the directory. A major difficulty in this procedure is that it requires a large number of clerical hours, and therefore is rarely used.

Shortened Systematic Method. This method is far less time-consuming. Pages within the directory are first selected on a systematic basis, following the procedure already outlined for use in the alphabetic directory. When the nth page of the book is selected, all telephone listings that fall within the particular geographic area of coverage are included, and the residential listings falling into the area are listed. If the selected page has no listings within the desired area, the next eligible forward or backward page is used. On each appropriate page, a systematic method of selecting residence listings is then feasible.

Stratified Method. This method is used by Market Opinion Research when a crisscross directory source is indicated, according to Louis Meier. An official municipal map is used to mark serpentine lines along streets. Each street is placed in a quadrant of the map. Streets are selected by quadrant, on a visual basis. Residential listings are counted for each street as it is selected.

This is not true random sampling, but it probably works reasonably well. The stratum is by quadrant. Additional subareas can be part of the stratum, if this happens to be desirable.

Problems in Using Crisscross Directories

None of these sample-selection methods, even though all seem far better than those available for personal and mail surveys, is without fault. There are at least five problems in the use of crisscross directories.

There Is No Standard Definition of Coverage. Some of the areas are covered as cities; some are parts of cities; some are counties; some are the even larger units, the Standard Metropolitan Statistical Areas. They would be much easier to work with if they were all accumulated on the standard basis of geographical definition.

Relatively Isolated Cities May Be Omitted. A moderate-sized city not close to a larger metropolitan center may be entirely skipped in the listing, largely because there is a restricted market for sale of such a list. (Most are used for personal selling and direct mail.) Athens and Chillicothe,

Ohio, both are missed, but Bowling Green, with a lower population than either, is included because it is close to Toledo.

These Directories Have at Least as Many Unlisteds as the Alphabetical Directories. These directories depend in part for their source upon alphabetical directories, and to that extent include as many unlisteds as the alphabeticals. In addition, those that do depend on the alphabeticals alone are even more out of date, since they are published after the alphabeticals.

These Directories Cannot Be Used for Demographic Selection. It might be considered feasible to use such directories to locate an ethnic group, for instance, since a particular ethnic group might center in a particular portion of a community. Income again is a specific demographic one might be tempted to try to isolate through the use of these geographically restricted lists.

Not so. Helen Wippich Greene of Valley Forge Information Service reports having tried the criss-cross-directory approach to contact families of Spanish extraction. It didn't work. The areas selected contained too high a proportion of non-Spanish families. And in most cities neighborhoods are too mixed economically to try to hit a particular income level efficiently, she reports.

The Method Is Expensive. Helen Greene also points out that the use of crisscross directories for sampling in telephone surveys is expensive. Even the most efficient of the sample-selection methods requires a huge amount of clerical time.

THE USE OF OTHER CONSUMER
LISTS FOR SAMPLING

The Marketing Information Center of the Reuben H. Donnelley Corporation is another potential source of a telephone sample.[12] Over the years, Donnelley has supplied marketers with lists of names, addresses, and telephone numbers of families throughout the United States, chiefly for mailing purposes. These lists are compiled from the 4700 telephone directories (and in some markets, the crisscross directories) published by various telephone companies. Within six weeks after publication of a new directory, Donnelley claims it has added 99 percent of the new residential listings and deleted those who have moved away. Donnelley estimates that its files contain essentially "all" listed residential telephone households, although some small independent rural directories may be missing.

Basically the Donnelley list of 53 million households is a summary of all alphabetical directories. But it is more than that, and that is why it is separately listed. In addition to the household's name, address, ZIP code and phone number (with area code) there are more than 50 other measurements: details of automobiles owned by the household, length of residence at the address, estimated family income in current dollars, estimated age of the household head, and some forty different census variables obtained from the block group, enumerative district, or tract in which the address is located.

Burke Marketing Research, Inc., works from a computer file of all listed telephones, updated annually. The basic file is arranged geographically, so that Burke can obtain subsamples of virtually any geographic unit desired. Any duplications have been eliminated.

The problem of not getting precise coverage of a civil unit, such as a county, is eliminated with the Burke set-up. It has been shown that both exchanges and telephone-company lists cross various civil-unit lines. With the Burke sampling procedure, it is possible to define exactly what civil units are wanted in coverage. These can correspond (for the first time in telephone surveys) with other marketing measurement units, such as Nielsen areas, Standard Metropolitan Statistical Areas, counties, sales territories, etc.

While the system is of obvious benefit in local surveys, the data can also be utilized to develop a national probability sample. The CMAS System (Custom Market Area Sampling) offers an advantage here. The arrangement of the numbers in the file is so ordered and weighted as to represent properly the denser population areas according to numbers of households—rather than numbers of telephones. Thus in Burke's national probability sample, Los Angeles County (which has about 52 percent of its telephones listed) and Ramsey County, Minnesota, (which has about 96 percent of its telephones listed) are each properly represented according to numbers of *households*.

Since this list is put together from lists published by the telephone company, it has the disadvantage of excluding unlisted numbers. When Burke wants to include the unlisted, it adds a digit to the number selected (a method further discussed a bit later in this chapter). However, to a slight degree this destroys Burke's ability to confine the sample completely to the specified area. The new number created sometimes is outside of the desired civil area.

SAMPLING FROM RANDOM-DIGIT NUMBERS

The differences between dwellings and individuals with listed telephones and those with unlisted telephones have been shown to be striking and significant. In the author's opinion, there is a need for some sort of random-digit-dialing sample on every telephone survey, unless it has previously been demonstrated that it makes no difference in results. There is a very real risk of misleading information if unlisted telephones are not included in the sample.

Are there problems of cooperation from the unlisted? These practically don't exist. Of all the major professional telephone research firms that were approached in connection with putting together the material for this book, only one indicated that it ran into difficulty with objections from those unlisted homes receiving calls. Instead of an objection, it is more common for the person to ask: "How did you get my number?" The response, "It was generated by a computer," is typically sufficient for the caller to continue. There simply is little or no resistance.

The obvious way to generate lists of random numbers is to get a list of all exchanges in operation, and then, with or without control of the number of digits to be generated for each exchange, simply to select four-digit numbers to be used. But the obvious way is an unworkable way, and this can be easily demonstrated.

There are presently 35,000 telephone exchanges (the first three numbers or letters following the area code). Each has a capacity of 10,000 specific lines or numbers (from 0000 to 9999). Thus total national capacity is 350,000,000 numbers. There are some 67,000,000 telephone households; 19 percent of the available numbers are now utilized by residences. Thus a completely random set of four-digit numbers for each exchange would result in four of five calls going to numbers not in use by residences. All methods of random digit selection for use in telephone surveys must—in one way or another—control for this situation. Otherwise the cost of telephone surveys would be unreasonably high.

Random-Digit Sampling from Alphabetical Directories

The most common method for random-digit dialing with the use of alphabetical telephone directories is the addition or subtraction of one or more digits from numbers selected in the directory. For example, suppose that in area code 419, exchange code 352, the number 0981 came up. If the system were to add a digit, the number 0982 would be used.

Some research firms add a digit; some subtract one. At least one firm uses an interval of three. Another uses a modification of ten numbers from the one selected in the book.

Lee Hite, of MARC, argues that the addition or subtraction of only a single digit contains a built-in bias towards listed numbers; he is certainly right that there is more chance of getting a listed number if only a one-number change is selected as compared with perhaps a ten-number change.

But this is the last stage of sampling. Firms which use this method of random-digit samples for a national sample have earlier stages of sample selection. Most of them are stratified.

MARC uses a three-stage probability sample. It first stratifies all the counties in the United States by region and by size of population. The second stage is selection of the counties within the sample. The total number of households in each county are entered, and the cumulative number of households, county by county within each cell (of the two strata) is entered. One number for each five interviews is then randomly selected. When this number corresponds to a household number sequence of the county list, the county becomes a part of the sample. The more populous counties come up with more selections, and thus there is a built-in self-correction for population size. By a semiannual updating process, new counties and new phone numbers are continually being added. In the current MARC data base over 95 percent of all the counties in the continental United States are represented.

The final stage is selection of telephone numbers. First, the telephone company provides the area code for the county, all three-digit telephone prefixes (exchanges) for the county, and all pertinent telephone directories. Then, all these directories are sampled for residential telephone numbers, although this is not the sample used for the survey; it is simply a sample to show the bands of numbers within each exchange that are in actual use. Finally, computer-generated ten-digit telephone numbers are generated. Any computer-generated number which falls within 100 digits up or down from the spread of those calculated in use from the directories will be printed out; all others are screened out.

Trendex has a national sample which is really only slightly different from this. It uses an 84-point sample stratified by area, by community size. It goes to the appropriate alphabetical directories, and sometimes uses random-digit dialing by upping the directory choice by 1, 10, etc.

Opinion Research Corporation has a national sample selected from 360 counties in the contiguous forty-eight states (six subsamples of sixty counties each). Minor political divisions are selected as Primary Sampling Units within each selected county. These are selected with a probability proportionate to population; this determines which telephone books are used in drawing the sample. Telephone numbers of apparently residential listings are randomly selected, with an equal number from each Primary Sampling Unit. A fixed-quantity digit is added to the listed number drawn.

Marketing Information Service has one of the more sophisticated systems of using directories to end up with random digits. Basically the company uses a stratified cluster (area) sample with samples of differing sizes in different areas. Their procedure is essentially for local areas, but could readily be modified to accommodate national samples.

A random sample of exchanges is selected, using a template. The template is simply a piece of heavy paper with holes cut in it to allow certain listings to show through. The holes are selected by drawing random numbers between 1 and the average number of listings per page.

This is used to provide a frequency distribution of exchanges. The number of interviews is then assigned to each exchange proportionate to this distribution. Series of random four-digit numbers are then selected by exchange.

Problems with Random-Digit Numbers Created from Directory Listings. The greatest problem—and there is no measurement at present as to how great it is—is that new exchanges are missed. Thus if a new exchange is added by a telephone company to accommodate a new development, this will be missed since it did not get into the telephone book as yet. Since alphabetical directories are published annually, on the average this means that new exchanges created within the past six months are omitted. There would seem to be two kinds of sampling bias resulting. First, a segment of the new home buyers is omitted; if purchase of household equipment were the subject of the survey being done, this could cause some error. Second, since people moving into new housing tend to be younger, rather than middle-aged, an age bias could be caused.

The other problem is a practical one faced by the research firm conducting the study. Many useless calls are completed. Jim Sammer, of Walker Research, says that many calls are completed to telephone booths, service stations, and morticians, to mention just a few. This problem results in increased costs to the buyer of such a survey.

Random-Digit Samples Not Using Telephone Directories

A few research firms use random-digit samples without dependence on telephone directories to avoid the problem of bias resulting from use only of listed exchanges. All companies utilizing this sort of sample prearrange their lists by area, size of the list, etc. The Research Information Center, Inc., utilizes such a sample. Hilda Barnes, president, reports that in any national study the universe is defined as people living in telephone homes in the forty-eight contiguous states. (Similar techniques, she reports, are followed in studies that are less than national in scope.) Survey cases are allocated to each state according to the number of resident telephones there. Within each state, telephone exchanges are selected with equal probability from all exchanges in the state. Four-digit random numbers are selected by the computer for each sample exchange, with an equal number of such numbers in each exchange. Completed residence telephone calls within each exchange therefore come out proportionately in relationship to the actual number of resident telephones within that exchange.

Chilton Research[13] has a slightly different approach. It employs a two-stage national sample. The first stage is selection of the exchanges in which work is to be done. The universe of central offices, obtained from the telephone company, is identified with the county each one serves. Standard Metropolitan Statistical Areas within four regions are classified by descending order of size. Nonmetropolitan counties are arranged in contiguous serpentine order (north to south—east to west) within region. Central offices are then cumulated county by county down the master list. Selection of the telephone exchanges is then done on a systematic, cumulative residence telephone listing.

Four-digit numbers are generated for each exchange. Then an equal number of these are selected for each exchange. Some 80 percent of nonworking numbers are eliminated without need for dialing by checking the central office of the appropriate telephone company to obtain banks of nonworking numbers. These data are put into the computer before the numbers are drawn, so that only numbers drawn outside of these banks will be generated; Chilton reports that about 40 percent of the ten-digit numbers which are dialed are households.

Walker Research is building a stratified national sample which does not depend on directories. However, Jim Sammer reports that they have not been able to get the cooperation of the telephone company in providing lists of working exchanges, so they won't depend on the telephone company either. Instead, they will do a national study annually, dialing various potential exchange codes to determine which are working exchanges. This sample will be a 2000-point sample stratified by population, by state, and by exchange. The last three digits of the number will be randomly generated.

Problems with Random-Digit Numbers Not Using Telephone Directories. There is one problem inherent in all such surveys: higher costs of conducting the study, which have to be passed on to the buyer. These higher costs result because unused and nonresidence incidence is higher than in dealing with numbers out of telephone books.

Another problem sometimes present is lack of cooperation of the particular telephone company. Where the telephone company will not cooperate fully, the program is in danger.

SELECTION OF THE RIGHT RESPONDENT

Once the residence telephone number has been selected for potential inclusion in the survey, there is still the question of who within the household is to be questioned specifically. More often than not, there is only one person in the household who is qualified. It may be the person who does the grocery shopping, the person who does the most driving, the person primarily responsible for purchasing tires for the automobile, the person primarily responsible for taking care of the cat, the adult male head of the household, the adult female head of the household, etc.

But in other cases—in population surveys, as Lee Hite terms them— there has to be some sort of random selection of the person within the household.

Kish[14] was the first to tackle this problem. In his classic paper of 1949, he presented a method for selecting one adult per household. All adult occupants of the particular household, with their relationship to the head of household, and his or her sex and age are determined. A number is then assigned to each. The interviewer is provided with six tables, each indicating the number of the individual within the household to be selected, varying with the total number of adults in the family.

Troldahl and Carter[15] introduced a modification in 1964. The impetus for this modification came from the increasing use of telephone surveys. The interest of the person at the other end of the telephone must be held long enough to complete the interview with the proper individual, and there was simply too much likelihood, with the time-consuming Kish technique, that the telephone would be hung up.

The Troldahl-Carter technique is simple. It asks only two questions before the interviewer goes to the tables to select the respondent:

1. How many persons 18 years or older live in your household, including yourself?

2. How many of them are men?

The selection technique allows for up to four adults and two of the same sex per household. There are four sets of tables which the interviewer uses in successive rotation to determine whether a man or a woman is to be questioned, and whether it is the younger or older male or female, if there are two of the same sex.

Dr. Barbara Bryant,[16] of Market Opinion Research, demonstrated in several studies conducted in 1973 and 1974 that the Trohdahl-Carter method produced proportionately too many female respondents. This was due largely to the greater mobility of males (they are more often not at home than females), and the disproportionate number of females in one-, three-, four-, and five-member households. With some pragmatic experimentation, Dr. Bryant came up with a series of tables paralleling those of the original Trohldahl-Carter method, but dropping out one of the four tables every second time around, so that this sequence would be followed in each seven interviews: Table 1, Table 2, Table 3, Table 4, Table 1, Table 2, and Table 3. A field test showed that this produced completed interviews with about the right proportion of adult males in terms of census data.

SOME MECHANICAL ASPECTS OF SAMPLING

At least two such aspects should be mentioned.

The Professional Telephone Survey Firm Always Provides the List of Selected Telephone Numbers to Its Interviewers

The professional telephone survey firm never, even when working from directories or other lists, has its interviewers look up telephone numbers. These are always supplied, for two important reasons. One reason is that selection of the lists calls for professional, meticulous, clerical talent, and the work should be done under supervision. Otherwise, there is too much risk of dilution of purity of the sample chosen. The other reason stems from the frequent use of WATS lines by the professional telephone research firm. It has already been stressed that the high rental cost of these lines means that there can be little "down" time; the research firm finds it essential to keep these lines in use as much of the time as possible. It cannot afford to take the interviewer away from his or her key job: using one of those lines.

The List Provided for Dialing Must Be Many
Times the Total Interviews Required

Market Opinion Research, for instance, in consumer surveys, provides
a list size which is anywhere from four to ten times the number of
required interviews. This sounds as though the completion rate is too
low. This is not the case, as many lines have been disconnected, many
are business telephones, and for many there is repeatedly no answer.

CALL-BACKS AND COMPLETIONS

The completion rate is the proportion of legitimate attempts which
yield a completed interview. Call-backs refer to repeated attempts by the
interviewer to get an interview. Call-backs and completions are closely
related. Since the completion rate reflects purity of the sample, the topic
is considered here rather than in Chapter 6.

A call-back may be made under any of several conditions:

1. When the respondent is too busy at the time of the original
   contact (and then an appointment is made)

2. When the correct respondent is not at home (and then the
   interviewer generally asks about a good time to call)

3. When there is no answer to the telephone ring

4. When the line is busy

The first two kinds are easy to handle, and need not be discussed.

There is no set pattern on how professional telephone research firms
handle the problem of call-backs, or even the set of conditions under
which call-backs are made. Most firms do not take a busy signal as an
attempted call at all. The Data Group Incorporated takes two busy
signals as one attempt. Some take the first busy signal as one attempt.

The timing of the call-back attempt also varies by firm. The Data
Group Incorporated uses a "differential" call-back procedure. The first
call-back attempt is made on a weekday during the day or evening, as
required. The second is made on the next weekday during the evening
or day (reverse of the first call-back attempt). The third is made sometime over the weekend.

Sylvia Barr, of Walker Research, says that her firm, after the first
attempt, generally makes one call-back. If the original call was made
during the day, the re-call is made at night. If the first attempt was at

night, the re-call is during the day. On some studies three attempts are made. The firm has some evidence which suggests that day—night—night might produce a higher completion rate.

The Advertising Research Foundation sets a standard of 80 percent completion as the minimum acceptable on studies which are to receive its stamp of approval. But the average survey for management action does not need such a level. The problem is the base from which to calculate completions, for not all dialings should be included. The Advertising Research Foundation suggests that the following be dropped from the base:

1. Confirmed nonworking numbers

2. Confirmed nonhousehold numbers (businesses, government, telephone booths, etc.)

3. Duplicate numbers

4. Ineligible households (no person of designated age or sex, for instance)

5. Estimated proportion of nonreached households that represent nonhouseholds

6. Estimated proportion of ineligible households among households whose eligibility is not established

Estimates for points 5 and 6 are calculated from the experience of interviewing.

These exclusions from the base seem sound.

How many call-backs should be made on a typical consumer study? This is not the right question to start with, but it is the practical question. The underlying question is: What completion rate should be aimed for?

The problem is answering this question is that the completion rate depends on so many variables. If the study concentrates on highly urbanized areas, since people in these areas are very mobile, completion rates per attempt will be less than if the study is only in rural areas. If the study is one primarily among the upper-income class, completion rates will be lower than those in a broader economic spectrum, for the same reason. If the study happens to be conducted during a bad-weather period, completion rates will be higher because people tend to stay at home more during bad weather. The number of telephone rings allowed by the research firm affects completions: the greater the num-

TABLE 4-3
Cumulative Completion Rate in Three Attempts in Two
National Studies by The Data Group Incorporated

	Attempt 1	Attempt 2	Attempt 3
Random Number Probability (Listings 15,718)	35.2%	56.3%	67.6%
Telephone Directory (Listings 4,812)	43.1%	58.9%	68.9%

NOTE: Nonworking numbers, nonhousehold numbers, and completed calls in which there was no eligible respondent have been eliminated from the base.

ber of rings, the higher the answering rate. The completion rate varies by sex, age, region, or other requirements for eligibility of interview. It varies by time of day required for the telephoning.

Despite all these caveats, there is a bit of hard evidence. Take a look at Table 4-3. In national studies conducted by The Data Group Incorporated, it is evident that three attempts, whether from a random-digit sample or a telephone directory sample, produce close to 70 percent response. We have taken data on completion rates of total completed interviews (not attempts) from another firm to come up with estimates that the fourth attempt will produce a completion rate of 71 percent, the fifth, 72 percent. At this level of call-backs, the productive rate increase becomes low indeed. For practical purposes it appears that two call-backs is the right place to stop. Costs rise too sharply without increasing completions significantly past that point.

REFERENCES

[1]*Phonefiche: Current Telephone Directories on Microfiche,* Wooster, Ohio, Micro Photo Division, Bell & Howell, undated.

[2]A. B. Blankenship, "Listed vs. Unlisted Numbers in Telephone Survey Samples," *Journal of Advertising Research,* vol. 17, Feb. 1976, pp. 39–42.

[3]G. J. Glasser and G. D. Metzger, "National Estimates of Unlisted Telephones and Their Characteristics," *Journal of Marketing Research,* vol. 12, Aug. 1975, pp. 359–361.

[4]Blankenship, op. cit.

[5]Glasser and Metzger, op. cit.

[6]D. A. Leuthold and Raymond Scheele, "Patterns of Bias in Samples Based on Telephone Directories," *Public Opinion Quarterly,* vol. 35, Summer 1971, pp. 249–257.

[7]J. A. Brunner and G. A. Brunner, "Are Voluntarily Unlisted Telephone Subscribers Really Different?" *Journal of Marketing Research,* vol. 8, Feb. 1971, pp. 121–124.

[8]Blankenship, op. cit.

[9]Blankenship, op. cit.

[10]"Surveys Altered Little by Exclusion of 'Unlisteds,'" *Advertising Age,* Oct. 11, 1976.

[11]Sanford L. Cooper, "Random Dialing by Telephone—An Improved Method, *Journal of Marketing Research,* vol. 1, Nov. 1964, pp. 45–48.

[12]*Probability Sampling Service: User's Manual,* New York, Reuben H. Donnelley Corporation, 1975.

[13]*A National Probability Sample of Telephone Households Using Computerized Sampling Techniques,* Radnor, Pa., Chilton Research Services, undated.

[14]Leslie Kish, "A Procedure for Objective Respondent Selection within the Household," *American Statistical Association Journal,* 1949, pp. 382–387.

[15]Verling Troldahl and Ray E. Carter, Jr., "Random Selection of Respondents within Households in Phone Surveys," *Journal of Marketing Research,* vol. 1, May 1964, pp. 71–76.

[16]Barbara E. Bryant, "Respondent Selection in a Time of Changing Household Composition," *Journal of Marketing Research,* vol. 12, May 1975, pp. 129–135.

QUESTIONNAIRE CONSTRUCTING AND TESTING

The questionnaire is the list of questions used when interviewing respondents. It normally is reproduced on sheets of paper, except where the CRT is used, in which case individual questions are flashed on the screen.

One major purpose of the questionnaire is to provide an instrument which will measure reactions through use of a standard stimulus. If during each interview, the investigator could decide just how the question were to be asked, the results would be meaningless because of a lack of standardization.

A second major purpose is to minimize response error; response error is an error by the respondent which provides incorrect or misleading information. Response error, such as faulty recall, can never be completely eliminated, but a serious effort must be made to hold it to a minimum. A poorly constructed questionnaire, with poor phrasing and sequence, contributes to additional response error.

A third major purpose is to minimize recording error. The duplicated questionnaire includes space for recording. Both nature of the phrasing and of the recording space and alternatives contribute to accurate recording.

There are three parts of the usual questionnaire: the introduction, the body or content, and the basic data. The introduction obtains quick cooperation from the respondent. The body or content of the questionnaire covers the subject matter inherent to solving the problem under investigation. The basic data include classification data (demographics, such as sex and age) and identification data (name, telephone number, city, and state).

Content covers a number of areas. One is facts and knowledge. These place an emphasis on accuracy of both reporting and recording. For example, a reporting question could be "What make of refrigerator do you have in your home?" or "What airline advertises, 'Fly the friendly skies of _____'?"

Opinions are another area. These represent the respondent's stated attitudes towards ideas, products, institutions, etc. This type of content requires an extremely careful questioning form to ensure that it really conveys the topic about which the attitude is being measured. The questions themselves must be unbiased. An example of a biased or leading question is "Do you like the friendly attitude of the cabin crews on airlines?"

Motives, another content area, are the real reasons underlying behavior or opinion. Such questions are unusually difficult to phrase. There must be a skilled use of probing for obtaining a deep-seated response, rather than acceptance of the first superficial reply. But the probing has to be of a neutral type.

In the measure of past behavior, passage of time may cloud memory. To improve recall, the question designer often uses memory aids. Sometimes, as with coincidental radio surveys, the errors of memory are eliminated or minimized through measuring methods that avoid memory and ask for immediate experience instead.

Occasionally, possible future behavior is asked for. Even the experts have a less-than-perfect record in this respect, for often respondents cannot predict what they will do in the future. Too many events change their thinking, and the farther into the future the respondents are asked to make such predictions, the greater the liklihood that the predictions will be inaccurate. It has been found, for instance, that if a cross-section of people are asked about their plans to buy a refrigerator within six months, the heaviest proportion with such plans typically report that the brand will be General Electric. Their buying, on the other hand, does not follow that pattern.

GENERAL TYPES OF QUESTIONS

Questions, according to their structure, can be grouped into three classes: open-ended, multiple-choice, and value-judgment questions.

Open-Ended Questions

These are questions for which the possible responses are not provided: the respondent constructs a reply without specific aid from the investigator.

The Completely Open-Ended Question. The question is asked in such a way that no limits are placed on the range of possible replies. Some examples are:

Why did you buy this brand? (Actually a poor question, used only to illustrate the question type)

Where do you plan to go on your next vacation?

What kind of work do you hope to get into when you are graduated?

One of the most common, and advantageous, uses of the completely open-ended question is questionnaire development where the researcher does not know enough about the probable range of replies, but ultimately hopes to end up with a question for which at least the main alternatives of response can be prelisted.

This type of question also permits the respondents to say exactly what they want, without placing any restrictions on their reactions. Finally, if quotable responses are wished, this is the way to get them. In practice, the open-ended question in the quantitative telephone survey has many more limitations than advantages. It is difficult to get the right amount of interviewer skill to ask it, especially with the neutral probe questions which are such a necessary part of the process. There is a much greater risk of interviewer bias. There is no way, even with the best of interviewers, that all the respondent's words can possibly be recorded, so excerpts of what the person says have to be selected. Psychologists know that we often hear what we want to hear, and it is likely to be so with the questioner.

The respondent often assumes that the interviewer understands the "obvious," but the interviewer may paint a stroke with a different color when writing the reply. The depth and length of the reply depends too much on the interviewer, and varies by the investigator. Those who interpret the written replies—translating the answers to numbers that can be entered into the computer—can attest to the difficulty of trying to decide whether a particular reply falls into one category or another. They can also tell about the difficulty of being completely consistent throughout a study in their interpretation; it is easy to shift one's interpretations over a time period. Also, the whole process of coding is laborious and time-consuming, and therefore expensive. One last disadvantage is that the use of the completely open-ended question overweights the replies of the higher socioeconomic groups. These are the more literate people, who know how to express themselves. This group gives the fuller, more elaborate set of replies to an open-ended question.

The Directed Open-Ended Question. This sort of question superficially appears identical with the completely open-ended question, but there is a subtle difference. The directed open-ended question is asked with a phrasing that directs the nature of the reply along some predetermined line. Some examples are:

What mechanical advantages does a Chrysler engine have?

What is there about the flavor of the product that appeals to you?

The evaluation of this sort of question parallels that of the completely open-ended question. On the advantage side it is easier to classify the replies, since they do not cover the side range of the completely open-ended questions. On the negative side, there is the possibility that the line covered may be of little or no importance to the respondent. In the case of the Chrysler engine question, the respondent may feel that basically the Chrysler engine has few mechanical advantages, yet he or she may mention the electronic ignition system simply because the question was asked.

The Restricted Open-Ended Question. This, too, superficially appears to be a completely open-ended question, but in reality, a finite limit of answers exists, whether on the questionnaire or not. Consider some examples:

What make of refrigerator do you own?

How many cups of coffee did you drink yesterday?

How long have you lived in Bowling Green?

What was the weather like yesterday?

This kind of question does not match the other two forms of open-ended questions in advantages and disadvantages. It is easy to ask. It does not inherently require a tremendously high level of skill on part of the questioner. It is not subject to the possible interviewer bias that the others have. It can be asked and recorded quickly. It can be coded easily.

Multiple-Choice Questions

There are three types: the dichotomous question, the subjective-choice question, and the objective-choice question.

The Dichotomous Question. The dichotomous or binary question offers two possibilities from which one is to be selected, and the two are at opposite ends of the same scale. Examples are:

Do you own or rent this home?

Did you read a newspaper yesterday?

Was your television set on yesterday?

Did you do any grocery shopping within the past three days (including today)?

This kind of question is fast. It is probably the very easiest type of question for the investigator to handle. There is little chance for interviewer bias. It is easy to get responses, for the respondent can generally tell immediately what the question is all about. It is simple to code in preparation for the computer.

On the negative side, there is the risk that a dichotomous question will be constructed from content which should not be used that way. In an attitude query, a question that might be asked is "Do you feel that the federal government is doing all that it can to hold down inflation, or do you not?" This has become a leading or biased question, because it does not offer the respondent the option of having no opinion on the topic. Another example of forcing the choice between two options when there should be more comes from a somewhat different field: "Did you have your television set on for more than an hour yesterday?"

The Subjective-Choice Question. Sometimes known as the cafeteria question, this lists a choice of answers which have been compiled from completely or directed open-ended questions, using the major answer categories received from a sample of people who have been the question in open-ended form. This step is taken so as to reduce interviewer error and simplify recording and coding. The answers may or may not be read to the respondents; if they are not read they are simply listed on the questionnaire or shown on the CRT for the investigator to indicate the reply category. In this case there is a category left for "all other" or "miscellaneous" replies—those replies outside the array of responses prelisted.

The major advantage to this form of questioning is ease of conducting the study (questioning, recording, coding). However, it runs risks. One or more important categories may be unintentionally missed. Studies have shown that when a list is presented, respondents will add such a reply if it is not on the list far less often than select the reply if it is on the list.

The Objective-Choice Question. This is the conversion of the restricted open-ended question to a question which prelists all known alternatives. Instead of stopping when the make of refrigerator is asked, all known makes of refrigerator are listed. The list may be included in the question, or at the end of the question (for use of the interviewer only).

The major advantage of this prelisting is ease of recording the reply and coding it. However, if it is a quantitative type of question, then presenting the respondent with the alternatives can lead to a bias of replies. If a question is asked about how many hours television was watched in the past 3 days including today, then the categories might be:

0

1–3

4–6

7–9

10–13

14–17

18 or more

In a quantitative series of replies such as this, there is a tendency of many respondents to select a choice somewhere towards the middle of the scale.

Value-Judgment Questions Sometimes known as rating questions, these kinds of questions are frequent in marketing research. A value judgment question asks for the respondent's degree of opinion about an issue or an object. There are two major types of value-judgment questions used in consumer and opinion research: the ordinal-scale question and the interval-scale question.

The Ordinal-Scale Question. This is a question in which the series of replies are ranked. For instance:

> Please rank these three brands of beer according to your idea of their price (from high to low): Lowenbrau, Carling, Pabst.

There is no attempt to measure the distance between the ranks. It is not possible to assign numerical values to replies; the only treatment possible is a summary of the number of times each brand was named as first, second, and third.

The ranking may be limited to a single comparison between two elements only, in which case it is often called a paired comparison question. An example is "In your opinion, which make of automobile gives greater mileage: a Buick or a Ford?"

The Interval-Scale Question. This question also ranks, but there is an effort made to hold the distance between the ranks equal. A simple example of this is the semantic-differential, which provides a 7-point scale, showing only the extreme word descriptions at either end of the scale, and the respondent is asked to choose the position along the scale which best represents his or her judgment or opinion. For example:

This product is

High priced ⎯ ⎯ ⎯ ⎯ ⎯ ⎯ ⎯ Low priced

High quality ⎯ ⎯ ⎯ ⎯ ⎯ ⎯ ⎯ Low quality

There are many additional forms that interval-scale questions can take, but it is unnecessary to present all of them here.

SOME GENERAL PRINCIPLES OR RULES OF THUMB
ABOUT QUESTIONNAIRE CONSTRUCTION

Questionnaire construction is an art, not a science. If twenty different research experts were given an outline of subject matter, and each asked to construct a questionnaire, there would be twenty different, unique questionnaires. Each one might be good, or even bad.

The form of the questionnaire takes depends partly on the nature of the content. It must always be built around the content, and conform to the requirements of the content, in terms of phrasing and sequence. If it is crucial to establish with a high certainty whether a person has seen a particular television show, then the recall questions will have to take up a large part of the questioning, and many probing questions about the detail of the show and/or commercials must be included to make sure that viewing really did occur.

The nature of the population being sampled on a survey also affects the form that the questionnaire takes. A personal health study done among the general population uses a far different vocabulary than one done among practicing physicians, where technical terminology is more common. A study done among lower-income people considers the simplicity of vocabulary to a far greater extent than one done among upper-income respondents.

The nature of the interviewers also affects the form that the question-naire takes. Completely open-ended questions should be included only if the interviewing organization has really first-rate investigators, and knows how to train them. Many professional telephone survey firms grade their interviewers, and not only adjust the questionnaire to the skill of the investigator, but match the skill of the investigator to the difficulty of the questionnaire.

Finally, the nature of the medium affects the nature of the question-naire. In this book we are concerned with telephone interviewing, not primarily the mail or the personal survey. Special considerations about the nature of the telephone questionnaire are so important that these are examined in a section which follows this discussion of general principles of questionnaire construction.

The Introduction and Opening Questions Must
Create Respondent Rapport

Respondent rapport must be created early. If not, too many interviews will be broken off. The completion rate will drop, and if the drop is precipitous, this could endanger the purity of the sample.

The introduction must be simple and to the point. It is something usually as short as, "This is Mrs. Smith, from Metro Surveys, in Philadelphia. We are doing a survey on _____, and I'd like to ask you a few questions."

The time required to answer the questions should never be misrepresented. This could lead to an early termination of the interview; even worse, over the long run, it could antagonize respondents against telephone surveys.

The opening questions must be simple and interesting. If it is essential to include dull questions or difficult ones—as it well may be on some studies—these should be placed well within the body of the questionnaire, after rapport has been established.

Questions Should Not Be Ambiguous

Questions should be phrased in such a way that they mean the same thing to every person being questioned. Some words or phrases may have different meanings to different people—they can be interpreted in different ways. Sometimes the wording may be difficult, or the vocabulary not understood. Consider this example:

What kind of cereal did you have for breakfast this morning?

This could be interpreted in at least four different ways. First, it might be interpreted as meaning *hot* versus *cold*. Second, it could be taken as concerning the form of the finished product: *flake, puffed, granule,* etc. Third, it might be the *brand* that the interrogator is after. Or fourth, it could be taken as meaning the nature of the grain: *corn, wheat, oats,* etc. The question should probably be a short series:

What brand of cereal did you have this morning for breakfast?

(Appropriate to each brand) Was that a flake or a puff?

The question "Is the electric utility in your community publicly or privately owned?" is ambiguous. If your utility *is* a profit-seeking company, some people might still report that it was publicly owned because shares are available to the public for purchase.

The completely open-ended question runs a particularly high risk of being ambiguous. The question "Why did you buy this brand of toothpaste?" is ambiguous because one person may answer in terms of an attribute of the product ("It cleans my teeth better."), another in terms of influence ("I saw it advertised on television."), a third in terms of personal tendencies ("We have to economize these days because of inflation, and this was the cheapest on a per-unit basis."). It would be far better to have three separate questions:

> What is there about the toothpaste, itself, if anything, which made you buy this brand?
>
> Was there anything you saw or heard about this brand of toothpaste that made you buy it?
>
> What personal or family factors, if any, made you buy this brand of toothpaste?

The researcher's own background can contribute to ambiguities in the questionnaire. Marketing researchers may slip into marketing jargon, which won't make much sense to most of the consumers with whom they are trying to communicate. Terms such as *markup, national brand, variety store,* or *direct marketing* are not likely to be understood.

Questions Must Be Psychologically Sound

Each question should be, where possible, related to specific experiences of the respondent. In one case[1] it was necessary to determine the amount of beer that people consumed. There were three difficulties: First, people cannot project such behavior over a long time period; the questions must be specific, otherwise answers will be ambiguous. Second, many people do not care to admit that they are beer drinkers. Third, heavy beer drinkers may not want to confess to the quantity of beer they put away.

The first difficulty is resolved by deciding to make any final measurement for a short time period. The second difficulty is resolved by asking three questions in rapid-fire sequence, after the interviewer has explained that this is for the study of people's brand preference within product classes. The first question is "What is your favorite brand of soap? toothpaste? beer?" There is no danger that the nonuser of a product will name a beer. There is no reason to do so, and the respondent will be identified as a nonuser.

The second question is "Now let's talk about the amount of beer you drink. Into which of these groups do you happen to fall, so far as beer drinking is concerned?" At this point the following display card is shown (in telephone interview it could be read):

Amount of Beer Consumed Weekly

A. HEAVY BEER DRINKER (over 60 bottles or cans a week)

B. MEDIUM-HEAVY BEER DRINKER (49 to 60 bottles or cans a week)

C. MEDIUM BEER DRINKER (37 to 48 bottles or cans a week)

D. MODERATE BEER DRINKER (25 to 36 bottles or cans a week)

E. FAIRLY LIGHT BEER DRINKER (13 to 24 bottles or cans a week)

F. LIGHT BEER DRINKER (7 to 12 bottles or cans a week)

G. VERY LIGHT BEER DRINKER (under 7 bottles or cans a week)

This question leads the respondent to think that no matter how much beer he or she typically consumes, there are others who drink more, and so there is no reason not to admit to the level of his or her drinking. Finally, the question that is asked is "How many bottles or cans did you happen to drink in the past 7 days?" These questions produced results paralleling gallonage figures reported in terms of government taxes within a area.

If a person must tell a little white lie to protect his or her pride, the person will often do so. If the most truthful reply is wanted, some method of removing the pride connotation from the question must be utilized. This was true in the beer example. Here is just one more example: Some years ago, Dr. George Gallup wanted to determine how many people had read a particular best-selling novel. Sales data for the book would not give an answer, since some copies, especially those in libraries, are read by more than one person. On the other hand, if he asked in a poll whether or not the individual had read the novel, pride would make a number of people say yes when they had not. So he simply asked, "Do you intend to read _____?" Those who had read it almost automatically reported the fact, and all the nonreaders were given a chance to salvage their pride by saying that they intended to do so.

Where Possible, Questions Should
Refer to Objective Behavior

The phrasing of the question should parallel the experience of the respondent, so as to measure, where feasible, specific behavior rather than broad generalizations made by the respondent. If, in the New York City metropolitan area, you ask, "What newspapers do you usually read?" the proportion naming *The New York Times* will be overstated. This isn't necessarily because respondents try to mislead.

If the question is phrased, "What newspaper did you happen to read yesterday?" then results paralleling circulation will be obtained.

Intensity of the Phrasing Influences the Reply

If a question is phrased extremely, it will show a skewing of the response distribution. It's generally better to use phrasing which is middle-of-the-road.

Here is an example of an extreme phrasing:

> Is the speed of the service at McDonald's all you could expect?

This is extreme because there are relatively few people who could not find they were delayed occasionally, if they dealt there long enough. So a better phrasing is this:

> Is the speed of the service at McDonald's reasonably good?

This much milder phrasing will obtain a substantially higher proportion of *yes* replies, and probably will provide a much fairer measurement of the relative public acceptance of the speed of service.

The Questions Should Be
Nonemotional and Unbiased

Some words and phrases are emotionally tinged and biased, causing positive or negative reactions to the words or phrases themselves, and overpower the total content of the question. Thus the reactions produced are more related to the word or phrase than to the question itself. A few such words and phrases are *civil rights, communism, big business, unions, power hungry, jet set, chauvinism, women's lib, old fashioned,* and *modern.* Most of these examples happen to fall in the category of words that would apply more to social and public opinion surveys than marketing, but they are no less real for that.

Even in marketing research, some words or brand names carry emotional connotations. The term "premium beer" attached to a brand in a survey may positively affect the replies, and the term "price brand" could negatively affect replies.

Length of the Questionnaire Must Be Relative to the Interest of the Subject Matter

As mentioned in Chapter 3, permissible length of the interview (therefore of the questionnaire) is largely a function of the inherent respondent interest in the topic and the questions. However, some users of marketing research believe that there should be a limit imposed by the user. Illinois Bell reports that its average questionnaire runs 7 minutes, though on occasion it has one taking as long as 35 minutes.

Personal Questions Should Be Well within the Body of the Questionnaire

This refers primarily to topics which are not often discussed openly with friends, let alone strangers. Questions about income, age, and bodily functions fit into such a category, yet each of these sometimes has to be included in a series of questions. Certain areas of opinion are sensitive, particularly concerning political or widely debated social issues. At the time that the residents of Boston were most uptight against busing, conducting a telephone survey on the topic and hoping to get sensible answers might have been difficult at best. Certainly such questions would have to wait until complete rapport had been established.

Questions Which Reflect the Respondent's "Intelligence" Should Be Well within the Body of the Questionnaire

If the question or a series of questions are apt to make the respondent feel "ignorant," "uninformed," or "unintelligent," not only must they be extremely carefully phrased, but they should never be asked before a high level of rapport has been established.

Suppose that the study asked about the respondent's knowledge of a number of federal agency functions, or included questions asking for brand or company identification of a number of advertising slogans. In either case, many respondents would have to give a successive string of "don't know" replies, and the average respondent would be somewhat embarrassed. If the researcher is not careful about introducing such questions, and placing them well along in the series of questions, there could be a high proportion of terminations.

Questions with Little Respondent Interest Must Be Well within the Body of the Questionnaire

The same admonition occurs with questions of a low interest level. If such questions are asked too early in the investigation, before a moderately good level of rapport has been established, some people will hang up.

What sorts of topics? Well, the details of what a grocery shopper takes into account when buying staples such as baking soda, sugar, detergents, etc., would be pretty low on a general-interest scale. So would a reaction level to the detailed parts of a proposed local ordinance.

Questions Should Be Asked in Proper Psychological Sequence

One question should lead to the next, setting up a train of thought. A sudden, totally unrelated question becomes somewhat difficult for respondents to cope with. It not only upsets them, but upsets their train of thinking, throwing them off. Many people do not answer the sudden, unrelated question, or they may give an "undecided" reply.

In one case a survey among employees of a particular firm covering attitudes about their fellow workers and supervisors was being conducted. It was necessary to gain the confidence of these workers before asking some of the sensitive questions, and the principal subjects of interest had to be introduced cautiously and gradually. The first few queries concerned the government and its effect on inflation. Questions followed about employment conditions in general, then about the respondent's own neighborhood and friends, and finally about several personal things. From these questions it was then relatively easy to ask questions such as:

How regular has your work been in the past year?

How long have you worked for your present employer?

Do you intend to stay with your employer in the future?

In another study the concern was to determine why people went to motion pictures, how they decided whom to invite to accompany them, and how they selected the particular show. Preliminary study indicated that those primarily interested in the company had to be questioned somewhat differently from those who selected a particular show. Those with primary interest in the picture were first asked how they had selected the particular film, with follow-up questions on how they selected their company and how they determined the particular time. Those primarily interested in general entertainment and company were first asked how they decided to go to the movies, how they happened to choose their company, and then how they decided on the particular show. The recall process was aided by asking the questions in the same order in which the decisions were made.

The Question Sequence May Lead to Response Bias

This occurs primarily with memory-type questions. If questions concern the recall of advertising detail that the person has recently been exposed to, these must be asked prior to the asking of any questions about brand recall or the buying of the product class. Such questions, asked first, artificially raise the level of correct recall to the advertising.

Bias in the reply to attitude questions can also be affected by question sequence. One questionnaire covering the topic of potato chips asked several questions about the purchase and consumption of chips. They were of a nature which made the respondent think primarily about regional and local chips. A number of questions, for instance, stressed brands in local stores. Finally, a question was asked about what brand the respondent considered best. This was intended to cover other than local and regional brands, but the direction of the earlier question made most respondents answer in terms of local and regional brands.

SOME SPECIFIC PRINCIPLES ABOUT TELEPHONE QUESTIONNAIRES

The principles outlined up to now have applications to all forms of questioning, including mail, personal, and telephone. However, the special nature of telephone questioning requires some additional, special care in constructing the questionnaire. There is no interviewer there in person to smooth out the rough edges and to persuade the respondent to continue if there are problems. The respondent can terminate the interview with a flick of the wrist and doesn't have to be bothered by the upset caused to the interviewer, who is not visible. The interviewer disappears from the scene forever once that telephone is hung up. With the mail questionnaire there are different problems, but if the respondent loses interest, there is at least the option of putting the questionnaire aside and returning to it some other time. No so with the telephone interview. Once lost, it is irretrievably lost.

The First Few Seconds Are Critical

The first few seconds determine whether or not the potential respondent is going to continue with the interview. While some suggestions for the introductory remarks on the questionnaire have already been provided, these first few seconds are so critical that some additional discussion is warranted.

Helen Wippich Greene, of Valley Forge Information Service, says that the introduction should offer enough information to create interest in being interviewed. One cannot blandly assume that the respondent should be grateful for the chance to respond to the questions. The potential respondent should be told, for example, that the manufacturer of an electric appliance wants to make its product more useful and acceptable to consumers generally, and that these questions will help the manufacturer do so.

The Question Must Be Conversational

Because of the lack of physical meeting of respondent and interviewer, the questionnaire must be conversational—it must be smooth and natural. It must be logical. It must go from the general to the specific; it must move gradually from one content area to another. It must not waste words.

Hilda Barnes, President of Research Information Center, says it succinctly: "It must flow."

Questions Cannot Be Condescending

In the personal interview situation it is possible to tell the respondent, "Let's play a game," and then present an involved or boring task to go through, such as responding to a word association test, in which the respondent is given a stimulus word and asked to respond as quickly as possible with a word or a phrase. The respondent doesn't have to play such games by telephone; it's too easy to hang up that receiver. Hilda

Barnes feels that regardless of the interviewing medium, any interview should avoid questioning techniques that are condescending.

Questions Cannot Be Involved or Stilted

Highly involved, stilted questions, even though never desirable, regardless of the method of conducting the survey, won't work at all in the telephone method. Replies to such questions may be obtained by the other methods (personal interview or mail), but by telephone the termination rate becomes excessive.

PRACTICAL EXAMPLE: A SOUP STUDY

While a great deal of thought and consideration clearly has to go into questionnaire preparation, as all of the preceding discussion illustrates, it is also true that evaluation of a draft questionnaire also requires a heavy dose of good old common sense. To demonstrate this, consider a hypothetical questionnaire.

The purpose of this hypothetical study is to determine the role that soup plays in lunches that are eaten at home. The sample is a national telephone sample of consumers, with interviewing conducted from 2 to 5 P.M. Figure 5-1 shows a draft questionnaire.

Comments on Draft Questionnaire

First, there is no introduction whatever. In view of the importance of the introduction, as discussed, this is an unforgivable oversight.

Question 1 is poorly placed. If age *is* to be asked (probably for later classification purposes), it should be well into the questionnaire, perhaps even at the end, long after rapport has been obtained.

Question 2 is too difficult to have been placed this early in the questionnaire. If the respondent is expected to check the pantry shelf—which is dubious strategy in a telephone interview—this should be indicated on the questionnaire. In any case, a question requiring such a high degree of cooperation—if it is to be asked—should come toward the end of the questioning. The question is ambiguous. It could cover cans (full strength and condensed), powder, cubes, or frozen. It is leading: it assumes that there is soup on the shelf.

Question 3 is out of sequence. An advertising recall question is rarely asked this early in a questionnaire. More warming up is required, and an inability to identify the brand, at this point in the questioning, could imperil continuation of the interview.

Soup Questionnaire

1. Into which of these age groups do you fall?
   18–30_____   31–40_____   41–50_____   51 or over_____

2. How much soup do you have right now on your pantry shelf?
   _____

3. What soup advertises, "Mm good! Mm good! That's what _____
   _____ soup is, Mm good!"? _____

4. What kind of soup did you have for lunch today?
   _____

5. How much did you have? _____

6. Did you have anything else with it? _____

7. How many people in your family had soup more than once last
   week? _____

8. Do you like soup very much, or do you eat it just because it is
   inexpensive and easy to prepare?

   Like soup very much ( ) Eat it because it is inexpensive and easy
                                  to prepare ( )

9. Who all ate this soup today? _____

10. Where did you get it? _____

11. How often do you have soup for lunch? _____

FIGURE 5-1

Question 4 is a most ambiguous question. What does the word *kind* mean? It could mean flavor; it could mean form. It is leading; it makes the assumption that soup was served for lunch.

Question 5, too, is ambiguous. What is *how much?* If an answer of "a bowl" or "a cup" is received, it is impossible to translate that into any standard measurement unit, such as ounces. If an answer of "a can" or "a package" is given, it cannot be interpreted either. Nor is it possible to solve the problem by asking about ounces. Unless this is a door-to-door personal interview, where it is possible for the respondent to show the container or serving dish, and ounces can be checked, by reading a label or using a measuring cup, the question had better be skipped. It will produce completely undependable, uninterpretable information.

Question 6 is ambiguous. Does it mean a snack (crackers or chips) to be eaten alongside or in the soup, simultaneously; or does it mean something more substantial, almost as a separate course, such as a sandwich?

Question 7 is poor from two standpoints. First, it seems quite a strain to put on the respondent's memory. In the second place, it doesn't mean much unless one knows the total family size.

Question 8 is a leading question. It presents the two alternatives as apparent opposite ends of a single scale, which they are not. The respondent may react favorably to both possible answers. In addition, the terms *inexpensive* and *easy to prepare* should not be presented as a single alternative. They are really quite separate entities.

Question 9 is too colloquial. While a telephone questionnaire should be conversational and flowing, it should not become so colloquial that it resembles an extremely low-key discussion between neighbors over the back fence. In addition it is not a precise sort of measurement. All family members should first be listed by sex and age, then those who had lunch at home the day of questioning, then those who had soup that day.

Question 10 is ambiguous. A respondent could properly answer, "off the pantry shelf," but that would not be very helpful. Is a store type wanted, or a specific store name? If it is the latter, there is still another problem. If the soup has been on the pantry shelf very long, the respondent may not remember where the soup came from.

Question 11 is also ambiguous. Where possible, people should be queried about their specific behavior, not asked to reply in vague, general terms about their behavior. What do terms such as *often*, *frequently*, *seldom*, and *occasionally* mean? How can summaries showing the proportion of consumers answering in each category be interpreted?

Also, what about homemade soup? If it is to be excluded, as it probably should be, then how should the answer of someone who opened a can of chicken broth and added noodles be handled? This is perhaps a procedural point requiring interviewer instructions rather than a questionnaire modification, but it is a problem all the same.

Finally, this questionnaire is not psychologically well arranged. Among other things, all questions about a particular activity should be placed together; the most obvious area requiring this is the discussion of today's lunch.

Revised Questionnaire

Figure 5-2 shows the questionnaire as it might be revised to meet all the objections raised to the draft. The point is simple. While questionnaire construction may not be easy, questionnaire evaluation and rebuilding may be considerably simpler.

QUESTIONNAIRE TESTING

Questionnaire testing (or pretesting) is the trial of the questionnaire with a limited number of respondents, to find out whether it works, and where it doesn't, how to modify it so that it will.

Purposes

One of the purposes is to make the questionnaire a more perfect instrument. This gets back to the point that questionnaire construction is more an art than a science. No one can be sure, when first putting a questionnaire together, that it will work perfectly. Suzanne Verdone, of Burke Marketing Research, says that "testing provides assurance that investigators and respondents interpret the questions correctly."

Closely related is checking the adequacy of any interviewer instructions provided on the questionnaire. Suzanne Verdone points out that a questionnaire may contain small but important errors in skip patterns, questioning sequence, etc., but the author is too close to the material to see them. These will be caught by the test interviewers. Eugene Telser, vice-president, Custom Research Service, A. C. Nielsen Company, feels pretty strongly about the need for this sort of pretesting. He says:

> There are some people who feel that they can sit at their desk and "write questionnaires." I have yet to meet any geniuses of this type who can really produce. Every questionnaire which I have seen which has not been pretested has had some serious flaw in it. The main purpose of pretesting is developing unambiguous lines of questioning.

Helen Wippich Greene of Valley Forge points out that checking the ease and accuracy of recording replies is another specific aim.

A second purpose is to obtain an indication of the kind of material that the study will uncover. Suzanne Verdon says, "It makes sure that the survey provides the types of answers needed." She gives an example.

The following questions were asked on a recent Burke study:

> In just the past 2 months, how many times have you eaten any barbecued food which was prepared at home?

> In just the past 2 months, what types of barbecued food have you eaten which were prepared at home?

The purpose of these questions was to determine the extent to which the respondents prepare food at home using a barbecue style sauce. During the pretesting stage, it became apparent that respondents defined barbecued food as anything which is cooked outside on a charcoal grill. Consequently, the questions were changed to the following more direct means of attaining the answers needed.

> In just the past 2 months, how many times have you eaten any food that was prepared at home using a barbecue sauce?

> In just the past 2 months, what types of food have you eaten which were prepared at home using a barbecue sauce?

Suzanne Verdone also points out a special application of the pretest in obtaining advance knowledge of the kind of reply that will be received. These replies can be used for a more meaningful prelisting of responses on the questionnaire, of rating scales, and of comprehensive frequency groupings.

A third purpose of the pretest is to help in making a cost estimate for the study. The time per interview can really be checked only through some sort of actual trial. However, this sort of test can be done relevantly only when the questionnaire has been pretty well finalized, when most of the "bugs" have been removed.

A fourth purpose of pretesting is to estimate the proportion of those approached who qualify. Frequently, in telephone research, not every contact is a qualified contact. The study may require interviewing only those who have eaten dry cereal for breakfast this morning, those who live in single-family homes with siding, those who do their own laundry at home, those who drink beer.

Frank McHugh, president of The Data Group Incorporated, says that one purpose of the pretest sometimes is to check the method of getting respondent cooperation. His firm conducted a study about sanitary protection among teenaged girls. It was realized that if the mother overheard some of her daughter's replies, there could be concern and upset on the mother's part. So the original time was spent on the telephone with the mother, getting her cooperation to interview the daughter, without revealing any of the detailed nature of the questions

Revised Soup Questionnaire

INTRODUCTION. Good afternoon. This is _____, of the Standard Research Company, calling from _____. We are making a survey on prepared soups, and I would like to ask you a few questions.

1. Did you, personally, eat lunch at home today?
   Yes □   No □
   (GO TO Q. 2)   (GO TO Q. 8)

2. Did you, personally, happen to have prepared soup—*not* homemade—for lunch today?
   Yes □   No □
   (ASK Q. 3)   (GO TO Q. 8)

3. What flavor of soup was it? (CHECK WHICH)
   Bean _____
   Bouillon _____   Onion _____
   Chicken broth _____   Oxtail _____
   Chicken gumbo _____   Pepper pot _____
   Chicken noodle _____   Scotch broth _____
   Chicken rice _____   Split pea _____
   Clam chowder _____   Tomato _____
   Consomme _____   Vegetable _____
   Mushroom _____   Other (specify) _____

4. Was this prepared from a can, a powder or a cube, or a dry mix?
   Can (Condensed □ or Regular □)
   Powder or Cube □
   Dry mix □

5. In terms of measuring cups, about how much soup did you, personally, eat at lunch today?
   ¼ cup □   ¾ cup □   over 1 cup □
   ½ cup □   1 cup □

6. Did you have any snack to go with the soup at the very same time you were eating it, such as saltines, other crackers, potato chips, or the like?
   Yes □   No □
   (ASK Q. 7)   (GO TO Q. 8)

FIGURE 5-2

7. (IF YES TO Q. 4) What was it?
   Saltines □   Potato chips □
   Other crackers □   Other (specify) □

8. Will you please tell me all the members of your household living at home, by sex. Please tell me the age of each, starting with the oldest.
   (RECORD BELOW) (CIRCLE AGE OF RESPONDENT)

9. (ASK FOR EACH FAMILY MEMBER) Did _____ eat lunch at home today? (RECORD BELOW)

10. (ASK FOR EACH FAMILY MEMBER WHO HAD LUNCH AT HOME IN Q. 9) Did _____ have soup for lunch?

	Q. 8 Age	Q. 9 Yes No	Q. 10 Yes No
MALES	_____	□ □	□ □
	_____	□ □	□ □
	_____	□ □	□ □
	_____	□ □	□ □
FEMALES	_____	□ □	□ □
	_____	□ □	□ □
	_____	□ □	□ □
	_____	□ □	□ □

11. During the past 7 days, including today, how many times have you, personally, had soup for lunch?
    7 □ 6 □ 5 □ 4 □ 3 □ 2 □ 1 □ 0 □

12. When you last bought soup, at what kind of store did you purchase it?
    Chain supermarket □ Independent supermarket □
    Independent grocery □ Other (please specify)_____

Revised Soup Questionnaire (cont'd.)

13. Please tell me how much you like soup generally. A rating of 7 means that you *like it about as much as you possibly could;* a rating of 1 means that you *dislike it about as much as you possibly could.* The numbers in between stand for feelings in between. Now, where would you rank your liking for soup, between 7 and 1?
    7 □ 6 □ 5 □ 4 □ 3 □ 2 □ 1 □

14. Compared with most other foods you prepare at home, would you say that preparation of soup is:
    one of the easiest foods to prepare □
    easier than most foods to prepare □
    about the same as other foods to prepare □
    less easy to prepare than other foods □
    least easy of any food to prepare □

15. Compared with most foods, would you say that soup per serving is:
    one of the most expensive □
    more expensive than most □
    about the same price as most □
    less expensive than most □
    one of the least expensive □

NAME OF RESPONDENT _____   DATE _____

ST. & NUMBER _____   INTER'S INIT _____

POST OFFICE & STATE _____

TELEPHONE NUMBER (INCLUDE AREA CODE) _____

FIGURE 5-2 (cont'd.)

to be asked (this might have led to premature discussion between mother and daughter, thus coloring the daughter's replies).

Sometimes the pretest leads to additions to content of the questionnaire. An important aspect of the topic may come up as an unsolicited comment by one or more of the pretest respondents.

The Pretest Method

Nature of the Interviewers. The nature of the interviewers for the pretest depends partly on the specific purposes of the test. If the test is chiefly to determine interview time and incidence, then it is clear that typical, average investigators should be used to get typical, average results. As Ann Fenton of MARC puts it: "For costing the study we use average interviewers." Louis Meier of Market Opinion Research says: "We use good interviewers, but not the most rapid or the slowest, so that we obtain a fair estimate of production rate in addition to the other benefits of testing." Hilda Barnes of Research Information Center says that her organization uses 4 or 5 average interviewers for the work.

Not all those conducting professional telephone surveys completely agree. Sarah Huneycutt of Opinion Research Corporation typically uses 4 interviewers, 2 of whom are superior, and 2 average. Sylvia Barr and Jim Sammer, of Walker Research, report that their firm tries to use 3 interviewers, one the most senior and experienced, one average, and one relatively new.

Eugene Telser of Nielsen believes that the project director on the particular study should personally act as a pretest interviewer. He says:

> It is his or her words that need to be checked out. Pride of authorship often precludes a given individual from making necessary changes as a result of someone else's pretest. It is no different from reading your own speech aloud before you give it—sometimes what you wrote sounds pretty imbecilic, and you're the only one who can tell it.

Number of People Questioned. There is no standard pattern as to the number of respondents included in a pretest. It varies by research firm, and by difficulty of the study. It may be as low as 5 or 6, or as high as 50 or 60.

Helen Wippich Greene of Valley Forge says it will be as few as 6 when the pressure is on, or can be as many as 60 if the study is extremely complex and the client approves the budget for such extensive testing of methods and questions. Market Opinion Research varies between 10 and 20. Sarah Huneycutt, Opinion Research Corporation, uses 10 as a minimum.

Monitoring. The professional telephone survey firm always monitors the pretest calls. This is the only way anyone other than the interviewer can obtain a full understanding of all the interactions between respondent and interviewer. It is the only way to get an understanding of all the nuances of the reply. It is the only way to perceive where the respondent is having difficulty in understanding, or coming up with a reply.

The monitoring is always carried on by someone of supervisory status within the research firm. Often it is the project director (the person responsible for study design, sheperding the study through the research firm, and reporting) who does the monitoring, rather than delegate it to the interviewing department, because pretesting can be crucial to a successful study. Sometimes the client will monitor, though with a firm such as Walker Research, located in Indianapolis, it is relatively rare for the client firm—often hundreds or thousands of miles distant—to visit the city for that purpose. But it is possible for remote clients to monitor even from their offices. MARC and Walker use long-distance calls for this purpose.

Chilton Research, like these other firms, has monitoring facilities within its offices. Since Chilton has the CRT, it has one major advantage in pretesting. If the monitoring shows difficulty with one or two questions, these can immediately be reprogrammed, so that by the next time these questions come up on the screen for the interviewer to use, they will have been changed. No printing of new questionnaire forms is required.

Debriefing. In debriefing, which is not too common following the pretest, the project director or interviewing supervisor reviews the questionnaire, question-by-question, with the interviewer. Trouble spots are looked for and discussed. The interviewer's ideas as to how the questionnaire might be improved are solicited.

Figure 5-3 is the Interviewer's Test Report used by Walker Research to debrief. It is well thought through and has been found by Walker Research to be a valuable part of their pretesting.

Frequency of Pretesting

Pretesting is not used as often as it is probably desirable. Pretesting should probably be used on every study where any untried questions have been added to a questionnaire. Yet this is not done as a standard with all research firms.

To be sure, some do it on every study. The Data Group Incorporated and Research Information Center are two of these. But Suzanne Verdone of Burke reports: "Ideally every questionnaire would be tested before interviewing is scheduled to begin. However, due to the last-

FIGURE 5-3

Interviewer's Test Report   Project #

Interviewer: _____ Date _____

Number of interviews completed _____

Number of partial interviews _____

Average time per interview _____

1. Questions respondents could not understand and/or could not answer in desired frame of reference: List and explain what problems seem to be.

_____
_____
_____
_____
_____

2. Questions where answers were not serious or too glib or evasive.

_____
_____
_____
_____
_____

3. Questions which worked especially well.

_____
_____
_____

4. Other special difficulties.

_____
_____
_____

5. Any other remarks.

_____
_____
_____
_____
_____

minute nature of many research projects, pretesting is sometimes not practical." Walker Research doesn't test as often as it would like, partially because one of the advantages of the telephone survey is speed, and most of the time clients demand that advantage. Jim Bacharach of Trandex says that complicated questionnaires should always be tested. "But it depends on client interest and our reaction to the questionnaire." At Chilton, if there is no time to pretest, the project director monitors the first night's work.

REFERENCE

[1]A. B. Blankenship, "Creativity in Consumer Research," *Journal of Marketing*, Vol. 25, no. 6, Oct. 1961, pp. 34–38.

INTERVIEWERS
AND INTERVIEWING

Most of the operations in telephone surveys—sampling, data processing, and the rest—can largely be handled by standard, repetitive steps. Not so with interviewing. This is the most humanized part of the study, in the sense that much judgment on the part of the worker is required. This is also the key to quality work in a telephone survey; without quality at this point the survey loses value. It is also the key to production; it is the one area which, because it is so humanized, can be either highly efficient or highly inefficient. It has the greatest single potential for error.

This chapter contains a twofold discussion. First it talks about interviewers: how they are recruited, selected, and trained. Then it considers interviewing: the principles, selection of interviewers for the particular project, specific training for that project, supervision, motivating, and retraining, as required.

INTERVIEWERS

Recruiting

Recruiting, selecting, and providing general training can be a big, continuing operation if the firm is large-scale. Research Information Center has 180 stations, with 132 in operation daily. Research Information Center has a staff position devoted exclusively to the recruiting, training, and development of the interviewing staff. A certain amount of interviewer attrition occurs naturally, but some of it must also be forced. Hilda Barnes feels that interviewers do not necessarily improve with age or experience; very often, the opposite occurs. Interviewers are constantly monitored and retrained when appropriate. A continuous program of training and development is followed at RIC.

Recruiting is done by one or more of four methods: newspaper display advertisements, references from present interviewers and employees, local outside sources, and employment agencies.

Newspaper Display Advertisements. This is the most commonly used procedure to attract the attention of potential interviewers. Sylvia Barr, of Walker Research, says:

> We stress and feature our telephone number in ads. While we show the address, we want to save their time and ours through telephone screening. We find out if they are seeking full-time or part-time employment—we want only part-time. If part-time, do they need a steady income? We can't guarantee that. How did they hear of us? If it was only through the newspaper ad, we will have to give them a full explanation of what we do, including frequency of the work, rate of pay, etc. During the conversation we observe how the person handles himself. The person should be mature. The nature of the voice itself is not too important.

Ann Fenton, of MARC, reports that they, too, use newspaper ads, and their ads give the firm's address as well as the telephone number. In their telephone screening, they watch for speech impediments. They also eliminate those who are not available for the right hours, and those who do not really want this kind of work. Research Information Center also asks the applicants to telephone in, for the same reasons that MARC does. Both Burke and Trendex make use of a standard display advertisement.

References from Present Interviewers and Employees. At least two firms— The Data Group Incorporated and MARC—use this method of getting lists of new potential interviewers. Present interviewers and other employees presumably know what is expected in this kind of work. They also know people who, at least superficially to them, are able to fill the bill. It does seem to make some sense; in a preliminary way some screening has already been done by the time the firm receives the suggestions.

Hilda Barnes, of RICI, feels that interviewers are not necessarily the best judges of other potential interviewers. Her firm neither encourages nor discourages this practice.

Local Outside Sources. Some firms go to local outside sources, such as colleges or universities, psychologists, and marketing people. This kind of source is promising as long as the source will give the problem some thoughtful consideration, rather than merely making suggestions to get rid of the questioner. However, the research firm learns over time which sources do provide promising leads. MARC uses this system effectively.

Employment Agency. So far as known, only one research firm—Valley Forge Information Service—uses a particular employment agency as one method of screening applicants before an interview is conducted by a staff member. The firm started out by using this method in order to recruit large numbers of people in a short period of time, and it worked, so Valley Forge has seen no reason to abandon this method.

The Selection Method

Before getting into the specifics of the selection methods, we will first consider briefly the characteristics that are looked for in a telephone interviewer.

One characteristic is a *telephone voice;* some term it a telephone personality or speaking ability. Helen Wippich Greene, of Valley Forge, says that voice quality is important. Michael Cohen, of Metro Survey Service, refers to it as a "respectable-sounding" voice. Certainly, as Greene mentions, the interviewer should be a good user of the English language. The interviewer should be articulate.

Some argue that the voice must not have an accent. James Bacharach, of Trendex, tells the amusing story of "the New York lady with the worst accent I ever heard when I interviewed her in person. But when you heard her on the telephone, it just didn't come through at all."

The interviewer should be *dependable.* It is crucial in this kind of work (where production schedules and keeping the WATS lines busy are so important) that people show up when they are expected, or give ample notice when they cannot.

Telephone interviewers must also be *productive.* In this sort of work it is not good to have workers who take their time between calls; they must get back to dialing just as soon as they can. They must keep busy during their assigned work hours. Michael Cohen, of Metro Survey Service, terms it "a sustained motivation for working."

Another highly important characteristic is *trainability*. The interviewer must be educable. He or she must be willing and able to absorb and follow directions. As Sylvia Barr of Walker Research puts it: "The person must take instructions well." Any failure to follow instructions will hurt the quality of the interviewing.

Finally, the interviewer *must be able to record well*. He or she must have good handwriting; the quality of the reply recorded doesn't matter if the research firm has difficulty in deciphering it. In addition, the investigator must be able to provide verbatim reporting of comments, so that it is really the response of the respondent, not of the interviewer, and so that the comment reflects the coloring given by the respondent.

A research firm uses three devices to select people who seem worthy of training: the personal interview, (in a few cases) testing, and trial interviewing.

The Personal Interview. All firms personally interview those they are considering for selection. Burke relies almost entirely upon this system to judge the degree to which applicants possess characteristics looked for. A personal judgment is made following the interview. A standard application form is typically filled in.

Testing. Chilton makes use of a three-stage series of tests. First is a listening test, in which prospective interviewers are given a one-page document which describes interview-recording procedures. The prospect listens to a tape-recorded interview and jots down the replies, attempting to follow the instructions previously supplied. The recordings are then objectively and mathematically scored. The second part of the testing procedure involves the playing of a tape of an actual interview, running about 20 minutes. At key points a moderator breaks in with an explanation. This is really a training device, explaining the principles of good interviewing, and it becomes the base for the third portion of the testing procedure. This is the actual conducting and recording of an interview by the prospect. There is a standardized, thirty-question questionnaire, and again, the results of the test are scored on an objective and mathematical basis.

Ann Fenton reports that MARC uses learning-rate predictability and personality tests to weed out those who would make poor interviewers. Market Facts has tried using an intelligence test, but found that it did not separate the better interviewers from the others.

Trial Interviewing. Market Facts argues that "the real test comes at the telephone," and all professional telephone research firms will quickly reject an applicant who, after some little period of training, simply cannot perform satisfactorily. Eugene Telser, of Nielsen, reports that they have the applicant make a series of practice interviews starting with simple dichotomous interviews and working gradually through several steps into very complicated ones. "Our interviewing supervisory group," he says, then selects the people who in their judgment are qualified." One pioneer in telephone work is reputed to have instructed the applicant to sit down at the telephone with a telephone book and to make a call. The applicant who did it passed. The applicant who just sat there failed.

What proportion of applicants make it through the screening process? With Metro Survey Services it is estimated at 2%; at Burke 5 to 7%; Chilton 5%.

General Training

General training typically consists of in-house instruction and practice interviewing.

In-House Instruction. Most training programs depend in part on a training manual, which includes topics such as the background of marketing research, the improvement of the voice personality, introduction to the interview, conducting the interview, the handling of open-ended questions (where no answer categories are provided, but the respondents are allowed to phrase their own replies, which are then recorded), the handling of probes (usually used in connection with open-ended queries to get a greater depth of reply, more answers, or explanations of answers), the handling of other specifics, sampling, and WATS lines and their use. A photograph of an actual training session at Walker Research is shown in Figure 6-1.

Walker Research introduces their president on a videotape presentation. The rationale is that the training group is more impressed with the seriousness of the program, and since they might run into the president anyway, it makes sense to let the group know who he is.

Most of these in-house programs take a day or more. At Chilton and MARC, it is a day. At Walker, it is closer to a day and a half. At Burke it extends over 3 days.

Practice Interviewing. Depending on the firm, the respondents used in practice interviewing may be other trainees, employees in the office, real respondents over local lines, or real respondents over WATS lines.

FIGURE 6-1.
An interviewer training program in progress. *(Walker Research, Inc.)*

In most cases there is monitoring by a supervisor or trainer, and the interviewer gets a critique both of the call and of the recording.

The time period for these practice calls runs from several hours on up. At Trendex, nearly 100 interviews are done on different kinds of studies before a person goes onto an actual study.

Kinds of People Who Seem
to Make Good Interviewers

Different professional telephone survey firms report somewhat different kinds of people among those who perform well.

Women. All firms agree that the majority of their professional telephone workers are women, though this doesn't necessarily mean that women make better interviewers than men. It probably means only that more women than men are available for such work. At Market Opinion Research, some 90 percent are women. The stereotype of the personal interviewer is a married woman between 30 and 50 years old.

Working Mothers. Sylvia Barr, of Walker Research, reports that often times the typical "working mother" is an individual who is returning to the work force after several years of being a full-time homemaker and mother. A relearning process is involved for these individuals so they may adjust to a work situation. In this initial period, working mothers may sometimes have difficulty receiving instructions and directing their attention to specific work situations.

College Students and College Graduates. At least two firms believe that college students or college graduates tend to make better telephone investigators. Barr reports that Walker Research has many college graduates. Research Information Center depends heavily upon college students. However, with college students, there are often problems of availability and turnover. With the student group, classwork and examinations come first, and they are typically not available over holiday periods, when they return home. In addition, since most of them are looking primarily for spending money, the appeal to work loses significance during some periods.

Those Looking for Unusual Financial Satisfactions. Ann Fenton, of MARC, comments that her firm has found that many of their good interviewers are people who are working to earn money toward some specific goal, such as home improvements or a trip to Europe. These kinds of incentive, it would seem, could work equally well whether the interviewer worked over a long time period, or for a brief period in a firm where a higher turnover rate was common.

Young People. Sylvia Barr, of Walker Research, reports a high proportion of young people on their interviewing staff, and many other professional telephone research firms say the same thing. If it is true that this is a job calling for constant effort on part of the interviewer, then a younger, more physically fit person could take the strain better.

A Real Mix. Some firms report a real mix of types on their interviewing staff. Sarah Huneycutt, vice president of Opinion Research Corporation, says that they have young people, old people, men, women, and various ethnic groups represented. Trendex also varies. Their continuing staff includes one retired school teacher of 65, one part-time artist who wears jeans, and a "real lady." Take your choice!

The Firm Locates in an Area Where It Can Get the Kind of Interviewers It Wants

In the past, the marketing research firm was most often located in the central area of a city where there was a concentration of its customers. With the professional telephone survey firm the location requirements are far different. If the firm is really top-notch, being located close to the customer is no longer so important as being located close to a good source of the type of people it is seeking as interviewers. Walker Research moved from a central location in Indianapolis to a developing suburb, in part to get interviewers. Michael Cohen, president of Metro Survey Service, explains that they selected their Frankford (Philadelphia) location because it was near the middle-class area from where they wanted to recruit their workers, and because the area was safe at night for the late shifts.

Some "Mechanics" of Interviewers

Pay Scales. Should there or should there not be differential pay scales for workers? Most professional telephone research firms use differential scales. One method of differential pay scaling is by the competence of the particular worker. The Data Group Incorporated and Walker, for instance, each have three classes. There is the novice or trainee, there is the senior interviewer, and there is the interviewer specialist.

Another method of handling the scales is by longevity. Longevity per se does not seem too good a basis, unless the firm is really equating longevity with competence. If so, it means that the worker who never attains topmost competence should not be kept on the staff.

Some firms use incentives, that is, special rewards given for specific contributions. For instance, if a worker beats the expected completion rate under especially difficult circumstances and remains error-free, one firm offers a cash incentive or free refreshments. Another firm offers a higher rate for its night shift. While it is not a monetary incentive, at least two firms follow the old system developed by Andrew Carnegie in those early days of steel production: they post production rates daily for all interviewers on a project.

Establishing flat rates for everyone is not common, and it seems to make sense that it is not. People do vary in their skills, and professional telephone interviewing is no exception. Why shouldn't competence, meaning quality and production, be rewarded?

The Physical Facilities. While the physical facilities provided by each firm for the conducting of professional telephone interviews vary, there is some consistency in the list of elements provided. Basically there are two areas: working facilities and a lounge area for rest breaks.

Typically, there is one large room, or a number of small rooms composing the interviewing area. Chilton has one large room, subdivided into banks of telephone locations. At the other extreme, Research Information Center has smaller rooms, each containing ten to twelve interviewer locations.

Each telephone interviewer is provided with a booth, or roomette, most typically a three-sided affair with partitions running up high enough so that he or she is out of sight and sound of the person working in the next booth. The booth provides enough flat, horizontal surface for all questionnaire and other work materials. A clock is visible so that the investigator knows the time in the time zone that is being called. Sometimes the clock is located within the individual booth.

Each booth is located within sight of the supervisor's area (which may be a small room with a glass for observation, or simply an open area of the interviewing space). The purpose of this clear view of each investigator is to see what the interviewer is doing. The supervisor has to have an understanding of the rate of production while the work is in progress, and must make sure that the worker is not wasting time between calls.

Figure 6-2 shows a section of the interviewing area at Walker Research. Hanging on the wall in front of each investigator is a WATS zone map and instructions on how to handle certain standard interviewing situation. The working materials are spread in front of the investigators.

Figure 6-3 is a close-up of a worker in one of these booths. The close-

FIGURE 6-2.
Several interviewers working in their booths. *(Walker Research, Inc.)*

FIGURE 6-3.
An interviewer working in her booth. *(Walker Research, Inc.)*

up demonstrates two more points. One is the use of the head set with attached mouthpiece, freeing both hands of the investigator; this device, too, is in common use at the professional telephone survey research firm. It means that at all times the worker can write, can shift materials, or dial. The other is the use of a push-button telephone. In all locations where these are available, the survey firm makes use of them, because pushing buttons is so much more rapid than dialing.

The other physical aspect of the working area which does not show in these photographs is the monitor system. The monitor system, as explained in the early definition of professional telephone surveys, enables the person doing the monitoring to break in and listen to any of the interviews occurring within station-reach of the monitor set, without any noise on the line, so that neither the interviewer nor the respondent is aware of such a cut-in. (Of course, the interviewer knows about the system, but is unaware as to just when the cutting-in takes place.) Some firms have special monitoring rooms, so that a client or a project director (as opposed to the supervisor) can listen in.

Many professional telephone survey firms have lounge areas for their telephone interviewers. When telephone interviewing is conducted the way it should be, the work can become very tiring. The worker must stay on the job constantly if those WATS lines are to be fully utilized, and if the speed and low-cost advantages of the professional telephone survey are to be achieved. Regular breaks are often provided, and the worker can go to the lounge, which is furnished with comfortable, relaxing chairs, perhaps a few tables, sometimes soft, piped-in music, and vending machines offering hot and cold drinks, sandwiches, candy, and cigarettes.

Records. Most firms maintain records for each investigator, and these records usually list, for each project worked on, the quality level achieved, the production level, and any other fact the firm believes helpful in assessing the long-term performance of each worker.

INTERVIEWING

There are many aspects of the actual interviewing on a job that must be considered: selection of the workers to be assigned to a particular project, training for the project, timing of the calls, provision of a dialing sheet for use of the investigators, the actual dialing, the introduction to the respondent, and supervision and monitoring.

Selection of Workers for a Particular Project

This is the obvious first step in getting the interviewing rolling. Many jobs will require no particular selection; almost any investigator on the staff will be able to handle the particular assignment satisfactorily. However, let's consider some of the special situations that do require particular types of interviewers.

By Project Difficulty. The more highly skilled workers will be used for the more difficult projects. Use of such staff is necessary when interviewing physicians, engineers, or other such highly specialized groups who are difficult to reach, and difficult to keep on the line very long. Ann Fenton, of MARC, says: "We will use senior staff interviewers on the most difficult assignments, including executive interviewing."

By Difficult Area. The more skilled interviewers must also be assigned to work geographic areas which are difficult. Los Angeles, Miami, and Manhattan are considered among the worst of these. Sylvia Barr, of Walker Research, says that Manhattan is so tough that clients often suggest it be omitted for prelisted studies.

By Need for a Special Language. Fred Currier, president of Market Opinion Research, stresses the need in *any* telephone survey to build trust early in the interview. His firm, for instance, uses bilingual workers for studies concentrating on Spanish names as the frame.

By Unusual Requirements. Hilda Barnes, of Research Information Center, recalls the girdle study their firm conducted a short while back. "In that study," she pointed out, "we had to use, for obvious reasons, all women interviewers." Barnes' firm has a staff composed of about 40 percent male interviewers, so the selection process became important.

By Accent. The question of accents has no simple answer. An interviewer with an extreme accent does run the risk of not being understood and may have to repeat questions for the listener, which would add time to the interview. It is not inconceivable that some people are alienated by certain accents. To judge how much of a problem an accent would be in a certain part of the country is not easy, but it would be safe to say that there are fewer potential problems when the interviewer has a local accent.

However, a Southern accent may not be a problem. Sylvia Barr says that a Southern accent is not a problem in any area of the country, and Ann Fenton, MARC, says that Southern accents are particularly acceptable in the East. There may be another kind of risk associated with a Southern accent, though. Sylvia Barr says that some interviewers with a Southern accent have a longer interview time.

Lynn Brown, president of Creative Marketing Enterprises, tells an amusing anecdote which worked in reverse. Brown is not Southern; he comes from northern Ohio. At any rate, he was making calls to Georgia. On one of these he was connected to a Southern youngster; he asked for the mother. The youngster called out to his mother: "Hey, Mom! There's a man on the phone with a Northern accent who wants to talk to you!"

Training for the Project

Training for the specific project generally occurs in three stages: briefing of the interviewers, practice interviewing, and beginning the actual assignment.

Briefing of the Interviewers. The briefing of the interviewers may be done by the client, by the project director of the research firm, or by the field supervisor of the firm. It will typically cover topics such as the nature of the sample, the sampling process, a statement of the anticipated completion rate per hour, how the questionnaire is to be handled, the handling of special situations which might arise, and, where appropriate, IBM coding and self-coding of open-ended replies. Unless there are too many interviewers working on a single assignment, this is usually covered in a single meeting with all interviewers present who are going to be working on the project.

Practice Interviews. Several practice interviews are then typically done with another interviewer, or perhaps with the client, project director, or a field supervisor. These continue with the supervisor critically evaluating the handling of each stage of the interview. Practice interviewing goes on until the supervisor is convinced that the particular interviewer is handling all procedures properly.

Start of the Assignment. The workers then begin the assignment. The early stages of the actual field work often are more heavily monitored than later stages, to be sure that any errors in procedure are corrected early in the field work.

Timing of the Calls. There are two timing aspects that will be considered here: the time of day and holidays.

Time of Day. Professional and business samples are typically telephoned during local business hours, generally 9 A.M. to 5 P.M. It is often productive to telephone business executives at their offices between 5 and 7 P.M. The secretary usually won't be there to screen the calls, but the boss may still be in the office. Of course this works only where there are centrex numbers, or where the switchboard remains open. Interviewing with consumers generally starts no earlier than 3:30 or 4 P.M., so that the sample will include employed men and women, who most commonly are at work during the day.

None of the firms queried begins calling before 8:30 A.M., local time, and with most the starting time is 9 A.M. None of these firms begins an interview after 10 P.M., and most do not begin one after 9 P.M., local time. "A recent study by Burke," says Suzanne Verdone, "shows that the not-at-home rate for female heads during daytime hours is 48% vs. 31% during evening hours."

The closing hour can be late if an appointment is made. When Burke calls later than 9 P.M., which is rare, interviewers begin by saying: "I hope it isn't too late to talk with you."

Research firms using WATS lines still make calls during local lunch or dinner times, though telephone companies, supersensitive to respondent backlash, typically do not do so.

These kinds of hourly time practices mean that the bands of WATS lines can be kept busy starting at approximately 9 A.M. in the Eastern time zone to a little after 9 to 10 P.M. in the Pacific time zone. If the research firm were located in the Eastern zone, it could run its calls from 9 A.M. Eastern time through 12 midnight Eastern time. Such a long interviewing day clearly indicates a need for shifts of workers, and this is the way that most firms work things to keep those WATS lines going. There is some disagreement on how long the shifts ought to be. They range anywhere from 4 hours to 7. Market Facts reports that its workers must work short shifts with frequent breaks to remain effective. Market Opinion Research says that 3½ to 4 hours is the most effective working period. A shorter period than that, it is argued, is inefficient. If the period is longer, the voice gets strained and the work gets sloppy.

Weekend Hours. All professional research firms agree that weekend interviewing with consumers is entirely practical. Most work for the full day on Saturday, but not Saturday night. Most seem to avoid Sunday morning, but interview Sunday afternoon. However, Hilda Barnes, president of Research Information Center, has her shop conducting interviewing until 10 P.M. on Sunday night. "Sunday night," she says, "contrary to conventional wisdom, is about the best time of the week for effective and efficient interviewing."

Research Information Center breaks another cardinal rule of interviewing research, and gets away with it. Says Hilda Barnes: "We have found that, similar to Sunday evenings, the last day of a three-day weekend is usually very productive."

Avoidance of Holidays. In house-to-house interviewing it has been traditional to avoid interviewing pretty much between December 15 and January 4 or 5. The reasoning has been that people are too busy during that period, and do not want to be bothered. Other holidays traditionally avoided include the Fourth of July, Thanksgiving, and Labor Day. Religious holidays, such as Good Friday, are traditionally avoided, in house-to-house interviewing. What about the avoidance of holidays when conducting a professional telephone survey?

There is minimal avoidance. It is largely again because of that big overhead factor that the research firm keeps paying for, whether or not used: the WATS line. All firms avoid Christmas, New Year's Eve, and New Year's Day before noon. A majority avoid the Fourth of July, Thanksgiving, and Christmas Eve. Some avoid Memorial Day and

Labor Day. A majority also try to avoid a week or more before Christmas. Michael Cohen, of Metro Survey Service, indicates that his firm is one of these, "although," he says, "we make an exception for kids. They are easy to interview during this period. They're likely to be at home, and they don't mind being interviewed."

Adjusting Timing to Meet Local Conditions. At least two frequent local weather conditions that affect interviewing plans are important enough to consider. One is rain; the other is a snowstorm.

"When we have an assignment to call farmers during warm weather months," says Ann Fenton, of MARC, "we first check out sample areas to find out where it's raining. Then we start making calls in those areas. Farmers do not work out in the fields when it is raining."

At Walker Research much the same sort of thing is done when there is a snowstorm. If the research firm hears of a snowstorm in Denver, interviewers are instructed to concentrate on Denver calls. People will be at home, and the completion rate will rise.

Provision of a Dialing Sheet

Most research firms provide each interviewer with a list of numbers to be called. Since most of the dialing sheets, regardless of the firm conducting the survey, are very similar, it is necessary to show only one. Figure 6-4 is a dialing sheet from Walker Research, Inc.

WATS CALLING CENTER DIALING SHEET
Walker Research, Inc.

Band number _____   Area _____   City _____

	Telephone number		Busy	N.A.	Refused to begin or continue	No eligible response	Disc/ non- usable business	Terminate	Complete	Date	Int.
1											
2											
3											
4											
5											
6											
23											
24											
25											
	Totals										

Form 201 (3-75)

FIGURE 6-4.
A dialing sheet. *(Walker Research, Inc.)*

Note first that the *band number* is specified—before the interviewer gets the sheet. This refers to the WATS band number, so that it is made simple for the interviewer to push the correct button on the set for the appropriate WATS band. The *area* is also spelled out before the investigator is given the sheet. So is the *city*.

The first column on the sheet has also been filled in, by the sampling department. Each pre-selected *telephone number* is listed. Number by number, the interviewer attempts a dialing, and indicates, for each completed dialing, whether the number was *busy*, whether there was *no answer*, whether there was *refusal to begin or continue*, whether there was *no eligible respondent* (for instance, if only an automobile owner would qualify), whether the number was one that had been *disconnected* or was a *business number*, whether the interview was *terminated*, or whether it was *completed*. There are also spaces to indicate *date* and *interviewer* initials.

The Dialing

The big issue in dialing is how many rings to allow before considering it a *no answer*. Different firms have varying standards. The number of rings varies from 4 to 8, with most between 4 and 6 because the telephone is usually in some convenient location. The general feeling seems to be that if the telephone is allowed to ring too long and *is* finally picked up, the person who answers will be annoyed. The person was either too far from the telephone to answer sooner or involved in some activity which he or she would have preferred not to interrupt. "In either case, says Sylvia Barr, of Walker Research, "we have created a poor interview situation." Helen Wippich Greene, of Valley Forge Information Service, says that "In New York City, where a majority of people live in apartments, you don't need as many rings."

There are some hard data showing the relation between various numbers of rings before an answer. Figure 6-5 shows these data, collected by General Foods, on studies over many different areas in April 1971, with approximately 40,000 dialings. There seems no reason to think that conditions have markedly changed today.

The bottom line, showing the totals, is the real one to look at. Some 14.8% of the calls are completed after the first ring. Then a cumulative total of 37.9% are completed after the second ring, 52.1% after the third ring, and 58.2% after the fourth. The next two rings pick up a total of only 2.4% additional. It seems clear that four rings is usually the right number for efficiency; after that, too few additional calls are added to warrant keeping the WATS lines and the interviewers tied up. Each

FIGURE 6-5

General Foods Telephone Dialing Study, April 1971

City	Number of Rings Before Answer						No Answer After 6 Rings	Total
	1	2	3	4	5	6		
Cincinnati	15.6%	23.7%	16.4%	6.1%	1.7%	0.3%	36.2%	100.0%
Portland	13.5	23.4	14.0	6.6	1.5	0.0	41.0	100.0
Denver	15.7	20.6	12.6	5.0	1.7	0.2	44.2	100.0
Syracuse	22.7	19.7	12.9	7.8	3.1	0.8	33.0	100.0
Omaha	13.5	26.9	17.7	5.8	1.6	0.1	34.4	100.0
Minneapolis	12.4	25.5	15.1	5.5	2.1	0.4	39.0	100.0
Sacramento	9.5	20.8	8.4	2.6	0.5	0.1	58.1	100.0
Buffalo	16.7	27.7	16.1	8.5	3.7	1.1	26.2	100.0
Atlanta	13.5	19.4	14.6	7.4	2.6	0.1	42.4	100.0
Average, all cities	14.8	23.1	14.2	6.1	2.1	0.3	39.4	100.0

NOTE: These data are based on approximately 40,000 dialings done in conjunction with a number of day-after recall tests. Interviewers were instructed to count and tally the number of rings before the phone was answered. The interviewing was done from 9 A.M. to 9 P.M. local time.

ring takes some 5 seconds. The first four rings obtain 96% of all calls completed after six rings!

There may be exceptions. One research firm argues that the number of rings allowed should be longer for warm days or in sunny climates, where often the respondent is outside.

Introduction to the Respondent

The professional telephone research firm typically has a fairly standard introduction that it trains its people to use. There rarely is a reason to change this. The first step is introducing oneself and the firm.

While this phase of the introduction will vary slightly from one firm to another, it will generally go something like this: "Hello, this is (interviewer's name), calling from Trendex, in Westport, Connecticut." Let's talk briefly about each element.

While most firms seem to use the actual family name of the interviewer, a few do not, in case an interviewer has a difficult or unusual name. Metro Survey Service uses names such as Smith, Jones, White, Brown, and Black. It is possible to use a whole host of easily recognized names generated simply by taking male first names and applying the suffix "-son": for instance, Robertson, Davidson, Dickson, Richardson, Johnson, Donaldson, Ericson, Williamson, Michaelson, Jackson, Frederickson, Harrison, Thomason, and the like. Or else it is possible to take a first name alone, sometimes pluralizing it: Johns, Roberts, James, Richards, Davids, Williams, Harris, Thomas. Sylvia Barr, of Walker Research, reports that her company has its younger female interviewers introduce themselves as *Mrs.*, because the company feels this projects an image of more maturity.

Naming the city the interviewer is calling from is an important part of the introduction. Long-distance calls are impressive to most of us, even those of us who make and receive many of them. Only the other day the author received a telephone call in which the caller introduced himself as associated with a periodical the author had not renewed, and mentioned that he was calling from a city some 500 miles away. It *was* impressive, even though it was obviously a WATS-line call. Such a statement underscores, without the caller's saying so, that the call is important. In the professional telephone survey, it attracts the attention of the respondent.

The name of the firm is important, too. It implies that all is honest, direct, and aboveboard. A few years ago the author received a telephone call from an interviewer in a city a short distance away, who identified herself, and then said that she wanted to get reactions to a number of publications. When asked to identify the organization doing the field work, she said she could not do so. She was refused the interview. If the firm doing the interviewing is not willing to be identified, the respondent has a right to be suspicious and refuse the interview. However, all professional telephone survey firms have the interviewer identify himself or herself during the introduction; the example is merely to stress the importance and need of doing so.

James Bacharach, managing partner of Trendex, tells of an interesting twist his company uses in identifying itself. After mentioning the name of the firm, the interviewer says: "Have you ever heard of our firm?" Regardless of the reply to this question, Trendex has found this to be a real icebreaker, and it gives the interviewer a chance to say quickly that the firm conducts surveys among people like the respondent.

The introduction should also say briefly what the topic of the survey is. The approximate time the questions take should also be stated, and should be stated with reasonable accuracy. (If the respondent does not presently have the time to respond, then this is the signal for the interviewer to ask for a time when the respondent might more conveniently reply and to set up an appointment for the interview.)

Handling Difficult Situations

Not all potentially difficult situations can be identified in advance; some become apparent only as the survey proceeds. However, two types of difficult situations, and their solutions, can be briefly reviewed here.

Sensitive Topics. Topics that are possibly sensitive can usually be spotted in advance. Sylvia Barr talks about a case in point.

> We received an assignment to interview men, who were going to react to a trial of men's underwear that we would send them through the mail. Most of our interviewers are women, so we had our interviewer first call the wife or mother, and then talk with the male subject. We successfully mailed the product, then completed our telephone follow-up with the men without trouble.

An earlier example has already told about the case where teenaged girls were to be talked with about their sanitary protection; the mothers were talked to first, to set the stage and prevent repercussions. It worked.

Unlisted Numbers

This subject, too, has been previously reviewed, so it needs only brief comment here. Almost all professional telephone survey companies report no difficulty with obtaining cooperation from those with unlisted numbers (when the sampling technique is one that includes these, as outlined in Chapter 4). Many such respondents don't even comment. When someone does, at least two of the firms have the interviewer say that the number is computer generated, and that ends the problem!

DATA PROCESSING

Data processing is converting every response recorded on every questionnaire to a number, entering all such numbers in a data processing machine (the computer), and obtaining figures (keyed back to the descriptive answer terms) which show the number of times each response was entered. This simplistic definition provides a good starting point for discussion.

This definition excludes nonelectronic machines, hand tabulation, and other tabulation methods, since these are used by the professional telephone research firm only for highly specialized application.

The purpose of data processing is to put meaning into the data. When the responses have been entered onto the questionnaires, merely the raw material of the survey is there. All surveys deal with figures. Data processing establishes what these figures are. Imagine a ten-question interview, conducted with 2000 people across the country. If one were to leaf through these questionnaires to attempt to get a picture of the survey results, one would end up with little more than vague impressions, and many would be wrong. Tables and other statistical measurements are needed.

The full-line professional telephone research firm has its own in-house facilities for data processing. (The firm that specializes in professional telephone *interviewing* does not, any more than it has methods of pulling telephone samples.) There are four distinct operations in data processing as outlined here: editing, coding, card punching, and computer running.

EDITING

Editing is the inspection and modification or correction of the recorded replies on the questionnaire. The overall purpose is to make the material more meaningful than it would otherwise be, and to make clear to all those involved in the succeeding stages of data processing just what the meaning of each reply is.

Survey data, in its raw form, is never perfect, no matter what the interviewing skills of the survey firm may be. All surveys contain some recording error.

Most professional telephone survey firms begin the editing process almost immediately after the interview has been completed, so that the interviewer can, if necessary, recontact the respondent for clarification, omission, etc. This field editing is usually done both by the interviewer, on completion of the call, and by the supervisor, at periodic intervals. When field editing is done, it cuts down on the editing that precedes coding.

The Specific Purposes

Editing, altogether, whether some is done at the field level, or whether all is done at the precoding stage, serves four purposes: the increase of consistency or accuracy, the increase of completeness, the improvement of clarity, and the provision of uniformity.

Increase of Consistency or Accuracy. The specific purpose in this case is to eliminate replies which are obviously inconsistent or incorrect. However, the conservative professional survey firm eliminates a reply when it cannot be sure how to make a correction; it corrects only when there is some convincing evidence that the modification is really warranted. There otherwise would be too fine a line between obtaining survey results and obtaining survey results that were really a figment of someone's imagination.

Let's see how this works. In a whiskey study, one question asked about the last brand of whiskey purchased, then asked the respondent about the type. In one case a buyer of Dewar's replied that the type was bourbon. Since Dewar's makes only Scotch, it is reasonable to edit out the bourbon reply, and enter in Scotch as the type. Why? Simply because a person is far more likely to be sure of the brand than of the type of whiskey purchased. (The author, since he spent eight years of his adult life in Canada, still has trouble remembering that in the United States there is no rye whiskey; the closest thing to it is blended whiskey.)

Consider another case: In a study undertaken about the food industry, the question was asked: "Do you think that the food industry is doing all it can to hold down prices?" One response was *no.* A subsequent question inquired why the respondent felt that way. This particular respondent replied, "They are paying too much to the farmer." The answerer obviously didn't understand much about economics: that food processors had to pay the farmer the going rate, and had very little control over the matter. So this answer was edited out as not being relevant. Note that in this case there was no interviewer error; this was a response error that an interviewer could not be expected to screen out.

Here is still another case. A vacuum cleaner study asked about brand owned and the type of outlet from which it had been purchased. One respondent mentioned Electrolux and reported that it had been purchased through a discount store. Now Electrolux is sold only through door-to-door selling. Once again, the safe assumption was that the brand was being reported correctly, but there was a memory failure or a slip of the tongue about the purchase source.

This type of editing also makes it possible to eliminate the incorrect asking (and therefore incorrect replies) of contingent questions. A contingent question is one that is to be asked only when the reply to a preceding question falls within a particular scope. In one study the top screening question concerned whether the respondent smoked cigarettes. Five succeeding questions, to be asked only if the person was a smoker, concerned attitudes toward the physical effects of smoking. If any questionnaire had been discovered (they weren't) having answers to these five questions when the reply to the smoking question was *no,* the questionnaire would rightly have been eliminated. (This is again the conservative approach. Better to discard the questionnaire entirely than to make the unfounded assumption that this was really a smoker.)

The Increase of Completeness. Even the best interviewer sometimes fails to fill in the reply to a question. While most such omissions are spotted at the field level and corrected there, the precode editing process also provides an opportunity to complete replies where omissions occur. The method is referral to another part of the questionnaire.

In a study conducted among women concerning the silverware they owned, the brand and pattern of the silver set(s) was asked about. The respondents knew these and could report them. Then there was a question about type: sterling or plate. Some respondents did not know which of these the pattern was. But in the research house office it was possible to fill this in, since the firm had been provided by the client with an exhaustive list showing brand, pattern, and type for all brands on the market.

Here is another example. One study inquired about the brands of television known. In a later question, the respondents were asked about what makes of television set had ever been owned by the family. A few people named additional brands. In this case the research house was quite right to add these brands to those named in the earlier question. These people were *familiar* with the additional brands; they simply had not thought of them at the time of the question.

Such editing requires careful consideration. The editing instructions must be prepared only with knowledge of what each question is really designed to measure. If the earlier question in this case had been designed to measure brands *thought of*, then no additions would have been made.

The Improvement of Clarity. This aspect of editing is aimed at removing ambiguity, wherever that may be possible. However, if the ambiguity cannot be resolved, it is better to delete the answer entirely than it is for the research firm to make assumptions about what the firm thinks is meant.

Consider an example: One survey—the same whiskey study referred to earlier—asked the respondent's opinion as to the largest-selling Scotch whiskey in the United States. Some respondents named more than one. What should be done in this case? There are three alternatives.

First, the total reply could be eliminated, on the basis that the person had really not answered the question. Second, both could be accepted. Third, the first named could be taken. In the particular study the first named was taken as the reply to be used. The client wanted neither the column of replies to total more than the respondents nor the particular respondent's answer to be edited out completely. The rationale was that the respondent probably felt, however slightly, a little stronger about the first one named, otherwise it would not have been the first named. The logic is debatable, perhaps, but the point is that there must be a consistency in the approach. Probably any of the three possibilities would have been equally defensible.

Provision of Uniformity. While the designers of questionnaires always do their best to see that the question phrasing and possible answers will obtain comparable replies from one person to another, they do not always succeed. A question may ask approximately how many miles an automobile owner gets to the gallon. A checklist may provide for replies ranging all the way from 5 to 45. However, a careful respondent who really keeps good records may reply 15.5, and no encouragement by the interviewer will get the person to modify the response. The good interviewer therefore will write in the specific answer.

But now there comes the problem of handling this response in the editing process, to make the reply fit into the scheme of things without distortion. Note how this is a policy issue that cannot be resolved easily ahead of time, because it has not been anticipated.

The Steps in Editing

The first step is to get ready for editing of the particular project. This typically requires the project director in the research firm to go over a number of questionnaires from the study. He or she makes notes on problem areas of the questionnaire at which the editors will be expected to take extra care. From these observations a brief but pertinent set of written instructions on editing will be developed.

The next step is the actual editing itself. The supervisor personally instructs the people on the editing. In the editing procedure, the editor must look at the total questionnaire, for it is not so much the individual pieces but the interrelationships that must be examined.

The careful professional telephone survey firm does its editing with a red pencil. The purpose is to make sure that the original recorded reply and the editing can be distinguished, should this be necessary.

A critical attitude is required on the part of the editor and the editing supervisor. This cannot be stressed strongly enough; that is why it is repeated. Editing must be conservative. Editing must be absolutely supportable; if it is not, it is the unethical manufacture of raw data. If there is any question about whether it is supportable, it is not!

CODING

Coding is the assignment of a number to each reply on the questionnaire. It is a step to getting the raw material in shape to be entered into the computer.

The Need

When the computer is used, all data entered into the system are numerical. The usual professional telephone survey firm utilizes the punch card as the medium for getting the data ready. Some understanding of the punch card is necessary for explanation of the coding process.

A sample of a punch card is shown in Figure 7-1. There are a number of observations to be made about it.

It has 80 columns. Each one of the columns has positions in it for numbers 0 through 9. What is not obvious is that there are also two additional positions, ordinarily referred to as X and Y (to avoid the confusion of double digits with the single digits). These positions are at the top of the card.

Here is the way the card is used to record answers to a questionnaire. Let's say that there is a simple question: "Do you have an automobile?" The obvious possible alternatives are *yes* or *no*. A *yes* reply may be assigned punch 1 in column 25; a *no* answer may be assigned punch 2 in that same column. Now clearly not all reply alternatives are that limited. An open-ended question may end up having thirty-five (or more or less) possible answers, once the range of replies is known. If there are thirty-five possible replies, then more than one column (with its twelve alternatives) will have to be used. (Three columns are not really necessary, for it is possible to use combinations of punches in the two columns for coding purposes, such as 1-1, 1-2, 1-3, etc. Since most computers will accept input containing only a single digit per column, code planning must be done with this in mind.)

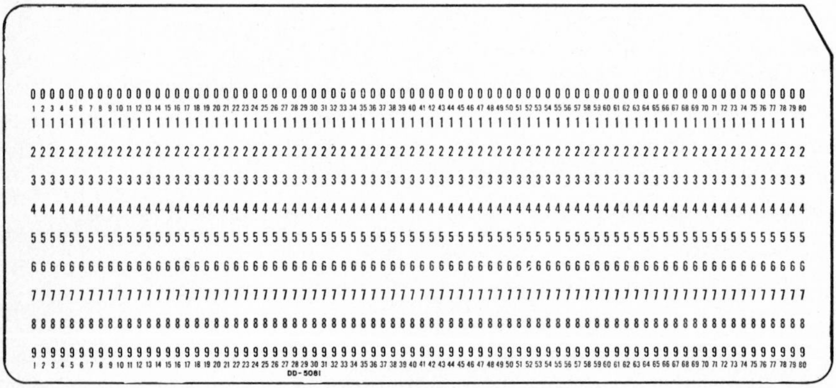

FIGURE 7-1.
A punch card.

The Process

Deciding Where to Place Codes. Some codes are precoded right on the questionnaire. Answer categories are listed on the questionnaire, and the interviewer checks or circles the reply, beside which is a small set of numbers, such as 12-1, which indicates that this reply is to go into column 12, punch 1.

Where there is no precoding, the code must be entered somewhere, and entered by hand. One possibility is to enter it directly on the questionnaire. Another is a special code sheet, designed to accompany the questionnaire. Perhaps most common is the standard code sheet, a sheet containing eighty spaces, each one numbered in succession, to reflect column numbers. Space is then left for a code to be entered beside each column numer. This is probably the most common coding sheet in the professional telephone survey field, because it is standardized. One of the great advantages of the professional telephone survey is its speed, so any standard device is a help in producing that speed.

Research Information Center does things a little differently. It uses an optical scanning system of coding. In this system there is a sheet of paper with 960 small squares entered on it. These are organized in eighty lines, each containing twelve positions, and each line and position is numbered. These represent the columns and punch positions within each. When the appropriate square is filled in with a pencil, it later is placed in an IBM 3881 Optical Mark Reader, which reads the material directly onto magnetic tape. The scanning machine includes a generalized editing feature that rejects incorrectly coded records. These are immediately referred back to the respondent's original questionnaire and corrected.[1] John F. Uhles, vice-president of Research Information Center, says that this method of handling the coding offers several advantages. The most important are the reduction of coding error and the increase in coding speed. Less time is spent in cleaning and consistency checking. In addition, the time lag between the coding and the data processing is minimal because the questionnaire information is read directly onto tape as soon as it has been coded. Given this time reduction, preliminary information is easily obtainable at any point in a study's progress and final data tabulation can occur quickly after interviewing is complete.

Determining the Codes. There are at least four different varieties of code: identification codes, automatic codes, numeric codes, and open-end codes. Each requires somewhat different handling, although the basic methods of establishing the codes are fairly similar, regardless of which type of code it is.

The first method of establishment of codes is the situation in which the useful categories of code are known in advance. In a national survey, for instance, the codes representing each geographic region can readily be spelled out in advance.

The second method is by reference to earlier surveys. The firm will have consistent methods, for instance, of designating such facts as sex, age, and income. The research buyer may have done a previous survey on the same topic, using many or all of the identical questions, and for comparison, will want to have the same set of codes used for identical questions.

The third method is a test tabulation. This is tabulating, by hand, a small segment of the total replies to the particular question, to get an idea of the nature and clustering of replies, so as to set up the coding structure. It is crucial to select a sample of returns that is reasonably representative. For instance, in a coffee study, where regional brands are important, it would be crucial to make sure that a sample representing all geographic areas were taken. (This is usually not a problem in WATS-line professional telephone surveys, since most research firms are working all brands every day that a survey is in process.) How many questionnaires should be examined? That is a little difficult to say. It depends on how easy or how difficult the particular code is to establish—on how much variability there is in the replies. The greater the variability, the greater the number of questionnaires that must be examined. One way to handle the actual tabulation is to have experienced personnel write down each response to a question on a separate card. If there are identical responses, then a tick mark is made on the appropriate card. The advantage of using a card system is the flexibility it offers when the codes are to be set up. Shuffling and reordering cards is a simple matter, even if there are as many as 200 of them.

Identification codes are those that identify the individual questionnaire, and some of the basic demographics of the particular respondent. Most professional survey research firms have standard items that they use for identification, and standard ways of handling the coding. The project number becomes the first code. While the nature of this coding varies by firm, the project number usually is not merely a sequential number adding a digit to the last one, but rather is designed to indicate information such as the year, the client, and the type of study. Four or five columns may be used for this purpose, and they are generally the first few columns on the card. The questionnaire number is always coded on the punch card, and obviously must be placed on the questionnaire as well. There is rarely a study in which it is not necessary for the professional telephone research firm to go back to an individual questionnaire for a reason of making a correction or change on the punch card. (This is usually handled by having each questionnaire numbered ahead of time, with an automatic numbering machine, or having the questionnaires numbered, in sequence, as the editing or coding process begins.)

Then there is other information which is usually standard for the research firm, such as geographic area, sampling point, sex, age, and family income. There may also be some "special" information, basic to the particular study, that is to be used for breaking out replies to questions. In one study concerning airline travel and attitudes toward airlines, frequency of commercial airline travel of each respondent was asked, and this was used to divide respondents into several equally sized groups of frequency. It became a basic factor used in analysis of replies to other questions, and a most useful one, too.

Automatic Codes. Automatic codes are those which have been determined in advance and need no special attention at the time of coding. Precoding falls into this category. Sometimes even open-ended questions are precoded. In honesty, this author does not recommend the procedure. It would seem to encourage poor work.

Several risks are involved. One is that the preliminary work to establish the codes may not have been extensive enough, and therefore the list of alternative replies established is not sufficiently extensive. Material was presented in Chapter 5 suggesting strongly that if an important alternative is omitted, even if space is provided for the write-in of other replies, the frequency of replying with that answer will be decreased. In addition, there is a great risk in entrusting the interviewer with proper handling and categorization of open-ended replies. As will be shown, the setting up of open-ended categories is a difficult proposition at best, and the classification of replies into the proper category is also tricky. There is no chance for the interviewer to check with the supervisor, and besides, the supervisor is a specialist in interviewing, not editing or coding. The very use of open-ended replies lists at the interview level goes against the concept of the professional telephone survey. The professional telephone survey is specialized: it should be a production line, with each specialist doing his or her bit. Suddenly the interviewer is being required to be a specialist in open-ended coding as well.

Open-Ended Question Codes. In open-ended question coding, a great deal of the detail of individual responses is given up in order to compress, summarize, and categorize, so as to get an understanding of the overall result. Sometimes, to preserve a bit of the original flavor, the professional telephone research firm selects some of the richer or more illustrative replies and reproduces these separately from the tabulation.

Setting up codes for open-ended questions is not simple. It may be one of the most difficult operations in survey research, if the classifications are to be sound ones, and the open-ended questions are really open ended (wide open). There are at least five requirements.

First, the classification must be *articulate*. Here is the problem. If only a few groups of responses are used, a number of relatively different kinds of replies must be included within each group. On the other hand, if each category is made very, very specific, then a really large number of categories will be the result. The solution: the use of "articulate" categorizing. There is a gradual development of classes. At the start, only a few groups of responses are defined. Each group is subdivided, and the process is carried on as far as necessary.

In articulation, the broad headings of replies are shown, perhaps in underscored or capital letters. Under each heading then comes a list of the specific forms that this category encompasses. The reader of such a table can easily get the overall implications by reading the numbers attached to the major categories, and the fine points of the comments by reading the subscript material.

Second, the classification must be *psychologically adequate*. The selected categories must represent the best possible scheme for comparison of the responses. However, it is possible to have the classifications too elaborate, and this leads to problems. There will be an increase in error. There will be an increase in the cost of processing.

With a psychologically adequate system, no response will be left outside of an answer category. Every class used will be significant. The categories will not be overlapping. The classifications are mutually exclusive.

People drink beer. They comment on their reasons for doing so. If these comments are simply listed in the order in which they come in, they will apparently vary all over the lot, and not make a great deal of sense. People drink beer to make themselves feel good, yet if they drink too much beer, it may do them physical harm. People drink beer to be sociable among others. People drink beer because it has a good flavor. Confusing? Well, if all the reasons given are classified under only a few headings, then the patterns of replies make a great deal of sense.

Headings of *Social Reasons, Flavor Reasons, Physical Effects, Reasons of Economy* might solve the whole set of problems.

Third, the classification must be *logically correct.* There can be no inclusion of groups which have been added together under different methods of classification. For instance, a classification of camera types in a marketing research study could not include Kodaks, automatics, instants, and 35 millimeters. There are actually four sets of classes represented there: brand, amount of automation, immediate versus darkroom development, and film size.

Fourth, the classification must be *psychologically pertinent.* The respondent must be considered. The classifications should represent a basic group of reasons as seen from the respondent's viewpoint. If a marketing research study were to inquire why people ate at McDonald's, the answers might be very diversified, spreading over an exceedingly wide range, such as "to save money," "when I am in a hurry," "because the food is good," "because I like the shakes," "it is nearby," and so on. Left alone in a strung-out pattern of this sort, the replies do not show a pattern. But now let's classify them under headings which make considerable respondent sense: *Good Food, Convenience, Price.* These are psychologically pertinent categories, and the specific replies falling under each can be specified and listed.

Finally, the categories must be *consistent.* There must be no chance that individual coders will code differently; the categories should be obviously tighter than that. If there is a chance that coders may classify an item in different ways, the categories are clearly not consistent or unique.

Numeric Question Codes. In numeric questions, the classifying process involves placing a variable series of responses into a meaningful array. There can be statistical treatment of numeric replies only if the replies are counted within clusters or class intervals. The basic problem is the setting up of class intervals. The class interval is a range consisting of a portion of the answers.

Let's give an example. If you ask ten automobile owners the age of their cars, you may get a sequential series that reads: 4, 1, 7, 3, 8, 2, 1, 6, 5, 1. Now the array shown that way has no meaning. There is no way you can treat it statistically unless you feel like going to the trouble of adding the figures up, and dividing by 10 to get the arithmetic mean. But you wouldn't do that with 1000 cases very easily. No, the way is to array the numbers by size:

Age	#
1	3
2	1
3	1
4	1
5	1
6	1
7	1
8	1

Now the array makes a little more sense, and it would be possible, if one cared to do so, to make the classes 1 or 2, 3 or 4, 5 or 6, 7 or 8, and end up with still fewer categories. In the example given there is no possible reply of zero, but in many kinds of numeric question there is. Where so, the zero is usually assigned a specific category of its own, for it is lack of possession, behavior, or whatever the numeric question is asking about. A zero is qualitatively distinct from all other numbers.

The setting up of class intervals is not an easy, automatic task. While it is not typically as difficult or involved as is the process of setting up classifications for open-ended questions, it still requires considerable thought and care. There are a few principles to be followed.

The categories must be *representative of the particular series*. Unless the researcher is pretty careful, the data may be distorted through use of unrepresentative class intervals. Let's give a simple example. Assume that the data range from 1 to 10, and that there are 2 cases in each class. Now assume that the class intervals selected were:

1–2
3–5
6–10

These intervals do not do justice to the raw data; they distort the raw data. Obvious, isn't it? Well, it isn't always that obvious in marketing research. People's behavior tends to cluster around specific numbers. Take the case of the simple question on a television survey: At what time did you first turn on your television set yesterday? The class intervals would have to be set up in a fashion to take into account that most people turn on the set at the beginning of a show, and therefore the intervals would have to show separately the hour and half-hour times slots throughout the day.

Again, a question about how much was paid for an item must

consider whether or not psychological pricing is common for the particular item in question. (Psychological pricing is the practice of using the digit 9 at the end of the price to make the price seem less: $39.99 instead of $40.00.) If psychological pricing is common, then use of a category such as $35.00–$39.99 would not represent the data because most of the answers falling in the range would be concentrated at the uppermost limit of the category.

Only a test hand tabulation will indicate the nature of the array of answers. In the numeric test tabulation each individual reply will have to be recorded to get an understanding of where the answers cluster. The class intervals should be built around these points.

The categories must be *logical*. Suppose that a question has been asked regarding how long ago a particular type of grocery item (for example, fresh meat) was purchased. Let's say that there is a clustering of answers around 4 days. This is no indication that the class interval should then run from 1–7 days, for that would kill the usefulness of the array of replies. It would be too broad a group, even though technically meeting the requirement of being a representative class interview. Some good common sense has to be applied.

The categories must *tie in with purposes of the study*. There are many possible ways in which the purpose of the study may affect the class intervals, but let's look at only one way. In a study among beer drinkers, asking about their beer-drinking preferences and situations, it was desired to analyze results by heaviness of drinking. This meant that the beer drinkers were to be divided into three groups: heavy, medium, and light drinkers. But the amount of consumption required to divide the drinkers into the three groups was not known ahead of time. Thus the actual class intervals for last week's consumption had to be kept fairly small, so that a first run through the computer could show where the splits had to be made to get fairly equal-sized groups. (The desire for equal-sized groups was to maximize reliability of results within each of the three groups. It makes more sense to have three equal-sized groups rather than one large, one medium, and one small group. Reliability of results is related to sample size.)

The categories must be *mutually exclusive*. It is truly surprising that a point like this one has to be made. Yet too many market research tables violate this principle. Too many show a category of income as $10,000–$15,000, and another of $15,000–$20,000, and so on. Where does an income of $15,000 fall under such a scheme?

When appropriate, class intervals should be *of equal size*. If all the previous requirements have been met, and this one, too, can be imposed, it should be. But this particular requirement is more of an ideal than a requirement, for there are many situations in which the class intervals simply cannot be of equal size.

Equal-sized intervals make the whole pattern of results neater, easier to digest, easier to treat statistically. They mean that there are fewer worries about the statistical treatment. But the researcher really has to be careful in applying this concept.

For a simple example, suppose a consumer gives a reply of zero to a question of how much ground beef has been purchased in the last week. The zero answer puts that consumer into a completely different category from all respondents who give a number of pounds; the zero answer indicates a nonpurchaser for the time period. The categories set up for the purchasers will show some groupings, but the size of their class intervals will be different from the nonpurchaser's.

Preparation of Coding Book. The professional telephone research firm prepares a coding book for each study. This book shows, for each question, the response categories, the column or columns assigned for those answers, the individual column codes applicable to each, and the standard basic coding. The page concerning the individual question indicates whether only single replies are acceptable or whether multiple replies are accepted. If only a single reply is acceptable, then the code page for the particular question also instructs the coder what action to take when a multiple reply has been recorded (such as taking the first reply only).

The particular page will also indicate the base for the question. If only users of a particular brand are to be asked a follow-up question, the appropriate page for the question will so indicate.

Coding. The most accurate coding is done when one person works on one question at a time. This way the coder becomes thoroughly familiar with the coding structure and the answers. The coder's mind is not thrown off the track by going to more than one array at a time. To be sure, if two questions are identical, and have the same set of codes, there is no reason why the coder should not handle both simultaneously, but this occurrence is not frequent.

Coding is typically done in colored pencil (usually red) so that it is easily distinguishable to the puncher.

The coding supervisor makes sure that all coders thoroughly understand the set of codes on which they are working. The supervisor makes sure that all coders use the same interpretation and make the same decisions in identical problems. It is up to the supervisor to direct the

FIGURE 7-2.
Coders at work. *(Walker Research, Inc.)*

entire procedure and to see that coding meets the accuracy standards of
the particular firm.

Most firms do not do a 100 percent check of the accuracy of their
coding. Research Information Center starts with a thorough check of the
first portion of the work on each question; as the company determines
that the accuracy level is acceptable, it gradually cuts down on the
amount of verification. This is the way that most of the firms in the field
operate.

PUNCHING

Punching refers to placing punch holes in the card. The operator of the
punching machine looks at the entered codes and their columns, and
does the appropriate punching. The operator does not need to know
anything about research or the research process. Punching is a process
which is even more mechanical than typing from a typed rough draft.

For the puncher has only to read the column number and punch location. There simply is no judgment in the process. The typist, if alert, will catch such things as misspellings and inconsistencies. But the puncher cannot and is not expected to recognize errors.

Most firms offering professional telephone surveys include the punching operation as a part of their processing system. However, as already pointed out, the optical scanning system of Research Information Center skips this step. There are other methods of skipping it, too. Another is Porta-Punch, and this is similar to the computer terminal keyboard in front of the interviewer at the time that he or she is making the telephone calls. In the case of Porta-Punch, the interviewer actually has a portable puncher at the time of the interview, and punches the keyboard appropriately in each column as the respondent provides a reply. As we have already seen, with the CRT and computer terminal, the interviewer simply depresses the appropriate key (according to the instructions on the screen) and the response is entered into the computer. Each way the process of a separate punch operation is avoided. However, neither system is common today. The CRT computer terminal setup is available only at Chilton and at the TELSAM centers of AT&T, described in Chapter 9.

There admittedly is a worry about systems that avoid specialized punching. If the interviewer makes an error in the punching, there simply is no way of catching it on a total basis. Samplings may be made of the accuracy, but they are only samplings. When the author was a partner of a marketing research firm, that company made a study in which it compared the punching made by interviewers at the time of interview to a tape recording of the interview. There was a 4 percent error, and the company rightly concluded not to proceed with the Porta-Punch.

The purpose of card punching is to get the coded information into a physical condition that will provide entry into the computer system.

The Equipment

There are two machines in the punching system: the puncher and the verifier.

The punch machine accepts in a hopper a stack of unpunched cards. One at a time, the cards fall to the horizontal surface of the machine. When one arrives there, it is ready to be punched in column 1. When the puncher depresses the punch key, the number is punched and the card automatically moves to the next column position, similar to a piece of paper moving across the typewriter.

FIGURE 7-3.
A key punch operator translates a coded questionnaire into data code. *(Walker Research, Inc.)*

The verifier is used to check the accuracy of the punching. The operator places the already punched card in the machine, and begins to read the material from which that punching was done, perhaps the questionnaire. The operator depresses the appropriate key, just as if punching the card. If the hole is in the same position the operator has depressed, the card moves to the next column. If the hole is not in the same position, the machine locks, and this indicates that either the operator or the puncher has made an error. A quick check determines whether the original punch is right or not.

Costs and Practices

Despite the fact that complete verification doubles the cost of punching, since in effect the operation has to be performed twice, most professional telephone survey firms do exactly that. They feel that a complete verification is desirable and necessary.

THE NEW SHORTCUT IN CODING,
PUNCHING, AND VERIFYING

Chapter 2 described the on-line entry of computer input by the interviewer, done with the help of a keyboard and a cathode-ray tube, which permit direct entry into the computer at the time of the interviewer.

National Family Opinion, with its centralized telephone interviewing facility, has the first cousin to this set-up, and will likely be as far advanced as Chilton is by the time this book is in print.

At National Family Opinion, information is read off the interview form by the person entering the data into the computer, though this is not the interviewer. Card punching and verification are not needed. The numerical data are entered from the questionnaire via the keyboard. The cathode-ray tube then displays the coded information, so

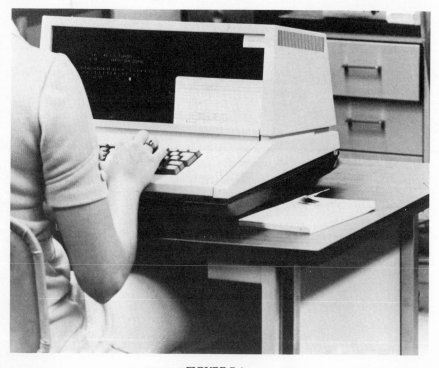

FIGURE 7-4.
A puncher entering data onto a cathode-ray tube just prior to computer entry.
(*National Family Opinion, Inc.*)

that the operator has a chance to visualize what is going into the computer before it is entered there. Only after the operator verifies the accuracy of the information is it actually entered onto the magnetic tape for computer processing. National Family Opinion reports that the system has dramatically reduced input errors, and has decreased worker hours and project time. This method of getting survey data into the computer is unquestionably the method of the future. It shouldn't take too long, either, for it has so many, many advantages. It is simply another step in bringing the survey process out of the cottage and into a highly efficient production line.

COMPUTER PROCESSING

Computer processing is entering the data into the computer, providing the computer with instructions on what is desired, and getting the output from the computer, largely in the form of tabular material.

Nature of the Facilities

There are two parts of the equipment in computer processing: the hardware and the software.

The hardware is the computer itself. There are many computers available to perform in the field of marketing research, and the specific names and varieties are beyond the scope of this book. Whatever the machine, the central processing unit (the CPU) is its heart. There is a memory or storage unit which holds data until they are needed in processing. There are main trunk lines over which information flows into the heart of the computer. The operator corresponds with the computer via a printer keyboard. The computer accepts input through a card-read punch, that is, the information on the card is read by a reader which translates the information into a digital system compatible with the computer. The output is generally in table form. The typical printer can print some 2000 lines per minute.

The software is the program used to prepare and systematize material for the computer. The typical professional telephone research firm has a program available. While there are several "canned" programs useful in marketing research surveys, one of the most popular is Disktab, developed by Donovan Data Systems. As one professional telephone survey research firm put it: "It's not too easy a system. But it provides more extras." The extras the firm is talking about consist mainly of statistical treatments.

The Process

The particular professional telephone survey adjusts the program it has to the needs of the particular study. Chiefly this adjustment consists of instructing the machine on the number and nature of "breaks" required in tabling the results to each question.

A break is a factor by which to look at the results. For instance, a break to a question might be by sex. This means that results to the question are separately examined for males and females. The various demographic factors (region, sex, age, income, etc.) are the most commonly used breaks, but there are many, many other possibilities.

But before the computer begins any of this actual analysis, the cards are counted against the questionnaires. This step is to avoid duplication or omission.

The next step is cleaning. This is a mechanical extension of editing as the final step in elimination of inconsistency and error. There are three types.

One is *out-of-field cleaning*. This is a check for punches outside of the range of codes allocated for the column. Another is *not-applicable cleaning*. This refers to a check to make sure that contingency questions have not been asked of people who were not supposed to have been asked those questions. A third is the *internal consistency cleaning*. In this case checks are made to locate any material which is clearly inconsistent within a questionnaire. A person who reports an occupation of college professor should have more than a high school education.

Following the cleaning, the computer is ready to go to work to turn out the tables. A table is a compact layout of numeric data, designed to make its major content apparent rapidly. It is self-contained, i.e., complete by itself. There is at least one table produced per question.

The title of the table denotes what is in that table. The question, along with its number, appears on the table, sometimes at the top (under the title), sometimes after the arrays of figures in the table. The base TOTAL INTERVIEWS is indicated, and the appropriate number is shown. Coming down the page, NO ANSWER may be indicated, with a number, and the next line down reads TOTAL RESPONDENTS, again with the number indicated. This is typically the base, and right below it appears 100%. Each response category then appears in turn down the page, with a percentage indicated. Most research firms have programs that show whole percentages only, and round off total responses to 100 percent. Breaks are shown going across the page. A sample of a table is provided in Table 7-1.

TABLE 7-1
Any Study Name

Example 1A-Standard Table Presentation—Frequencies and Vertical Percentaging to Tenths, Standard Titling and Table Number Locations.

	Total	Age			Education				Household Income				Locality	
		18-34	35-49	50 +	Some High School	High School Grad.	Some Coll.	Coll. Grad.	Under 5,000	5,000 to 9,999	10,000 to 14,999	15,000 and Over	Urban	Rural
Total respondents	500 100.0	218 100.0	117 100.0	165 100.0	100 100.0	136 100.0	117 100.0	147 100.0	158 100.0	179 100.0	100 100.0	63 100.0	250 100.0	250 100.0
Used and brand (net)	492 98.4	215 98.6	115 98.3	162 98.2	98 98.0	133 97.8	117 100.0	144 98.0	153 96.8	177 98.9	100 100.0	62 98.4	246 98.4	246 98.4
Used brands A, B, C (net)	218 43.6	93 42.7	55 47.0	70 42.4	47 47.0	62 45.6	44 37.6	65 44.2	68 43.0	80 44.7	45 45.0	25 39.7	111 44.4	107 42.8
Used brands X, Y, Z (net)	280 56.0	120 55.0	58 49.6	102 61.8	57 57.0	75 55.1	72 61.5	76 51.7	90 57.0	98 54.7	57 57.0	35 55.6	135 54.0	145 58.0
-A-	87 17.4	40 18.3	24 20.5	23 13.9	15 15.0	26 19.1	17 14.5	29 19.7	29 18.4	28 15.6	20 20.0	10 15.9	45 18.0	42 16.8
-B-	96 19.2	46 21.1	23 19.7	27 16.4	22 22.0	28 20.6	16 13.7	30 20.4	26 16.5	36 20.1	21 21.0	13 20.6	51 20.4	45 18.0
-C-	56 11.2	19 8.7	15 12.8	22 13.3	14 14.0	17 12.5	12 10.3	13 8.8	19 12.0	25 14.0	8 8.0	4 6.3	31 12.4	25 10.0
-X-	132 26.4	50 22.9	32 27.4	50 30.3	20 20.0	37 27.2	36 30.8	39 26.5	44 27.8	38 21.2	32 32.0	18 28.6	77 30.8	55 22.0
-Y-	84 16.8	33 15.1	19 16.2	32 19.4	27 27.0	26 19.1	14 12.0	17 11.6	31 19.6	33 18.4	13 13.0	7 11.1	32 12.8	52 20.8
-Z-	88 17.6	46 21.1	14 12.0	28 17.0	13 13.0	18 13.2	30 25.6	27 18.4	23 14.6	34 19.0	20 20.0	11 17.5	42 16.8	46 18.4
All other	48 9.6	22 10.1	13 11.1	13 7.9	11 11.0	12 8.8	12 10.3	13 8.8	15 9.5	19 10.6	9 9.0	5 7.9	21 8.4	27 10.8
Don't know/no answer	8 1.6	3 1.4	2 1.7	3 1.8	2 2.0	3 2.2		3 2.0	5 3.2	2 1.1		1 1.6	4 1.6	4 1.6

Your company (or client's) name

Total respondents are still the base in open-ended questions where one respondent may give more than a single reply. In this case the computer program normally adds a footnote to the effect that columns may total over 100 percent because some respondents gave more than a single reply.

Some questions produce answers which include a category of "don't know." There is some question as to what to do with these don't-know replies. The alternatives are to remove them from the base (the argument is that they clutter up the results) or to show them as a response category.

When the meaning is unclear, the don't-knows should probably be removed from the base. For instance, a consumer answering "don't know" to a place-of-purchase question for canned soup *did* buy it somewhere, and leaving such replies in the table of percentage items doesn't help make the answer array clearer. It is right to leave the don't-knows in the percentaged figures when the meaning is really clear. If the question is "What brand of microwave oven advertises itself as the Radarange?" then a don't-know is a perfectly acceptable reply, and gives the sponsor of the study information that is being looked for.

The final use of the computer is the generation of statistics about results of the survey. These fall into four types: measures of central tendency, measures of dispersion, bivariate analysis, and multivariate analysis. This book is not intended to be a statistical treatise, so comments on these will be limited. Not too many research buyers (only the most sophisticated) ask for some of the advanced programs that are available.

Measurements of central tendency are often asked for, however. Most common is the arithmetic mean, commonly referred to as the average. (This is the sum of all the values in the table divided by the number of cases.) Occasionally the median is called for: this is the value of the middle case in the array. Sometimes the standard error is requested. This is a measure of how much variation there is in terms of dispersion from the particular percentage figure. It is utilized chiefly to find out whether there are significant differences in one percentage figure from another, so as to determine whether the percentage variations between sections of the country, for instance, can be considered as statistically different from one another.

Bivariate analysis shows the relationship between two factors. Its most common form of measurement is correlation. Correlation shows the relationship between a change in one variable and a change in another. The "breaks" described earlier in the discussion may suggest an indication of such a relationship, but do not attach a specific single measurement of how close this relationship is. The correlation coefficient provides this. Most professional telephone research firms can provide correlation coefficients where these are requested.

Multivariate analysis goes a step beyond. Multivariate analysis provides a measurement of the relationship of two or more variables against the aspect being measured. For example, multivariate analysis could measure statistically the way that brand of replacement tires purchased is related to awareness of the brand, price of the brand, convenience to the dealer, and many other factors.

Multivariate analysis takes many different forms. One is multiple correlation, which is the determination of the statistical relationship of each of a group of variables to the particular element which is the basic measurement, as in the example above. Canonical analysis is essentially the same sort of measurement, except that there are multiple factors in both directions. Thus it would be possible to determine, by occupational level and income (the dependent variables) how factors such as age, educational level, early family demographics, and other factors (the independent variables) were related to one another.

Factor analysis is still another multivariate tool. In this case a large group of variables is reduced to a few, by measuring interrelationships. Responses to a list of thirty-six questions in a test comparing two unidentical coffees may be reduced to four or five basic groups of factors.

Discriminant analysis is a spatial representation or mapping of attitudes toward companies, brands, or other aspects. This sort of analysis is particularly useful in defining market segments which are looking for or using particular brands or services, for reasons otherwise not easy to identify. Discriminant analysis shows the clusters and segments of the population falling into the particular area. It shows their location on the map, and it measures their size.

REFERENCE

[1] *Standards of Operation*, Phoenix, Research Information Center, Inc., 1976.

REPORTING

An advertising agency research director recently had a marketing research firm conduct a survey on attitudes toward a number of brands in a particular product field. He specified that all he wanted was tables of results; he would put together his own report for the client.

When the computer printouts arrived, the research director happened to be out. But the account supervisor, one of the principals of the firm, was not. He happened to spot the material from the research firm on the desk of the research director. Knowing and curious about the survey, he took the liberty of opening the package, and immediately rushed with the material to the client. Neither one could make much sense out of it all. They could read results, question-by-question, and they could see the results of the breakouts, but there was no summary, no pattern that they could perceive. What was missing was a *report*.

A report is a formal or informal presentation of the survey findings, perhaps along with the implications that these carry for marketing management action. The facts in a survey remain without value until they are communicated accurately and effectively to those who make the action decisions. It is curious that good reporting is a major area of weakness for many researchers. One of the greatest criticisms leveled at marketing researchers is just that.

There should always be a report. There should be a record which puts together the findings of the survey. It should always be a written report, though as will be shown later, it may also be an oral presentation.

Who should prepare the report? Should it be the research firm? There are certainly some arguments favoring this viewpoint. One is that the research firm will have an outside viewpoint. It will have no axe to grind, no fears of angering someone within the client organization by telling the truth. On the other hand, if the market research department within the client firm prepares the report, and shows, for instance, what a poor job the marketing department is doing in some aspect of its work, this could stir up considerable personal resentment.

The outside research firm, too, has perhaps a greater opportunity to display imagination. Here we are thinking primarily about recommendations for action, where the outside firm has not been working, day in and day out, on the marketing problems faced by the particular product or brand. Internal client personnel, unless they are rotated fairly often from one brand to another, have a tendency to become stale, to run out of ideas. The outside research firm is not so likely to face this situation, since it does not do that much continuing, intensive work on a single brand. In fact the experience the outside research firm has on other products for other clients may contribute to its thinking for the particular brand.

There is still another point favoring a report by the outside research firm. The old adage, "A prophet is without honor in his own country" is often true. An expert may be a person who is a hundred miles from home. The deep, inbred familiarity of the marketing staff with the marketing research staff within its own company often means a taking for granted a feeling that the particular marketing research person, while competent, is not all that much of an expert in marketing. This is most often an incorrect view, but it is understandable.

On the negative side of having the outside research firm prepare the report is the argument that the research firm will lack the in-depth understanding necessary about the company, the product field, and the particular brand.

All right. Should the report then be prepared by the client research department, working from the statistical material produced by the research firm? There are advantages. One is the inside understanding of the total situation—the industry, the company, the product field, and the brand. Another is the understanding of those who will be getting the report, for there is a chance to tailor the style of the report to the key people who will receive it. There certainly is also the fact that company researchers will have constructive ideas that develop partially as a result of their background with the firm.

There are also negatives. The in-company viewpoint is restricted. If the research report is written by a member of the company research department, it will tend to stress what the company wants to hear. It will be restricted, most likely, to recommendations (if these are included) which the researcher consciously or unconsciously believes are likely to be accepted. The company researcher is conditioned by experience with the company, and this conditioning is bound to make the researcher hold back on concepts which seem to go against company thinking, even though some of these concepts might be very fine indeed.

The other negative of having the client researcher do the report is that after a long time on a brand, the researcher may begin to run thin on imagination. After working as a researcher for six years on a deodorant, what new ideas are likely to be seen as growing out of a research study?

The report, as has been stated, should always be in written form. Occasionally it is desirable to have it in oral form as well. Since the constant here is the written report, most of the remainder of this chapter concentrates on the written report. Much of what is said in these sections also applies to the oral report. However, there is a separate section, toward the end of the chapter, which considers the oral report separately, and shows its unique aspects and considerations.

CONTENT OF THE REPORT

There will never be a standard report. The nature of each report has to be tailored, for each marketing research survey study is unique; therefore every report is unique.

For one thing—assuming it is the telephone survey firm that has been requested to do the report—the client company will undoubtedly specify, at least partially, the nature of the report that is desired. A buyer who is in the research department of the client may specify, for instance, that only a description of the method is wanted in the report. This description will be utilized in the report the buyer puts together for the buyer's own management. On the other hand, a full report, including recommendations, may be requested.

A second factor is the problem: the nature and the complexity of the report. Most consumer product tests—in which consumers try unlabeled products and give their reactions—are fairly simple and direct. The report can therefore be of the same nature. But a study of market segmentation, describing the different perceptions people have of various brands and the different ways people use brands, may be far more complicated. Macleans toothpaste, a British product, ran many blind product tests against the leading brands of American toothpastes before they finally decided to enter the market. They lost, time after time, to the American brands they were testing against, until they got the brilliant inspiration to take a close look at the nature of the people who were selecting Macleans in the consumer product tests. The users tended to be people who wanted to keep their teeth white, and didn't object to the taste of the product (which most other people did not find very pleasant). Once the toothpaste manufacturer realized that it had a real market segment, it entered the market, and has done very well. But a report on this sort of research problem was much more complicated than that of just a simple product test.

Finally, the audience is a factor in affecting the content of the survey report. The researcher preparing the report should know the expectations of the major person or persons who will be getting it. This is not to say that the material should be slanted to distortion, but only that the content should or should not stress technique, should or should not be lengthy or short.

What should be included in the report? There is no final, definitive answer. However, despite that, we here recommend what we think should be included. Let's first dispose of those standard parts, unimportant but necessary, which can be taken for granted.

One is the title page. This should include the title of the survey, which is the self-contained description of what the survey was all about. It might be "A Consumer Product Test of Brand X vs. Brand Y." It will also contain the client name. How the client name is handled will depend on whether the client research department or the research firm is putting out the report. In the former case, the client name will typically appear at the bottom of the page. In the latter case it will appear, usually, right below the title, with a statement "Conducted for" preceding the client name. The name of the research firm may also be on the title page. It will be at the bottom of the page if the research firm is submitting the report. If the research department of the client company is submitting the report, the name of the research firm may or may not appear on the title page. (If it does not, it will be named at a later point in the report.) If it does, the title page will carry the name of the research firm under the title, with a statement such as "Conducted by" preceding the name of the research company.

There is another portion of the research report which can be considered as fairly standard and routine. That is a letter of transmittal. It is sometimes included, and is addressed to either the individual who was responsible for buying the survey (if prepared by the outside supplier) or the one who authorized it inside the company (if the research department of the client is preparing the report).

Finally there is the table of contents!

Now we get down to the more critical aspects of the contents. The way the contents have been arranged in this discussion is:

Introduction

Recommendations

Highlights of Findings

Discussion of Findings

Appendixes

There is nothing sacrosanct about either the topics included or the order. However, there seem to be many reasons, backed by experience of the author, for believing that this particular arrangement is unusually good.

One of the major reasons is that this is a nice, orderly, compact arrangement. The order parallels the newspaper order of reporting. It gives the busy executive the opportunity to stop at any desired point, with as much of a concept of the total survey as he or she cares to have. It begins—with the introduction—by telling the reader what the survey is all about. The next section tells what the survey suggests in the way of marketing action, and if the top executive wants to stop here, fine; the gist of the study has already been provided. On the other hand, the executive who wants to go on to see a little more of what is behind the recommendations can proceed on to the highlights, to learn something of what backs up the suggestions for action. And, if *really* intrigued with all this, the executive can go on into the discussion of findings and be filled in on virtually everything he or she would care to know.

The Introduction

The introduction is just that: it introduces the reader to the survey report. It outlines, *briefly*, the marketing problem that the survey is intending to solve (or help to solve). It states, also briefly, the research objectives of the survey (the kinds of information it is designed to measure). There is a very brief description of the method of the survey (the fact that the telephone method of interviewing was used, the nature of the sample in very broad terms, such as "a three-stage national probability sample, selected from telephone alphabetical directories," the dates of interviewing, and that the interviewing was supervised and monitored). The entire discussion in the introduction should rarely exceed one page. It is for broad, general information only.

Recommendations

As stated, the original problem should have alternative marketing decisions which the study is designed to aid. Sometimes, to be sure, the study is broad and general, and in that case the marketing alternatives are not known or stated in advance, but marketing recommendations may still grow out of the findings of the study.

The whole issue of whether or not recommendations properly should be a part of the report is examined in the next major section of this chapter. It is the author's strong opinion that they should.

Each recommendation should be buttressed with the fact or facts from the survey which lead to it.

Highlights of Findings

This is the third major section of the report. It telegraphs the overall results, so that the reader can pick up the gist of the findings without having to go through all the details. It is, in a real sense, the executive summary of findings, an abstract of the findings.

Discussion of Findings

This is the text section that looks at the details of findings. It may simply be a question-by-question review, or it may be organized into subjects or aspects of the questioning. The discussion of findings makes much use of summary tables, which are abstracts taken from the computer printouts, so that the reader who does not care to does not have to look at the computer sheets at all.

Appendixes

There are at least two appendixes in the usual research report: a detailed statement of procedure and detailed tables of results.

The detailed statement of procedure is a thorough description of exactly how the study was carried out. It talks in detail about the sample design and execution. If indeed a national three-stage probability sample from alphabetical listings was used, this appendix describes what those three stages were. It will mention the recency of the telephone listings. It will mention how names from each directory were selected. It specifies the level of call-backs and the completion rate achieved (and how this was calculated). The timing of interviewing is outlined—the dates and hours. Any special interviewing techniques are mentioned. In addition, a copy of the questionnaire is enclosed. Typically, interviewing instructions developed for the particular project are also included.

There is a good reason for including all these fine technical details. It is so that the study can be duplicated sometime in the future, should that ever be desirable. The easy availability of the total procedure will make this simple to do.

The detailed tables of results are typically all the computer runs. All such runs are included simply so that the report is an encyclopedia of the study. Should anyone ever care to look up a particular fact not discussed in the narrative portion of the study but one that has been tabulated, it is possible to do so in these tables.

THE QUESTION OF RECOMMENDATIONS

Should the report really contain suggestions for action or steps the business should take, based in part upon results of the study?

The Case Against Including Recommendations

Some make a strong case against the inclusion of recommendations. Here are the main reasons cited.

The Researcher Lacks All the Facts. The researcher's knowledge is limited to the results of the survey, according to this argument. And survey results alone should not lead to recommendations.

The last sentence is true, but if the researcher has only limited background knowledge of the company, the industry, and the brand, then something is badly out of whack. A researcher who is employed by the client company should have virtually the identical amount of information as those doing the marketing of the brand. The researcher hasn't been doing the proper homework.

If the researcher is not a member of the marketing research firm's staff, then the client researcher or marketer should have provided the researcher with a sound background before the study was undertaken. This is situation analysis, and covers an understanding of the marketing environment within which the problem is posed: the industry, the company, the company products, packaging, the markets, the distribution system, pricing and profits, and methods of advertising and other forms of promotion.*

---

*For a more complete discussion of situation analysis, see David J. Luck, Hugh G. Wales, and Donald A. Taylor, *Marketing Research,* Englewood Cliffs, N.J., Prentice-Hall, 1974, pp. 79–80.

The Researcher Is a Technician, Not a Marketer. This argument holds that the researcher is only a technician, not a practical marketer. If the statement is true about a particular researcher, it can probably be argued that this is not a topflight researcher. The best researchers are generalist researchers who really do know and understand the field of marketing. They can easily obtain the specialized help they need for the various aspects of research, such as sampling, statistical analysis programs, and interviewing.

The fallacy of this argument is most apparent when examining frequency with which marketing research people in manufacturer firms move out of research and into brand marketing.

It Is a Usurpation of the Line Function. According to this argument, marketing management has the responsibility for the line decisions on a brand, and it is the function of research to play only a staff role—to generate the facts.

In the first place, the sharp line between line and staff is breaking down, as company management is demanding more flexibility among its staff members. But even if there still is, in some cases, a rather distinct line, who cares? If having the researcher come up with recommendations helps to get a better job done, why not do that better job?

The Case for Including Recommendations

There is a more impressive case for including recommendations.

The Researcher Has a Superior Understanding of the Problem. The company researcher probably has a better concept of the problem than does the brand manager, since (though it is not discussed in this book) part of the job of a researcher is to define the problem. The company researcher has to go through all the steps in problem definition before it is possible to put together a sound research design. It is a part of a researcher's training. In the source of events, if the research firm is to write the report, all this background will have been given to the researcher in the research firm. If asked to come up with recommendations, the researcher will know more about the problem than the marketing person.

Also, the researcher will know more of the contents of the data than will anyone else. One of the real joys of the occupation is that for a brief period—until the results are communicated—the researcher knows more about the findings in a particular study than anyone else in the world.

It Is Valuable to Get the Opinions and Judgments of Someone Not on the Daily Firing Line. The marketing people in the company really should welcome the opportunity to get the viewpoints of someone whose nose is necessarily kept to the daily grindstone of marketing the brand. This is a real chance to get an "outside" viewpoint. It will be more of an overview, unclouded with the biases of daily work on the brand. It should be a relatively unprejudiced, unbiased view.

There Is No Compulsion for the Marketer to Accept All the Recommendations. Perhaps this is the most convincing argument of all; surely no one expects the marketer uncritically to accept all the recommendations made by the researcher. No sane person would do this. The marketer will have to consider each recommendation very, very critically, and will have to make sure that it does, in part at least, spring from the survey findings. The marketer will have to make sure that the recommendation makes good, practical sense and that it has a reasonably good chance of succeeding. Also, it should not cost too much. Unless it is a portion of a proposed entire new marketing program, the marketer will have to make sure that it will blend properly with the existing program. So there are all sorts of checks to be made.

It seems unwise not to take advantage of the generation of new ideas. There might just be some good ones generated.

One Other Consideration

There's just one other point: Should the outside research firm write recommendations? The question is whether the outside firm was selected to conduct the particular telephone survey because of its competency in professional telephone surveys alone, or whether its ability to provide marketing counsel was also taken into account. If it was selected only because of its telephone survey competence, then it might be unwise to throw the burden of marketing counseling on it.

STYLE OF THE REPORT

So often the writing in the research report is dull; sometimes it is downright bad. Those in brand management are often heard to complain about this. It has even been suggested that the very nature of the research process contributes to this. The researcher is a specialist who is more attuned to receiving communications than to doing his own communicating.

Here is an atrocious sample from a report:

> Purchasing behavior can be conceptualized as the vectorial resultant of conitive and cognitive forces in buying disequilibrium.

Translated into English, this merely means:

> People's thoughts and perceptions affect their buying.

The example has to give rise to another suspicion; Are some researchers trying to overimpress others with their knowledge? Use of many of the words in the example suggests so. If true, this is doubly bad. For not only does it make for a poor report, but it creates resentment against the individual researcher, who subconsciously is trying to make the reader look bad through an effort to impress the reader with the researcher's own expertise.

There are a number of rules of style which should be followed in the research report.

The Wording Should Be Clear

The words should communicate. Familiar words should be used. If a short word will fit the bill, it should be used in preference to a longer one. The phrasing should be direct. The active voice should be used in preference to the passive, where it can be made to fit. Phrasings should be positive rather than negative, where there is a choice. Technical jargon should be avoided unless using some technical name will avoid a long, involved discussion.

If canonical analysis has been used in the computer program, this term can be used by itself in the discussion of results, with a footnote saying that a full explanation of what this is is found in the technical appendix.

The Wording Should Be Brief, Concise

When the author wrote his first book, he had no contract with a publisher, though a publishing house had encouraged him by expressing general interest in the topic. After many months the 600-page manuscript was wrapped and set off to the editor. The author waited, very impatiently, for about five weeks, and then a bulky package arrived for him. With disappointment, he realized that the manuscript had been returned. But not all was lost; when the package was opened, there was a letter inside saying that the editor *would* accept the manuscript if it were cut in half!

Over the next several months (because the author was working in business, and the editing process had to be done on his own time) some heavy black penciling had to be done. It was a difficult task, for the author did not want to eliminate basic ideas, only nonbasic words, phrases, and sentences. Finally the task was done, the manuscript was retyped, and sent back to the publisher. This time it was accepted.

That manuscript was far more interesting than it had originally been, simply because there was scarcely an unnecessary word in it. It was short and pithy, and that's the way the writing in a research report should be, too.

Even the skilled writer will have to look for pet superfluities. Here are a few possibilities:

it is to be noted that

note the fact that

in order to

it is obvious (clear, evident) that

it is interesting to note that

as a result

The Writing Should Be Interesting

Churchill was a genius at creating vivid phrases. He gave us such inspirational or striking phrases as "blood, sweat, and tears," and the "iron curtain." But that was Churchill, and the author is not suggesting that the researcher should go this far, even if the researcher is capable of doing so. Such vividness could make the reader feel that the researcher is in the wrong business and would make a better writer than researcher.

The Writing Should Be Precise, Accurate

Too often the writing of even the good researcher is not precise. Frequently, a researcher writing about the results in Table 8-1 will say, "Men liked the product more than women." This is not precise; actually it is incorrect. What should really be said is "A greater proportion of men liked the product than was true among women." This is not

TABLE 8-1
The Proportion Liking and Disliking the Product

Q. On the whole, did you like the product or dislike it?

	Total	Men	Women
TOTAL INTERVIEWS	(2000)	(1000)	(1000)
NO ANSWER	(—)	(—)	(—)
TOTAL RESPONDENTS	(2000)	(1000)	(1000)
	100%	100%	100%
Liked it	45	50	40
Disliked it	30	25	35
Neutral	25	25	25

quibbling. The first quotation implies either of two things, neither one demonstrated by the table: that there was a greater intensity of feeling among men, or that men liked the product more than they liked women!

Precise writing will hang together and be cohesive.

The Writer Should Minimize Hedging

Too many researchers, largely because of the nature of their work, have a tendency to qualify statement after statement in the report. Now certainly the study has limitations; no study was ever completed that did not. These should certainly be stated. If they are not stated, the reader may notice and may lose confidence in the report entirely.

But once stated, they need not be reiterated at every point. Reiteration will destroy confidence, and it surely makes for dull reading.

The Writer Should Use Good Grammar

Fortunately there are not too many research reports that use poor grammar. The admonition belongs in the list, however. As the next generation of researchers move into line, poor grammar is going to move in with them. Unfortunately, they'll have to be trained in grammar on the job. The author, as a university professor, sees and hears poor grammar increasingly. Some examples:

that high of a total

you know

I mean

There is misuse of colons and semicolons, and the usage of apostrophes is incredible.

The Report Should Include Some Graphics

The old adage that one picture is worth a thousand words may be a slight exaggeration, but there is truth in the concept. For that reason the research report should use graphics in various forms. The aim of graphics is to show clearly and quickly what is in the text in numerical form, and possibly in a complex, complicated form. There will be some further discussion of the use of graphics in the discussion of the oral report.

PREPARATION OF THE REPORT

Preparation of the report is an art, not a science. No two researchers will ever turn out identical reports from the same set of tables; too much judgment and individuality is applied in the process of report preparation. But that doesn't mean that there are not some specific procedures that can be spelled out.

Perhaps an interesting way of starting this discussion is to give an example. The example is not from a telephone survey, but that doesn't detract from its usefulness.

The author was formerly a partner in a major marketing research firm. He was directing a large national study. Each interview ran a little over one hour in length, and in an hour's time a lot of questions can be asked.

As sometimes occurs in market research surveys, there were delays in processing the work, yet there was a very firm final delivery date. The field work, because of problems, stretched out for two weeks longer than the schedule called for. By the time the material was ready for data processing, another major study had slipped in ahead of it, so there were additional delays. The author had previously prepared his report outline, so he knew where he intended to use the results to each question.

The pressure was on to write the report, and remember that this was really a massive study, with hundreds of computer runs. As the computer runs came off the printer, two assistants began preparing summary tables from the runs. The author scanned these, placing those he wanted to use in one pile, those he did not in another. He made notes on each of those he did, highlighting what it showed. He took all these home, along with a dictating machine. After each three hours of dictation, the tapes from the machine were delivered to the office to two cooperating secretaries, who transcribed them in rough. After two days the dictation was all finished and transcribed; the author then went over the rough, editing it and smoothing it out. In another two days the report had been typed and duplicated. The computer runs were in one volume; the remainder of the report, totaling 156 pages, was in another.

Fortunately, most research reports are not this voluminous or done under this much pressure.

There are three major steps in preparing the report: analyzing the data, writing the report, and editing and rewriting the report.

Analyzing the Data

The method of data analysis has really been indicated in the example. The writer must first consider the purposes of the survey and then put together an outline of topics, from the survey to be discussed. Each survey question is classified under an appropriate topic.

Either the writer or an assistant prepares summary tables (abstracts of pertinent computer runs). The analyst then makes notes on each summary table of the major findings shown in it.

Writing the Report

Now the analyst is ready to begin writing. First the summary tables are sorted out by where they fit into the outline. Each pile is studied, by topical position within the outline, to see what general picture is starting to emerge. Then, in proceeding with the writing, the analyst develops that picture. The first part of the material then becomes the discussion of findings. This is the section from which abstracts are then made to provide the highlights of findings. At that point the researcher proceeds on to recommendations, if these are to be a part of the report. The highlights become the basis for recommendations; each highlight or pattern of highlights is related to the purposes of the study to arrive at generalizations. All the foregoing will be used as a springboard to recommendations.

These recommendations can sometimes be extremely creative. Let's review an example, although not from a telephone survey. Some years ago the author directed a study of gelatin desserts in Canada. It covered many, many different topics, such as women's attitudes and behavior about such products. The study was done for General Foods Limited, manufacturers of Jell-O.

The study on the client side was directed by Ron Rhodes, then a product manager, and Joe Doyle, then research manager, both now vice-presidents. When the results were in, the author wrote a report which he thought was reasonably good, including recommendations. But when Ron Rhodes saw the data, he immediately spotted two isolated facts which led almost automatically to a media recommendation. Most women, if they were going to prepare a gelatin dessert for dinner, did so late in the morning. Most women had a radio on in the house at that time. Therefore radio advertising in the late morning suggesting Jell-O for dinner that evening was a natural!

The more routine sections of the report should probably be prepared in advance, to get them out of the way. The title page, the Introduction, and the Details of the Method can all be prepared before data processing.

Editing and Rewriting the Report

Now the written material, before duplication, can be carefully edited to meet the style standards recommended earlier in this chapter.

THE ORAL REPORT

Occasionally, a study, as well as having a written report, is presented orally. Should there be an oral presentation? It probably depends chiefly on the importance of the study. An oral presentation implies that the study is far more than just a routine affair.

Forms of the Oral Report

While there is not always a clear line separating them, oral presentations seem to fall into three categories: an informal discussion in an office, with a limited audience; a semiformal meeting in a conference room, with a somewhat larger audience; and a formal presentation in a hall or auditorium, with still a larger audience.

Methods of the Oral Report

One method of the oral report is the reading or review of the written report. This is usually deadly. Very few people, including researchers, can read aloud that effectively very long. The method is not recommended, unless the researcher has had training or experience in acting.

Another method, closely related, is the completely oral report, for which the presenter has made advance notes and talks about the findings from these. This is not very much different from the reading method, and it rarely can be recommended for the same reasons. It usually is not at all satisfactory for complex material.

The most common method is an oral report with visual aids. The visual aids can take one or more forms: a blackboard or blank paper, with the presenter making notes for the audience in the process of giving the report; an overhead projector with acetate sheets, which can either be prepared in advance from typed or other duplicated material, or marked with crayon as the presentation proceeds; flip charts, showing text material, drawings, photographs, maps, tables, etc.; slides, which may or may not be accompanied by a sound track; or a motion picture or videotape. This list is pretty much in order of sophistication or complexity, and the more formal the meeting, the greater the chances that one of the more sophisticated methods should be used. It is the more formal meeting in which there is the greatest effort to impress the audience with the importance of the material, and the more sophisticated presentation devices aid that impression.

Two caveats about the oral presentation should be mentioned. The first: Don't distribute the written report in advance of the meeting or during the meeting—only at the end. Doing so will cause a loss of attention during the meeting. People who have read the report in advance may not even show up for the meeting; if they do, their attention is likely to wander because they know the story. If the written report is circulated at the start of the meeting, people will be leafing through it, rather than paying attention to the presentation. The end of the meeting is the *only* time at which to pass out copies of the written report.

The second caveat: Know your audience. When the author was director of market research for a manufacturer, one of the first major studies to be reported was planned to run for about two hours. Executives such as the chairman of the board and the president, as well as the vice-president to whom the author reported, were there. The author decided that there would be a coffee break with doughnuts between the two hours of the morning meeting. The vice-president showed his displeasure, with some remarkably audible comments about "our fancy research department." It was a little late by meeting time to learn that the vice-president didn't like coffee! Know your audience!

Preliminary Steps

There are three preliminary steps to prepare for the oral presentation: select the proper physical facilities, plan for the proper amount of time, and personal input of the presenter.

Select the Proper Physical Facilities. One of the first considerations in deciding where to hold the presentation is the size of the audience. The physical facilities must provide sufficient space to hold the audience, without crowding.

The space should have adequate ventilation for the size of audience and the length of time. There should be no telephones, or if there are and there is a switchboard, the operator should be told not to ring during the meeting. There should be no outside noise. There should be facilities to handle the kind of presentation planned.

Plan for the Proper Amount of Time

The amount of time must be carefully planned for two reasons. One is to let the audience know in advance about how much time to allocate for the session. The other is to know for how long the meeting place should be reserved.

While there are no hard-and-fast rules, generally the time planned should be at a minimum. The meeting should not drag on; some of the audience will lose interest, and, if their rank is high enough, may even leave. So a minimal time for the presentation should be figured on (so long as no injustice to the results takes place). On top of that, particularly if there is a chance that some of the findings or recommendations may be controversial or unusual (unexpected), time for discussion will have to be allowed. It may be wise to overallow for this; if it turns out that the meeting is completed before schedule, no one is going to object.

Personal Input of the Presenter

The presenter is the main key to how well the presentation comes across. He or she has two specific responsibilities when getting ready for the session.

Learning the Material. The presenter must know the material inside and out. The information must really be absorbed; it must be soaked up. A poor impression will be made if, when asked something, the presenter has to refer to the report. This is not to say that every statistic in the report must be memorized; that would be an impossibility. But it does mean that the presenter must have a general idea of what the results to each question are—whether or not the figures are used in the oral presentation—and some idea of the level of most of the remaining important information growing from the study. At the meeting, the presenter must be the expert on the results.

The presenter must also be the expert on the method and should have in mind the elements of the entire research design, even though he or she may not be able to cite all the details without going to the report.

Polish the Style. The style in the oral presentation is different from that in the written report. All principles outlined in the style for the written report hold here, but the total style is still different. The style here is similar to the newspaper headline. The important statement is made first, with conversational fill-in to back it up.

The style of delivery is important. The tone of voice is perhaps the most important single element. There must be enthusiasm. There must be variation in tone.

In addition, the vocabulary of the audience should be used. The researcher should know, from the nature of the audience, what that vocabulary is. A researcher would not talk about "respondents," a marketing research term, when "consumers," a marketing term, might be used.

Ideally, to prepare for the meeting, a script should be prepared. To test his or her delivery of the script, the researcher should tape-record the presentation, to find out where it is strong, where it is weak, and then make appropriate changes in content or form of delivery.

Organization of the Material

Organization of the material for the oral presentation is different from that of the written report. For the written report, it was suggested that the material be presented in an order so that the reader could stop at any point when feeling he or she had gotten enough, parallel to the way a newspaper story is written. With the written report there is no captive audience, and the busy executive has a right to stop reading the report after feeling that enough information has been obtained from it about the survey.

The situation is very different with the oral presentation. Here there is a captive audience unless the presentation becomes downright atrocious. These people have set aside a time period to look and listen. Under these conditions, the presenter doesn't want to toss all the goodies into the show at its beginning. The audience will become bored.

The presentation should begin with a statement of the problem and a brief review of the method used in the survey. The results of the survey should then be presented in much the same way that the discussion of findings is organized in the written report. Then the major findings should be reviewed in highlight from (and paralleling the highlights of findings in the written report). Finally, the climax of the presentation is reached: the recommendations. Thus, the presenter is taking the audience through the material in much the same sequence in which it was put together.

THE AUDIENCE

Who should receive copies of the report—or be invited to the oral presentation? The two questions are pretty much the same, except for routine deliveries of the report to places such as a company library.

Selected Top Management

There are generally people in top management of the firm who show unusual enthusiasm or curiosity about marketing research surveys. Depending on the company, this curiosity may go as high as the chairman of the board. Certainly all such management should be included, and if the report or presentation concerns a major study of real importance, all top management, regardless of general interest level, should be included.

Marketing Department

Those in the marketing department concerned with the particular product or brand should be included: the vice-president of marketing, the group brand manager, the brand manager, and assistant brand managers.

Research and Development

Those in research and development who work on the particular product line should be covered for all consumer product tests. Most such reports are usually only in written form, so this becomes a matter of circulating them.

Sales Department

The sales manager is generally included whenever the study concerns the movement of merchandise, such as tracking studies in a test market to track what is happening to the brand as the testing proceeds. (A test market—further discussed in Chapter 9—is one or more areas in the United States in which a product is introduced to predict its success if introduced nationally.)

Advertising Agency

All advertising research for a particular product or brand handled by the advertising agency should be reported to the agency. The people covered, depending on agency size, will be the account supervisor, the account executive, and the research supervisor (or equivalent titles).

EVALUATING THE REPORT

How good is a report? That's a question that needs answering, and there are several things to look for in arriving at an answer.

Does the Report Keep the Problem in Mind?

A very elegant report is not a good one if it misses coverage of the problem. The report should be studied to make sure that it does, indeed, answer the problems raised at the start of discussion.

Is the Report Objective?

To be truly sound, the report must be objective; it must be based upon the facts developed from the study. It is all right for the report to be speculative *if* the speculation is clearly pointed out as such.

Is the Report Properly Selective of Facts from the Study?

Few reports can discuss all the detailed tables of results generated by the computer. This would take too many pages, would be boring, and is not necessary. However, the report should be carefully studied to make sure that the writer has not been too selective in deciding what facts to use in summary. It is often possible to prove a point by ignoring some evidence to the contrary.

Is the Report Well Organized?

Is the organization of the report apparent, and does it make good sense? Does it help to pull the message of the report together so that the person exposed to it gets a balanced view of what all the results are like, and their significance?

Is the Report Well Written?

So much has already been said about this subject that no further discussion is required.

SPECIAL USES
OF THE
TELEPHONE SURVEY

Telephone surveys are very versatile. They can be used in almost every way that personal interview surveys and mail surveys can, except for the limitations outlined in Chapter 3.

The various applications of the telephone survey discussed in this chapter are those over and above mere substitution of telephone for personal or mail contact. Some make sole use of the telephone; others are combination studies. Some are rather general procedures; others are highly specific. Some are continuing services; others are ad hoc studies. Some can be conducted by any knowledgeable research firm or individual; others are services that must be purchased from firms providing a continuing service. Most are available to anyone; a few are proprietary.

So that the material in this chapter has the broadest implications for those interested in the professional telephone survey, any method utilizing the telephone approach is outlined, whether or not it comes within the definition of the *professional* telephone survey as defined in this book.

The major part of the chapter discusses by area of application the procedure or procedures used to solve marketing problems. The discussion includes procedures for broadcast audience measurement, television commercial testing, studies of consumer product reaction, tracking studies, and attitude studies. The chapter closes with a consideration of techniques broadly available for the collection of material to help solve problems in almost *any* marketing area.

BROADCAST AUDIENCE MEASUREMENT

There are several services offering such studies, and the techniques used are common property. Therefore, almost any professional telephone survey firm can undertake a similar study.

Arbitron Diary

Arbitron* offers a local radio and television measurement service through the medium of diaries, which are recording forms for various members of a family to fill in during the course of each day, showing the time, the channel (or station), and the name of the program. The sampling unit is generally a single county. The sample is computer generated from all telephone-listed households. The selected household is sent a preliminary letter informing them of their selection for inclusion in the study, and explains that an interviewer will be telephoning them about their participation.

At least five attempts are made to reach a household before it is dropped from the study. In television surveys a family diary is sent to all selected households (one family diary per set within the household). In radio studies, individual diaries are sent to all persons 12 years old and over within the family.

The reports show the rating (percent of total homes) in the audience for a channel or station by time of day, as well as the audience share (the percent of total homes tuned in at the time to the particular channel or station), with breakdowns by sex and age. The results are used by media buyers to aid them in selection of channels or stations and times. The cost to reach 1000 viewers or listeners is generally calculated by the buyer before making the choice.

---

*The procedures used by Arbitron are discussed in their individual reports. Old reports are available by writing the company.

Nielsen Station Index

The Nielsen Station Index[1] is somewhat similar to the Arbitron Diary procedure. Usually done on a county basis, the sample is a systematic selection of television households in the sample area. The sampling frame used is one of telephone-listed households compiled and updated by the National Data Center in Lincoln, Nebraska, although in larger markets Nielsen now uses random-digit dialing so as to include nonlisted households in its sample.

Telephone calls are made to selected homes, information about television set ownership is obtained, and cooperation for diary placement is obtained. Three attempts are made before the home is dropped from the sample.

Radar

This is a measurement done twice annually of the network radio audience. It is currently done by Statistical Research, Inc. Telephone homes are selected from a national list on a probability basis, and within each home falling into the sample, a random selection of a person 12 years old or older within the household is made. Completed sample size is approximately 5000.

This is a recall study, with the respondent being asked to tell the stations and programs listened to over a three-hour period. The telephone interviews are handled from central locations with monitoring.

Other Broadcast Audience Studies

The remaining broadcast audience studies are done on an ad hoc basis, as opposed to the ones described, which are syndicated.

Coincidental Studies. Almost any well-qualified marketing research firm can undertake a coincidental study, where the telephone interviewer asks about the television or radio station and program the respondent is presently tuned to. However, there are two firms which specialize in this kind of measurement: the Hooper Division of Starch-INRA-Hooper,* and Arbitron.[2]

This method generally uses the telephone book as the source of

---

*The activities of the former C. E. Hooper, Inc. firm in the measurement of coincidental radio audiences are outlined in Chapter 1.

listings, and a systematic sampling procedure (see Chapter 4) is followed. Calls are typically made between 8 A.M. and 10 or 11 P.M., local time.

Recall Studies. Like the coincidental studies, these can generally be conducted by any well-qualified marketing research firm, but there is at least one firm which specializes in the kind of study: it is Arbitron.[3]

In the recall study, discussed in Chapter 1, the respondent is asked what was heard or viewed during a particular time period. The telephone book is generally used as the source of numbers to be telephoned, with a systematic sample. In the case of Arbitron, up to six attempts to complete the call are made before the number is dropped from the sample. The method is particularly useful to cover early-morning or late-night shows (before 8 A.M. or after 10 P.M. locally) since calls cannot be made at the hour that the show or program is on the air.

TELEVISION COMMERCIAL TESTING

As the costs of time, talent, and production rise, the sophisticated advertiser is unwilling to "guess" that a proposed commercial will be effective. There is too much money and market position at stake. So the sophisticated advertiser has a research firm make a test of the effectiveness of the commercial; most of these tests involve a partial or complete contact of the sample via telephone.

There are three basic methods of research used to test commercials: forced exposure, seminormal exposure, and normal exposure. Each refers to the environment in which the respondent is exposed to the advertising material.

In forced exposure, the respondent is a member of a captive audience, often in a theatre situation. There is no easy way to avoid being exposed to the advertising material, so in that sense, this is a highly artificial way of testing commercials; we mainly watch television at home and have the option of leaving or tuning out when the commercial appears. In the seminormal exposure situation the programming is, in effect, forced down the throat of the respondent. However, since the viewing mainly takes place in the home, the person has the option of viewing or not viewing the commercial, having been asked only to watch the program. In the normal exposure situation, the person is free to choose any show, and therefore views both program and advertising at will, with all options open. Obviously, in terms of the viewing situation, the normal situation is by far the most natural one. All else equal, this is the kind of measurement most likely to produce valid measurement.

Forced Exposure

There are several ongoing research services using the forced exposure technique.

ASI In-Theatre Technique.[4] This technique is mainly applied to television commercial testing, though special studies can be contracted for radio commercials. Testing chiefly in Los Angeles, this is an in-theatre technique, where the commercials are presented along with a pilot television film which has not yet been exposed to the public, or with a film classic.

Recruiting is done partly by telephone. Some 40 percent of the people invited to the showing (and they are told only that it is the showing of a new film—there is no mention of the advertising) are recruited through the use of crisscross directories (to be sure to get them from specific areas). The remainder are recruited through personal contact in shopping centers or other areas with a high concentration of traffic. A one-session sample is 250 people.

When people arrive at the theatre, they are shown to seats. Two hundred seats have dial interest recorders, which the respondents can turn to show the degree of their interest in the material presented at the particular time. Also, 115 people have a BSR (Basal Skin Resistor) sensor attached to one hand to measure the amount of perspiration, an indication of emotional reaction.

Members of the audience first fill in answers to questions about their demographics, then to a series of questions about a free draw. They are asked which brand in a product category they want if they happen to win the draw, to be held at the end of the show. The moderator, using a canned approach (so there will be no variation from one session to another), describes what is about to happen.

Then the pilot film and commercials are shown.

Afterward, in a self-administered questionnaire, there is a new series of free-draw preference questions (with an explanation that one product category was inadvertently omitted from the first time around). Then there is a questionnaire which asks the respondent to play back brands advertised and the details of the advertising.

Three basic measures result from all this:

1. Interest and involvement. These come from the recorder dial averages and the scores of the BSRs.

2. Communication. This is the amount and nature of the brand and message recall.

3. Persuasiveness. This is the "increment"—the difference in the percent selecting the brand before seeing its ad, and the percent selecting after exposure. (Note that there is no awareness beforehand that the particular commercial will be shown, or awareness afterward of what the intention of the "draw" question is.)

Seminormal Exposure

Several services offer television commercial effectiveness studies where the viewer is asked to watch a particular program without any advance mention of the advertising, and later, following the show, viewers who have watched the program are queried about the advertising or their brand preferences.

ASI–In-Home Commercial Testing Service.[5] This is an on-air measurement of television commercial performance.

The first step is the telephoning of cable television subscribers in two selected markets. They are telephoned one or two days prior to the showing of a feature film (with little television exposure) and are invited to watch the show, which will appear on an unused channel. A total of 2500 are asked to watch, and all calling is done from a central location with supervision. A standardized questioning approach is used, and the potential viewers are informed of the special telecast: its title, the main stars, the time, the date, and the channel. There is no mention of advertising or of research.

The film is shown, with test commercials embedded.

The day after the showing, recall interviews are made to those invited. This is done by telephone, again from central locations, with supervision and monitoring of the work. A total of 200 people who have actually watched the show are questioned about their recall of product categories advertised, unprompted brand names, prompted brand names, and commercial content.

In-View.[6] This service, offered by Gallup & Robinson, is basically the same procedure used by ASI, with a few variations. For one thing, the location is fixed—it is always Philadelphia. For another thing, closed-circuit television is not used—the firm has reserved time on a UHF prime-time program. In addition, this service is ongoing. It does not require the setting up of a special study. The facilities are there and available to any buyer who wants to use them. Finally, the questioning procedure is just a little different.

Three hundred men and three hundred women are invited, by telephone, to view that evening's showing of the program. As a stimulus for viewing, the potential audience members are told that there will be a drawing for three $100 prizes among viewers. The sampling frame is all listed telephone households on the Pennsylvania side of the Philadelphia Standard Metropolitan Statistical Area.

Twenty-four hours after the program, interviewers telephone about 150 men and 150 women who watched the episode. These qualified viewers (qualified by having properly answered questions about details of program content) are then asked detailed questions to establish the level of perception (brand name registration), communication (playback of the detail of the commercial content), and persuasion (favorableness toward the buying of the brand).

The same basic invited-viewing method is offered in the measurement of attitude shifts correlated with exposure to the commercial. A separate sample of respondents is generated, with the same people being interviewed before and after exposure to the program. One hundred is the sample size. Several possible measurements are available; the user selects one of them:

1. Top of mind (the first three brands that come to mind)

2. Brand preference

3. Purchase intent

Whichever method is selected, the effectiveness of the commercial is judged on the basis of the difference between the replies before and after exposure. If Arrid were being tested and scored 30% on top of mind beforehand and 70% after, then the increment of 40 points would be the measure of commercial effectiveness.

Television Testing Company.[7] Commonly referred to as TTC, this is a joint venture between Audits & Surveys, one of the larger firms in the field of marketing research, and Teleprompter, the country's largest owner and operator of CATV systems. This, too, is a syndicated service.

Four markets are selected for a particular study (out of twelve available). Sample size is 800: 400 men, 400 women.

The first step is the approaching of people to view the show. The major method of approach is telephone calls made at random, using telephone alphabetical directories. This is supplemented by local television and newspaper advertising.

The questioning in advance of the program asks only brand attitude.

Several product categories are included to avoid placing respondent attention on a single category. Questioning following the show varies. One half of the sample are asked about exposure (to establish that they did, indeed, see the program), and then are asked about brand attitude. There is no mention of the commercial content of the show at all.

The other half of the sample, on the follow-up interview, after being checked for exposure, are asked about recall (brand and detail of the commercial).

Thus the method measures, in independent procedures which avoid bias, brand increment (difference in brand attitude before and after exposure of the test commercial of the brand) and recall.

Normal Exposure

There are two types of measurement which consistently use the telephone approach to measure commercial effectiveness with normal exposure (where the viewer makes an independent decision on what to view, and views at home). Every research measurement is made after the fact. The viewer is not forced to view the advertising and is not asked to watch the particular program.

Day-After Recall. One of these methods is day-after recall, usually referred to in the trade (advertising and advertising research) as DAR. This method was established by Burke Marketing Research, back in the early 1950s. However, the method is not copyrighted, and many marketing research firms today are fully capable of carrying out such a study. But Burke has the advantage of having done so many of these that they have been able to set up norms of what scores mean, percentile-wise, by product groups, so that it is possible for buyers to see where they stand quantitatively against others in the same category (without any identification of brand, of course).

Basically DAR measures the proportion of people exposed to a commercial who can play back the sales message of the commercial.

Here is the way it works. In one or more selected areas, a test commercial is used during time "owned" by the sponsor, during a regular broadcast of the particular show. The test commercial (and there may be more than one, for different brands, in the case of a multiple-brand advertiser such as Procter & Gamble) is "cut" into the slot occupied by the same brand or some other promoted by the advertiser. Prime time (7:30 to 10:30 P.M.) is most often used.

Within a period of 24 hours following the telecast, homes are dialed. Random (usually systematic) numbers are selected from telephone alphabetical directories. Program viewers are sought. Questions are first asked about recall of the show to establish that the respondent was really a viewer of the program. Usually 150 program viewers are sought, and, depending on the rating of the show, locating them is likely to require some 3000 dialings.

Those who turn out to be program viewers are then asked whether they saw a commercial for the product category and if so, for what brand. If necessary, an aided recall brand question is asked, to learn whether they recall advertising for the particular brand.

Total Prime Time.[8] Total Prime Time is a syndicated service offered by Gallup & Robinson. Basically it is a delayed aided-recall study. Here is the way it works.

Telephone interviews are made to obtain a sample of 3300 men and women in the Philadelphia Standard Metropolitan Statistical Area, similar to the manner in which the In-View Study is conducted. Two hundred interviewers are used. Prime-time viewers are read the preceding night's program schedule and are asked to reconstruct their viewing pattern on a half-hour by half-hour basis. Viewers exposed to any program segment are presented with a constant number of brand names (as cues) and asked for commercial recall.

Viewers claiming recall of a given commercial are then asked a series of open-ended questions. Verbatim comments are recorded to determine proof of commercial registration, communication of ideas, attitudes toward the commercial, and brand-buying attitude.

There are three basic measurements that come out of this procedure:

1. Attention value of the commercial

2. How well the commercial communicates ideas

3. How well the commercial creates a favorable buying attitude.

Single Show Surveys.[9] Single Show Surveys is another Gallup & Robinson service, this one custom tailored for clients who need to measure the reactions of a highly specialized audience (such as dog owners, mothers, weight watchers, high-income people).

Buyers of the service have many options. They select the timing (the date and broadcasting time) and the place (one or more of thirty-nine possible locations throughout the contiguous forty-eight states). In addition to the specialized nature of the audience, there is a choice of questions, which can be built completely or partially to the buyer's specifications.

Sampling is from telephone alphabetical books, and the sampling usually includes three or four cities. Questioning is done, via the telephone, the day following the particular telecast. With the exception of question modification and addition by the buyer, the questioning procedure is the same as Total Prime Time.

Basically, the method measures the same three elements in the TPT study. The major difference is the customizing.

READERSHIP STUDIES

Readership studies are a common form of personal interview surveys in which the respondent is taken through a periodical, page by page, and asked to report on those items which he or she has noted, read partially, or read completely. Two research groups offer this sort of study via telephone surveys.

One is Chilton Research, with its Ad-Chart.[10] A random probability sample of a magazine's entire circulation is drawn. Screening calls are used to turn up 100 people who have a copy of the magazine on hand. Advertising readership and information are then obtained. The person is queried as to whether he or she has noticed, started to read, or read half or more of the item. The job title of the respondent is obtained, and the respondent is also asked by product class whether he or she has purchase power. (Chilton uses this technique primarily for business publications.) Additional questions can be added at the choice of the client.

A second readership measurement service via telephone is offered by Belden Associates.[11] The service is called the Televisual Method.

A copy of the test issue of a magazine is sent to respondents with instructions to keep it sealed and ready by the telephone. Since the letter accompanying the magazine is crucial, the letter is shown in Figure 9-1; as can be seen, the letter pleads with the respondent not to open the envelope ahead of time.

When reached by telephone, the respondent is first asked a general question on magazine reading, then whether he or she received that issue of the particular magazine. The respondent is requested to remove the test issue from the envelope and is given an opportunity to leaf through the magazine quickly and say which articles "look interesting, whether you happen to have read them or not." (The purpose of this particular question is to reduce inflated claims of readership which otherwise might come later.)

Belden Associates

Research and Counsel in Marketing and Communications

Dear Mr. Smith:

Within a few days one of our interviewers is going to contact you. We will need your help -- just a few minutes -- in an interesting and unusual communications survey.

You are one of a few opinion leaders in your community we are sampling. The purpose is to discover how much of certain information you have time to read. The only way to find out is to ask you; in return, all we can do is tell you that your replies will contribute toward one of the country's great needs: better understanding of our industrial system. And we think you will enjoy the interview.

Enclosed is a <u>sealed</u> envelope that contains reading matter you will need to examine at a <u>particular</u> moment during the interview. There is nothing unusual about its contents, but if you were even to glance inside before the interview, it would spoil the research technique we are using.

Please keep the envelope sealed, and place it by your telephone so it is handy when the interviewer contacts you.

We are conducting the survey for one of America's largest manufacturers. Belden Associates, a professional research firm, guarantees to you that no sales attempts will result from this research, now or later. We will very much appreciate your talking with our interviewer.

Yours sincerely,

Ralph Bubis

Ralph Bubis
Executive Vice President

FIGURE 9-1

The respondent is told that "articles and pictures in different magazines are sometimes very much alike," and then is asked to make positive identification of the issue as one that was read. This is followed by a page-by-page inspection, in which the respondent is asked whether he or she has read anything on that page. Finally, there are attitude questions about the publication.

CONSUMER PRODUCT REACTION STUDIES

These studies ask people about their reactions to a particular brand or product. While the studies take many different forms, one form is the consumer product test, in which the respondent first tries a product, usually without its brand being divulged (so as to eliminate the halo effect of the name), then describes personal reactions through responding to a standard set of questions.

Perhaps the most unusual consumer product test (which happened to involve use of the telephone survey at one point in the study) was conducted by the author a few years ago. Thirty-seven groups of ten men each were invited to a beer-tasting party, each one held at the home of a representative of the research firm. The men would receive two bottles of beer to try, one labeled X, the other Y. Each man would also be given a self-administered questionnaire to fill in as he tasted the two brews—questions comparing the two in terms of flavor, carbonation, and the like.

After that, by instruction, the hostess would tell the respondents that the research firm had sent her enough beer to fill the refrigerator and she didn't know what to do with it all. She then would invite them to stay and drink it. Also at the instruction of the research firm, she was to encourage each respondent to drink as many bottles as possible and was to keep track—without letting the respondents know—of how many bottles each one drank. Some of the sessions ran until 2 A.M., and some of the respondents put away prodigous quantities of beer!

Each session was intentionally conducted on a week night. The following morning, someone from the research firm telephoned each respondent at work. The respondent was asked, on behalf of the research firm, whether he had been well treated the evening before. Then the interviewer said that since a lot of beer had been consumed during the session, the research firm wondered how the respondent was feeling. The presence and severity of a number of hangover effects was checked.

What was this all about? It was a controlled experiment on hangover effects. Three brands of beer were in the test. Any one respondent was drinking only a single brand all evening long. By checking—separately for each brand—the presence and severity of hangover effects by amount of beer drunk, it was possible to compare the hangover effects of the three brands. Knowledge of brand had nothing to do with the effects, for each respondent was drinking unlabeled bottles.

This study was a combination of personal interview and telephone, and such combinations in consumer product reaction studies are not new. In 1964 Payne[12] reported the successful use of a personal placement of a product, with a telephone follow-up to measure reaction. A 97% completion rate was attained.

Robert Baxter, manager of consumer research for Chrysler, reports that in the automobile industry, the major use made of the telephone survey is in conducting studies among owners of particular makes and models. These names are typically purchased from R. L. Polk and Company, who purchases them from individual states (the states obtain them through automobile licensing bureaus). If purchasers of Chrysler cars with particular features are needed, names can be obtained through the company's own records.

The automobile industry also uses the telephone approach to recruit automobile owners to come into a central location to a so-called style clinic, in which competitive, comparable new cars are on display and the respondent is to react to the outside styling and inside features.

Chilton Research conducted a study in which 3000 people were screened to locate 900 users of a particular product. Two different samples of this product were then mailed to each person. One-half were told to use *A* first, one-half to use *B* first. Then 700 users were telephoned to get their reactions to the first one, and 500 were reinterviewed following their use of the second. Results for *A* and *B* were then summarized.

This sort of study is common among the professional telephone research firms. It is fast, and it is relatively inexpensive, because screening to locate qualified testers can be done so rapidly.

TEST MARKET STUDIES

A test market (sometimes referred to as a market test) comes close to a controlled situation in which the marketer miniaturizes a proposed marketing effort to arrive at a prediction of what would happen if it were a national effort. Today the costs of undertaking a national marketing campaign are so great that the marketer is not willing to risk all that money without some advance indication that the effort will be successful.

In test marketing, the product and the marketing effort may be introduced in several metropolitan areas or in a region. The results of the effort are closely monitored.

There are two basic types of telephone surveys which can aid in the test marketing phase: tracking studies and a simulated test market, which cuts the time and cost of the test marketing operation.

Tracking Studies

Tracking studies are continuing studies designed to keep abreast of what is going on in the marketplace. They provide a series of pictures, rather than a single snapshot. While some involve more than consumer measurement, consumer measurement is the topic of interest in connection with this discussion of the telephone survey.

Several types of consumer information are typically collected. Top of mind and share of mind are measured. Top of mind is the first brand of the product that comes to the mind of the consumer in response to a question. This happens to be a very predictive item: it frequently is a predictor of later brand purchase. Share of mind is the proportion of people mentioning each brand when several brands are asked for.

Advertising recall is also typically asked. This includes recall of brands seen or heard advertised, where each one was seen or heard advertising, and a playback of the advertising content.

Finally, purchase and repurchase of brands are measured.

Let's put this series of pictures together. Suppose that a company were introducing a new product into a market, and it wanted to determine both how well the product was doing and the reasons for the relative success or failure. Top of mind and share of mind tell how hard the company is hitting the consumer. Advertising recall tells whether the advertising campaign is reaching people, and whether it is getting the story over to them. (It may be reaching people, as reflected in high brand recall, but it may be communicating poorly, as indicated by a low content playback.) The rate of trial of the product shows the degree to which the manufacturer is successfully persuading people to try the product, while the repurchase level shows the degree to which the product is sufficiently satisfactory to get people to repurchase. (The manufacturer's marketing efforts, if sufficiently strong and sound, can get people to buy. But they won't rebuy a product they don't like, no matter how good the marketing effort is.)

Warriner[13] describes how a telephone panel was used in tracking the introduction of a new product in test market. The product was a household commodity. Five hundred consumers were telephoned, at intervals, a total of eleven times each. They were asked, at two-week intervals:

1. Have you bought any _____ within the past two weeks (since I called you last)?
2. (If yes) What brand did you buy? _____
3. What size did you buy—large size or regular size?
4. (For each size mentioned) How many packages did you buy?

National Family Opinion is the largest mail panel operation in the country, with 150,000 cooperating families. In numerous cities across the country the firm has enough panel members to set up continuing panels for tracking studies. The company recommends a diary form to record purchases, utilizing its professional telephone interviewers on WATS lines to speed the reporting and to ask other tracking questions as required.

Chilton reports that increasing numbers of companies are using tracking studies.[14] Bortner and Assael strongly favor this sort of study, arguing that it offers flexibility (the questions can be changed to meet conditions) and that a data bank can be established. The major data are obtained through use of Chilton's WATS-line professional telephone survey facility.

Simulated Test Market

The Laboratory Test Market[15] is aimed at predicting what will happen in a test market. However, it costs far less than the $500,000 to $1 million marketing cost of the typical test market and can be completed in weeks instead of 6 months to a year.

Offered by Yankelovich, Skelly and White (the current firm name), it, too, is basically a theatre operation. Consumers, in groups of thirty to thirty-five, are taken into a theatre. There they fill in a questionnaire covering demographics and purchase behavior on a number of product categories (including those whose commercials they will see, although they don't know anything about that). Then a television film is shown, including the commercial being tested and other noncompeting commercials. At the end of the showing, they are given "seed money" (an amount less than that required to purchase the particular product) and are taken into a simulated store, where the advertised brand and its major competitors are on display and available for purchase. There is no forcing of the purchase; the respondent can buy or not, as he or she pleases.

There are then focused group discussions. After an appropriate time, the respondents are reinterviewed by telephone inquiring about product reaction (if they have purchased the brand), the reactions of other family members, the degree of satisfaction or dissatisfaction, the reasons for satisfaction or dissatisfaction, comparison with previous brands or products used, usage data, and their repurchase intentions.

The only real use of the telephone approach in this method, to be sure, is the telephone follow-up. But it is an essential portion of the technique, so the service properly belongs in this discussion.

ATTITUDE STUDIES

Various kinds of attitudes can be measured in the professional telephone survey. Four will be considered here: company attitudes, economic attitudes, opinions, and farmer attitudes. In all four areas there are ongoing studies.

Company Attitude Measurement

American Telephone & Telegraph Company, as shown in Chapter 2, conducts Telsam (Telephone Service Attitude Measurement) regularly. This is a proprietary study, though Robert Gryb, who directs the work for the participating companies, is quite willing to discuss its objectives and techniques. The study, conducted monthly, is contracted out to professional telephone survey research firms. Each operating company of the Bell System decides whether it will participate; this is really a series of studies rather than a single national study.

The questions center around:

1. Installation

2. Operator services

3. Business office

4. Repair

5. Dial (coin box service and local and toll transmission)

Each topic is handled as a separate study, and a sample of people who have recently experienced the particular area are drawn. Managers can have their own special questions asked, if they wish. There are occasional studies done for participating companies on procedural changes, such as the operator's method of handling a call. Sample size varies, depending on the organization structure of participating companies and their local needs.

One special feature of these studies is the speed with which results are processed and presented. Within the first day of the succeeding month, results are given to company managers. Minicomputers are used to display the questions on CRTs and transmit the results to a master computer for processing. Computer graphics are used in generating the reports. They are (1) the 12-month trend of the overall rating, and (2) key aspects of service. Also, numeric backup includes question-by-question answers for this month, for last month, and for the 3-month average.

Ohio Bell does some of its own attitude studies, also using the telephone as the information-getting device. E. E. Chapman, district manager of public relations, directs these operations. One continuing study is the advertising and rate attitude monitor. The purposes of this study are to measure the impact of Ohio Bell advertising and public attitudes during rate-increase negotiations. One hundred calls are made weekly (a total of 5000 a year), using a random computer-generated sample of residential telephone homes in Cleveland, Akron, Youngstown, Columbus, Dayton, and Toledo. Questions cover advertising awareness and recall, and attitudes toward telephone rates, service, and employee treatment.

The company also conducts a Public Overview Study. In this study the purpose is to measure public opinion trends toward telephone company service, reputation, and employee treatment. A total of 2300 randomly selected telephone homes are included.

Economic Attitude Measurement

The Sindlinger Economic Service has been provided by Sindlinger & Company for over 20 years; it will be recalled that this firm was named as the pioneer in the professional telephone survey field. The purpose of this service is to determine by national, regional, and market size the level of household money supply or consumer confidence as measured by current and expected income changes, as well as expectancy on employment and area business conditions.

The derived indexes provide an advance view of consumer saving and spending patterns and project consumer plans to buy housing, automobiles, and some nineteen other major durables as well as projecting the main scope of retail sales.

Correlations of these indexes with government and private sector data provide forecasts for over 150 business and economic data areas. Published reports provide analyses of the interrelationship of all economic/political data with cross-tabulations for all socioeconomic characteristics.

The sample, 5000 telephone interviews monthly with household heads, is a national probability sample of all telephone homes and is pulled from telephone books. All interviewing is done from offices of the firm in Wallingford, Pennsylvania.[16] Once selected for the sample, numbers are called and re-called until the interviewer is informed that the number is out of service or the party has moved. The service is sold on an individual subscription basis.

Opinion Polls

Opinion polls are increasingly making use of the telephone method. The research firm doing the major portion of the work for one of the two major presidential candidates in the last national election most commonly handled the work via telephone. Results were needed quickly, to guide the campaign planners, and it was less costly than house-to-house personal interviewing.

The New York Times and CBS News Survey[17] during that same campaign was also a telephone study, and this particular study even used computer-generated telephone numbers from a list of the working exchanges across the country.

Farmer Attitude Measurement

Chilton Research has set up a DEW (distant early warning system) study among farmers.[18] Its purpose is to provide monthly data on American farmers' current actions, attitudes, and intentions, so as to provide early warnings of significant changes in farm conditions and purchase requirements. Its aim is to be of use to manufacturers and suppliers of farm equipment, supplies, and services.

The sample is a random probability sample of 1000 farms monthly. The questionnaire covers plans, intentions, and actions on:

1. Crop planting and livestock production

2. Farm purchases, by dollar amount and type

3. Projected crop and livestock prices as they affect plans

4. Farm media usage

5. Financing and insurance

The interview runs about 30 minutes, and all telephoning is done from the research offices in Radnor.

BROAD APPLICATIONS

There are at least three applications of the telephone survey that cut across areas and can be applied to almost any topic of questioning, whether it concerns company, product, the economy, advertising, or whatever. The applications are validation studies, omnibus studies, incoming WATS studies, and the telephone group interview.

Validation Studies

It has been pointed out that validation studies are common and necessary to ensure that personal interviews, particularly of the door-to-store type, have been done and honestly done. Most validation studies today are done from a central telephone facility using WATS lines.

Omnibus Studies

An omnibus study is one in which more than one buyer participates. Each buyer submits questions and holds proprietary rights to results of those questions, but they are combined in a questionnaire with those of other buyers. If the buyer has only a short number of questions to field, it offers tremendous cost savings to combine the field work. Omnibus studies can also ask screening questions, with the option of making a separate telephone call, mail survey, or personal interview survey among those who qualify.

As of this writing, there are two omnibus facilities in the professional telephone survey area. One is offered by Trendex.[19] The field work is conducted the first week of each calendar quarter: in January, April, July, and October. Some 70,000 randomly selected households are drawn from 274 Primary Sampling Units, stratified by area and community size. If a sample of fewer than 70,000 is desired, arrangements can be made for a subsample.

To keep down questionnaire length, Trendex uses the first contact merely for screening purposes. If the buyer wants to ask a number of questions of those who qualify, a second contact will be made.

The other omnibus facility is offered by Opinion Research Corporation, under the name "Telephone Caravan." The company also offers a personal interview Caravan omnibus.

This telephone study is conducted monthly, with a national sample of 1000 adults 18 and over. The basic Opinion Research Corporation national probability sample (described in Chapter 4) is used to select starting points in known working exchanges. A computer then generates the list of random numbers to be used in the dialings.

Interviewing is done predominately during evenings and weekends.

Incoming WATS Lines Studies

The WATS lines previously discussed in this book are outgoing—that is, they are used for outgoing calls. But there's another kind, too, used for incoming calls. These are the free numbers starting with an 800. R. H. Bruskin Associates has developed a new telephone research tool using these.[20] One of the firm's clients has many thousands of such calls coming in weekly. Bruskin now offers a service whereby, when the incoming consumer is finished inquiring for information or placing an order, the operator asks whether the consumer would be willing to answer a few questions. Some of the applications, according to Bruskin, are mass screening to locate users of low-incidence products, questioning on product and brand usage, and obtaining information on shopping habits, store visits, etc. Respondent name, address, city, state, and zip code have already been obtained. Calls are reported to be a cross-section in terms of sex, age, geography, and economics. Costs are reported as being far lower than if the interviewer were to make calls to respondents. One does have to wonder, though, whether the self-selection process involved results in a homogeneity of a basic sort which might make the results questionable. It would help to see parallel results from a survey done both ways: from these incoming lines and from a cross-section on outgoing lines.

The Telephone Group Interview

The group interview has been a part of marketing research for at least the past three decades. It is used, usually in the early stages of questionnaire development, because it stimulates new ideas and provides dynamics in attitudes and opinions. Its primary use has been to develop hypotheses which can subsequently be tested in an actual survey. Goldman[21] has written the classic paper on group interviews.

Group interviews have traditionally been done in person, with a meeting between some six to twelve respondents and a moderator. In recent years there has been a little experimentation with telephone group interviews.

In London, for instance, Miln, Stewart-Hunter, and Marchant[22] describe a group session in which eight respondents, after having been asked to watch a particular television show, discussed commercials on the show. Tele-Sessions, a firm based in New York, formerly conducted a number of telephone group sessions. Lynn Losen, of American Can Company, conducted a group session with people located in different parts of the United States. Blankenship and Pearson[23] conducted a group interview with men and women in different parts of Ohio.

In the London session the hard-of-hearing, those with speech impediments, and those with thick regional accents were eliminated; these principles make good sense for all screening in group work.

Because there is only voice contact, not full personal contact, the moderator must spend a little more time on preliminaries than is true in the personal group session. Blankenship and Pearson, to help break the ice, asked their participants to draw a circle representing a table around which all participants were seated. The first name of each person was written, in succession, around the table; people were asked to call each other by first name, and did so. Each person was also asked to give his or her home before speaking, and was reminded not to break in on anyone else.

Blankenship and Pearson used a speakerphone to talk into and to listen to. This gave the moderators complete physical freedom, and also made it possible to tape-record the session directly with an electronic connection, thus minimizing voice distortion.

The major advantage of the telephone group session over the personal group interview is the low cost of getting widely separated people together. Respondents can be geographically scattered. Largely because of this, the group session is considerably less costly than a physical group session with the same respondents. Another advantage is that the environment is much more natural for the respondent: it is the home (or office). Also, many of the problems of arranging for the session are transferred to the telephone company. The conference-call operator telephones the participants ahead of time to remind them. In addition, there seems to be little tendency for an initially willing person to drop out, which is so often the case with the personal group interview. This is probably because the telephone group session requires a little physical effort on part of the participant. Still another advantage is that the meeting can be conducted at a time of day when people would be unwilling to leave their homes.

There can be one disadvantage, but it is a disadvantage of any telephone survey which uses a list of names other than those of telephone owners. Such a list will include inaccuracies, and if it is an old list, a lot of people will have moved. Directory Assistance, if the calls are scattered, is almost a "must" unless the work is conducted by a professional telephone survey firm that has all directories available across the country.

Another claimed disadvantage of the telephone group interview is that it completely misses nonverbal communication. Blankenship and Pearson believed that they observed some of this, but a firm that has conducted many such sessions claims that little if any communication is so lost. However, another firm argues that these nonverbal clues are important indicators of interest levels and meanings that a good group moderator is so dependent on. This firm argues that many personal group sessions are not only tape-recorded but videotaped as well, because of these nonverbal clues.

The final answer is not in. Telephone group interviews are still in their infancy, and controlled experiments are needed to compare them with personal group interviews.

REFERENCES

[1] Reference Supplement: Nielsen Station Index, Chicago, A. C. Nielsen Co., 1974–75.

[2] *Be the First to Know Today What They Listened to Yesterday!* New York, American Research Bureau, undated.

[3] *Television Recall Surveys,* New York, Arbitron Television, 1975.

[4] *A Synopis of Advertising Testing Services and Procedures,* New York, ASI Market Research, Inc., undated.

[5] *In-Home Testing Service,* New York, Audience Studies, Inc., undated.

[6] *Gallup & Robinson's Invited Viewing Syndicated Television Research Service,* Princeton, Gallup & Robinson, 1974.

[7] *Marketing, Advertising and Communication Research Employing CATV Technology,* New York, Television Testing Company, undated.

[8] *Gallup & Robinson's On-Air Syndicated Television Research Program,* Princeton, Gallup & Robinson, 1974.

[9] *Gallup & Robinson's On-Air Custom Television Research Service: Single Show Surveys*, Princeton, Gallup & Robinson, 1975.

[10] *New Ad-Chart Readership Service*, Radnor, Pa., Chilton, undated.

[11] *The "Televisual" Method of Readership Measurement*, Dallas, Belden Associates, 1968.

[12] S. L. Payne, "Combination of Survey Methods," *Journal of Marketing Research*, Vol. 1, May 1964, pp. 61–62.

[13] Robert H. Warriner, "Test Market Evaluation through a Telephone Panel," in Henry F. Brenner, *Marketing Research Pays Off*, New London, Conn., Printers Ink Books, 1955.

[14] Bruce Z. Bortner and Henry Assael, *Continuous Tracking Studies via WATS Lines and Personal Interviewing*, 13th Annual Conference, Advertising Research Foundation, Nov. 15, 1967.

[15] *Laboratory Test Market*, New York, Daniel Yankelovich, Inc., undated.

[16] J. Stevens Stock, "Surveying Consumer Buying Plans," *Business Record*, Dec. 1958, pp. 3–18.

[17] "2,025 Interviewed in Times-CBS Poll," *New York Times*, Oct. 31, 1976.

[18] "New Early Warning System Being Initiated to Cope with Agriculture and Food Crises," Radnor, Pa., *Chilton Corporate News*, May 2, 1975.

[19] *Try the Trendex Omnibus*, Westport, Conn., Trendex, undated.

[20] Described in *The Bruskin Report*, no. 79, Oct. 1976.

[21] A. E. Goldman, "The Group Depth Interview," *Journal of Marketing*, July 1962, pp. 61–68.

[22] D. Miln, D. Stewart-Hunter, and Len Marchant, *The Telephone in Consumer Research*, Special Groups Volume, E.S.O.M.A.R. Conference, Hamburg, 1974, pp. 229–264.

[23] A. B. Blankenship and Michael M. Pearson, *Guidelines for Telephone Group Interviews*, unpublished manuscript, 1975.

FINAL
CONSIDERATIONS
AND THE FUTURE

What is in the future for professional telephone surveys?

Chapter 2 outlined the reasons for the appearance and growth of the professional telephone survey. A recent study[1] showed that over half of those questioned in marketing research interviews were approached via the telephone, 26 percent by personal contact (in-home and mall interviews) and 20 percent by mail. In a recent speech Theodore R. Weiss,[2] consumer affairs supervisor of Illinois revealed that Gerald McCloskey, then president of the Market Research Association, had predicted in a telephone conversation that by 1980, 75 percent of all survey work will be done by telephone. "Personally," commented Weiss, "I think it will be sooner than that." It may well be. There are many pressures that seem likely to make it so. James Bacharach, managing partner of Trendex, says, "Monitored telephone surveys will become increasingly important. Personal interviewing will become more and more difficult. There will be increasing resistance to personal interviewing. The major problems of telephone surveys have been overcome: the proportion of homes with telephones and the problem of reaching unlisted numbers."

Decline of Mail Surveys

Mail surveys will almost surely decline in coming years, at least as a portion of the total interview pot. One reason is increasing postal costs. As of this writing, the first-class mail rate is 13¢. Carl C. Ulsaker,[3] in charge of labor and cost control for the U.S. Postal Service, predicted that the rate would probably rise to 23¢ by 1981; if recent increases are an indicator, his prediction seems low.

It also seems likely that there will be other problems with the postal service. Today we all know how overburdened the mails are; if this continues, service may be even further delayed and the mail survey will lose considerable attraction.

Finally, a mail survey cannot be turned into a production line in the manner in which the professional telephone survey has been; as discussed, the raw material of the professional telephone survey can be entered into the computer at the time of collecting it, and, if the programming has been done ahead of time, the end results of the study can start coming out of the computer upon completion of the last telephone interview. There is no way that the mail survey can ever become a production line similar to that.

Decline of Personal Interview Surveys

Personal interview surveys, at least the door-to-door variety, will also decline significantly in share of survey work. There are several reasons.

There Will be Further Cost Increases. Personal interview surveys of the house-to-house type are already significantly higher in cost than telephone surveys. These personal interviewing costs have already risen significantly over the past several years, entirely aside from the usual inflationary rises. The reason is a tax ruling by the Internal Revenue Service, made in June 1975.[4] The role of local supervisors in house-to-house calls has previously been outlined. Most supervisors are unincorporated firms, in which the proprietor works out of his or her home. In the past, many of these people never withheld tax and other monies, believing that they were dealing with their interviewers as contractors, not as employees. Under the IRS ruling, local supervisors *are* responsible for withholding under the Federal Insurance Contributions Act for social security deductions, unemployment tax deductions, and federal income tax deductions. What's worse, the ruling was made retroactive, so that the Midwest Survey Service, of Omaha, was assessed $85,000.

Ruling 75-243 holds that interviewers who are paid on an hourly basis to conduct market research surveys for a company are employees of the company if it hires from its list of people who want to conduct interviews on a permanent basis, issues specific instructions for conducting interviews, may select interviewing locations, sets quotas and deadlines for completion, does not permit interviewers to hire assistants or substitutes, and requires daily reports.

One immediate effect has been the demise of many of these small, local services. The retroactive decision forced many of these small operators into personal bankruptcy, since they lacked the means to meet the dollar demand. In itself, this contributes to a decline in house-to-house surveys, though only temporary. The gap is being filled by new individuals and firms who now start at once to make all the necessary withholdings.

The long-range effect to survey research is the more serious one: a rise in costs. It now costs more to conduct a business that specializes in door-to-door surveys, and there is only one place that the additional costs can come from: the buyer of the survey. One source[5] suggests that this means an immediate increase of 6 percent in total costs of a personal interview survey. On the other hand, the head of one research firm (who prefers to remain anonymous) puts it more at the level of 15 percent. Whatever the right answer is, it is a significant rise.

Completion Rates in Personal Interview Studies Will Decline Further. Chapter 2 talked about decreasing completion rates in personal interviewing and mentioned some of the reasons. There is even more concrete evidence.

Gale D. Metzger[6], head of Statistical Research, Inc., a firm which specializes in professional telephone surveys, pointed out that the decline in completion rates, in terms of studies his firm had conducted did *not* include telephone surveys. He gave three examples:

A national survey of 4000 respondents obtained a 67% response in 1972, 72% a year later.

Three different surveys in the Spanish community of New York City in 1972 and 1974 obtained response rates of between 94% and 96%.

A national tracking study in 1971, 1972, and 1973, with 12,000 cases each, showed no change in completions during the period, staying at about 80%.

John Weber,[7] in a master's paper at Bowling Green State University, gathered pretty solid evidence—though of a secondary nature—that the decline in response rates is occurring in personal interviews, not in telephone surveys. He sent a questionnaire on the topic to the heads of the fifty-five consumer research firms estimated to be the largest (estimates made by three people experienced in the research field). Thirty-three responded.

Table 10-1 shows that almost 80 percent report that completion rates in personal interview studies have dropped, one-third say that mail return rates have dropped, and almost half report that even telephone interview completion rates have dropped. There may be a telephone completion rate problem, but those in the field don't think it is so serious as the completion rate problem for personal interviewing.

There Will be a Demand for Higher-Quality Data. As the nation approaches a zero-growth economy (because of a no-growth population), marketing will become increasingly competitive. Manufacturers will no longer be able to grow simply because the economy is growing. They will have to create new products; they will have to enter already crowded fields and try to take market share away from competition.

Under these inevitable conditions, marketers will demand increasingly accurate marketing information. They will not be willing to risk marketing errors through surveys of questionable quality. It is already evident that telephone surveys are the answer, where quality of the

TABLE 10-1
Showing the Number of Survey Firms Reporting a Change in Completion Rates Within Past Five Years

	Personal Interviews	Telephone Interviews	Mail Questionnaires
Total Responding	27	29	18
Dropped	21	14	6
Rose	1	1	1
Remained the same	5	14	11

SOURCE: John Weber, "Completion Rates in Consumer Research: Problems and Proposed Solutions."

interviewing is a known factor, through supervision and monitoring. Only the professional telephone survey offers real quality control.

There Will be a Need for Faster Results. As marketing becomes increasingly competitive, there will be less time to make decisions. This, too, places a high demand on the telephone survey, for it has been shown that under proper conditions, the professional telephone survey is by far the most rapid method of collecting and producing data. The speed of the interviewing, the fast input into the computer (and increasing numbers of professional survey firms will be turning to an on-line system, where the interviewer keypunches the data right into the computer), and the automatic production of computer printouts upon completion of field work mean that the professional telephone survey far outdistances the mail survey and the personal interview survey.

CONCERN FOR THE FUTURE

The future increase in the use of telephone surveys is good for the field of marketing research—no question about that. But its coming rapid growth also presents problems—problems which are of deep concern to most professionals in the field.

There is a need for responsibility in conducting telephone surveys. The rights of the respondent must be protected by those authorizing and those conducting the survey. As Sanford Cooper,[8] president of Burke Marketing Research, Inc., says, "The business of consumer surveys comes with no guarantes that researchers will be permitted to solicit consumer opinions as freely in the future as they have in the past." He is referring to consumer resentment and the possible enactment of restrictive legislation, both of which will be considered.

In a 1975 Chicago meeting[9] researchers expressed deep concern about the problem of maintaining proper relationships with survey respondents. In attendance were representatives from the Advertising Research Foundation, the Bureau of the Census, the Council of American Survey Organizations, the American Marketing Association, the American Association for Public Opinion Research, the Americal Sociological Association, the Institute of Management Sciences, the American Psychological Association, the Council of Better Business Bureaus, and the Association for Consumer Research. Letters of support were received from the Conference Board, the American Management Associations, and the American Economic Association.

The concern is there, and properly so. Let's take a look at some of the specific concerns.

Misleading Uses of the Telephone Survey Approach

There are three ways in which the telephone survey has been used in a misleading way.

A Lead into a Sales Pitch. The telephone survey approach all too often has been used as a lead into a sales pitch, right over the telephone. The Walker survey[10] was a thirty-city survey, with a 300 sample, made by telephone using Walker Research WATS lines. The sample was selected by a random method, so that unlisted numbers were included. Either the male or female head of the house was interviewed, dependent on availability at the moment. If both were available, the woman was questioned. Admittedly this resulted in an overrepresentation of women, with a sample of 71% females.

Some 42% said that they had been misled, by having been approached in an apparent survey which turned into a sales pitch.

In a Roper study some eleven years earlier,[11] 27% reported that they had been thus misled. If these two studies can be compared, then this sort of misleading approach is on the increase. In the Roper study the major offenders were firms selling magazines, books, encyclopedias, screens, and storm windows. Weber found that two-thirds of the leading survey firms thought that sales disguised as surveys had had a strong effect on survey completion rates.

In a multi-community study,[12] one community had a 14% refusal rate on a coffee survey, while other communities were averaging only 2%. It turned out that several weeks earlier the telephone approach had been used for a sales solicitation in the one area.

A Means of Getting Sales Prospects. Here an apparently innocuous survey approach is used to get sales leads. One common method is to carry on an interview about purchases planned within the next few months. No sales pitch is made at the time. That comes later, in an entirely different contact.

Some years ago, when the author was with a marketing research survey firm, he was approached by a member of the research department of an advertising agency that had a major automobile account. He was requested for an estimate to conduct a study by telephone to locate people who planned to purchase new cars within the next twelve months. Names and addresses of those who planned to buy were to be turned over to the advertising agency, who would, in turn, give them to the auto manufacturer as sales leads.

The request for an estimate was turned down. Within the year the American Marketing Association had adopted a code of ethics for the marketing research field that stated that it was unethical to solicit for sales leads and unethical to turn over names and addresses of respondents without respondent permission.

Recontacting Without Prior Agreement with Respondent. Should the respondent *ever* be recontacted—even just for research purposes—without prior agreement? Suppose, for instance, as in a Trendex omnibus survey, the first contact is used to locate users of Rise shave cream. Then these users are telephoned again to find out details of their loyalty to the brand. Or suppose that all that is wanted as a recontact is a validation interview—to make sure that the reported call was really made. (The need for this in the professional telephone survey is doubtful, but the issue is still a legitimate one.)

There is some feeling that respondent agreement *should* be obtained in advance. There may be justification for this, although the author cannot see it. There is simply no evidence that people resent being approached a second time—none at all. Yet Solomon Dutka, president of Audits & Surveys, says that in a major audience study his firm conducted, respondents were asked if they could be recontacted if necessary. The validating agency—a separate firm—was given only the names of those people who agreed. If you were the buyer of research in this case, would you be happy with such a list? It almost invites interviewer dishonesty.

Overall Impression of Those Interviewed

What is the general feeling of those who have been interviewed? Do they feel that they have been mistreated, taken advantage of? Or are they generally favorable? Answers to these questions are surely important for the future of the professional survey.

Fortunately a majority of those interviewed are happy about the whole thing. But the results are not all that favorable. Sanford Cooper[13] reports a study that Burke conducted among people they had interviewed the day before. More than 50% were favorable about the earlier contact. But the Walker study reported a year later, found that among those previously interviewed, 74% had a pleasant overall impression. The difference between these two results is probably understandable psychologically. Psychologists tell us that we have a tendency to remember the pleasant and forget the unpleasant. So the longer ago the contact was, the more likely it is to be remembered pleasantly, all of which doesn't say too much for how well people are reacting to being interviewed.

Possibly of even greater concern is lack of conviction, revealed in the Walker survey, that marketing research does anything much. Some 43% (less than a majority) said that they were favorable toward the industry, that it was educational, interesting, or beneficial to the improvement of products or services. One-third were unfavorable. In a separate question, 6% said that the market research industry served no useful purpose.

None of these figures suggests that the public, tomorrow, is going to be so uncooperative in responding to an interview that a survey researcher should give up the occupation. But the data do strongly suggest that there is a core of a real problem, that those in the field are right to be concerned, and that they had better undertake a program of public education.

Invasion of Privacy

Justice Brandeis, almost a half century ago, said that "discovery and invention have made it possible. . . . by means more effective than stretching on the rack, to obtain disclosures. . . . of what is whispered in the closet." He might almost have been talking about the telephone survey.

What *is* invasion of privacy? To some, it is as simple as answering the telephone only to find that it is a survey or a sales solicitation. Some people clearly think that their telephone is for communication between friends and those they are doing business with.

Carlson[14] puts it well:

> The average telephone subscriber does not see himself as just another potential sampling point in one of our surveys. He pays a monthly rental for his phone and usually has a proprietary feeling about it. The day may come when he reacts to increasing sales solicitations and public opinion surveys by asking why he should help subsidize the sales and research activities of others.

For others, it is the asking of questions that are too personal. In the Walker study, 19% of those who had been interviewed thought that some questions (such as family income) were too personal. In addition, 2% objected to a question about age, 2% to a question about occupation, 1% about race, and 1% about education. If the list had been more inclusive, there would have been even more objection, for a total of 43% said that some questions asked in polls or research surveys were too personal.

Cooper[15] argues that it is not even necessary to ask the name of the respondent for validation purposes. (In the professional telephone survey, where random-digit dialing is used, the name of the family is not known; in fact in most cases, even where alphabetical directories are used as the sample source, the family name of the telephone subscriber is not given on the listing form provided to the interviewers.) In the Weber study, over a fourth of survey firms said that they thought the asking of personal questions had had a strong effect on completion rates. Weiss[16] says that Illinois Bell avoids asking questions about income, education, and ethnic background.

Mistreatment of the Respondent

There are several ways in which the survey respondent may be mistreated. One is by downright mistreatment from the interviewer. The other two ways are more subtle: The first is by an interview which lasts too long; the second is by inconvenient timing of the call.

Poor Treatment from the Interviewer. Among those previously interviewed, Walker found that 19% thought that the interviewer was not really interested in obtaining their opinions. One might speculate that in these cases, the respondents felt that the interviewer was handling them in a mechanical, routine way. If so, of course there would be resentment, whether mild or severe. Even more serious, the Walker study showed that 6% of those previously interviewed felt that the investigator was downright discourteous in some way!

Cooper makes a couple of suggestions. He suggests that the interviewer should not hold onto a busy respondent and that perplexing or vexing questions should be explained.

Interviews That Are Too Long. The Walker study among previous respondents found that 17% thought the interview was too long. While this is not a very high figure, if telephone surveys increase to the extent predicted here, this opinion could cause a significant rise in nonresponse. It has ominous overtones. Two-thirds of the survey companies in the Weber study felt that length had had a strong effect on completion rates.

Cooper argues that the shorter the interview, the better. Maybe he is right. At least it is safe to say that the interview should be absolutely no longer than it has to be to provide the input to help solve the problem.

Even worse than total length of the interview is the misleading of respondents as to the length of the interview. In telephone surveys, in particular, there is simply no reason to mislead the respondent about the interview length. The respondent should be informed at the start the approximate length of time the interview will take, and if the respondent at that point does not have sufficient time to go through the session, it is simple enough to arrange another time for the interview. Misrepresentation is not only dangerous for future respondent cooperation but simply unnecessary from the survey firm's viewpoint.

Poor Timing of the Calls. There is some argument that telephone calls are made at unreasonable hours—hours basically unacceptable to the respondent. Manfield[16], in a survey made among local supervisors, found that the supervisors reported many validation calls were made, by telephone, at what they considered to be unacceptable times: 11 P.M. or later, Saturday evening, and Sunday evening. However, as we have seen, 11 P.M. on weeknights and Saturday evenings are typically avoided by professional telephone survey firms, and there is evidence (as discussed in Chapter 6) that Sunday evening is not a time when people resent a telephone interview. The Burke study[17] found that 14% said the interviewing was at an inconvenient time. It is probably safe to say that the final score is not in. More evidence is needed in this area.

Surveys Are of Little Value to the Consumer

The Walker survey learned that 19% of those who have been interviewed think that such an interview is a waste of their time. And 40% say that the information gathered in polls or market research surveys helps the manufacturer sell consumers ideas or goods they do not want or need.

However, the Burke study reports that more than three-quarters of those who have been interviewed think that surveys aid the consumer. Clearly, final word on this whole area is far from being in hand.

DEVELOPMENTS IN THE FUTURE

What will happen to the professional telephone survey in the years ahead? This whole topic is speculation, but it seems worth pursuing. There are two areas to be considered: technological improvements and government restraints.

Technological Improvements

Four possibilities, technologically, come to mind. There will be technological changes far beyond any of those that can be predicted here, however.

Use of the Home Telephone as Direct Access to the Computer. The telephone dial is on its way out. Ultimately it will be replaced by the push-button set. Now the intriguing thing about the push-button set is that it can, even today, be tied in directly with a computer, as an input station (also as an output station, though that is not relevant to this discussion).

Technology to combine a normal telephone conversation with a computer input cannot be that far distant. If it does develop, then the respondent will be able to reply by pushing a button, rather than—as in the most advanced system current today—giving the reply to an interviewer, who has to interpret it and push a key for computer input. This should save time and therefore reduce costs. Admittedly there is also the problem that it may raise errors in input, for an interviewer can be trained to be careful in such punching, while the respondent will be relatively inexperienced.

While not quite the same thing, there are trends in this direction right now. A New York City television channel is experimenting with a system in which the MC of the program poses a question to the audience and asks them to call one telephone number if they vote *yes* on the issue, another number if they vote *no*. The telephone system has been set up to record the number of *yes* and *no* replies.

Changing Times makes a prediction along the same lines.

> The evening news is on. A Walter Cronkite or John Chancellor or Harry Reasoner reads off the headlines. A pause. Then a request to the millions out there watching: How do you feel about a specific issue of the day? In a matter of minutes the announcer reads off the results of this instant poll. A nonsense idea, you say? Read this prediction of Richard C. Wald, President of N.B.C. News, on how it will be ten years hence. "I hate to say it, but I think we will probably come into a period of instantaneous polling. . . . I am sure that within ten years there will be a mechanism by which some anchorman sitting somewhere can say: And what do you think of Henry Kissinger's plan to nationalize whatever it is? And he'll push a button, and within ten minutes a national poll sample will have been taken, and people will say what they think. . . . [18]

Computerized Screening. The late Robert MacMillan, of Chilton Research, was a visionary in telephone interviewing and made many contributions to the field, as earlier discussion has shown. One thing he predicted was computerized screening.[19] As explained in an earlier point in this book, many telephone surveys are designed to locate people who qualify for the particular interview: owners of home freezers, beer drinkers, those with electric toothbrushes, those who have been to a movie in the past week.

In the MacMillan vision, the process of screening will be computerized. The computer will dial the number, and, through a recording, will ask the screening question. If the answer shows a qualified respondent, through a designated *yes* answer, the equipment will then flash a signal to an interviewer to pick up a telephone and proceed with the interview. If the designated answer is *no,* the computer will play back a recorded message ending the interview with thanks.

Fantasy? Maybe so, but possibly not. In any case, enjoy an anecdote, though we cannot identify the research firm involved because it may suggest that an interviewer had developed too standard a patter. This interviewer *had* developed a fairly standard approach, and perhaps *had* become a little bored and boring in the process. Suddenly, at one point, a respondent said, "Is this a recording?"

"Certainly not," came back the indignant answer. "I am a *person!*"

Well, it might just happen that the voice the respondent hears sometime in the future will be a recording!

Actually there is already equipment which would need only a small amount of modification to handle screening. This equipment could handle calls by asking questions and tape-recording the replies. One such machine is the Con Mode, manufactured by the Conversational Voice Terminal Corporation in Chicago; and the other is the Ansafone, manufactured by the Dictaphone Corporation. Even without modification such machines could save interviewer time by enabling the worker to avoid asking questions and merely code or numerically punch the replies. For a nation that has developed atomic energy and put men on the moon, it would not seem a difficult task to mechanize even the coding or punching portion of the operation. There are already optical scanners, so why not audio scanners?

Computerized Dialing and Recording. An even more economical method would be a recorded series of questions. After each question was asked, in the case of answers with prelisted categories, the person could be read the (prerecorded) list of possible replies, and requested to push the appropriate button on the home telephone. If it were to be an open-ended question, responses could be recorded at the research station by a device much the same as the telephone answering and recording devices available today. In the case of short-answer replies, with pre-listed categories, the reply would immediately be entered into the computer.

If this comes about—and it seems that the technology is virtually there—it will offer tremendous cost and time advantages. Imagine a supervisor in a room with 100 of these devices. All the supervisor would be is a troubleshooter, much the same as supervisors of completely mechanized manufacturing facilities. The work would be far more rapid than it is even today and far less expensive in terms of constant dollars. The quality would be much more controlled, too.

The major disadvantage is the dehumanization of the interview. Unlike the present personal or telephone interview, there would be only a recording. The respondent has no way to break through to the consciousness of a person. This could well be resented. It seems highly likely that a good proportion of respondents simply would break off the interview before it had been completed.

Also, of course, there would be no interviewer present to ask about responses which were not clear. It would be like a mail questionnaire.

The Videophone. The videophone, already technically perfected, is a device that sends video images between the telephone caller and the correspondent. However, a market test showed that while people enjoyed it, they were not willing to pay the fee for the extra service, so it was never offered to the public at large.

If this *is* ever offered at large, and becomes popular, it could result in a whole new stage of the professional telephone survey. It could make the telephone interview almost as personal a matter as the present house-to-house interview, without its obvious limitations.

It would also mean that visual materials could be shown to the respondent, thus overcoming one of the major limitations of the telephone interview.

There is one other possibility somewhat similar to this, but not so advantageous. That is the possibility that the telephone research firm could make arrangements, in the local television area, to have the interviewer's image and voice come in over an unused channel. This is not very promising, however. For one thing, it assumes that the respondent telephone is in the same room as the television set. For another, it is only one-way visual communication, though it admittedly is more important for the respondent to see the interviewer than the other way around. Finally, it means that all interviews in a given area would have to be confined to a concentrated time period. (At present the interviewers can make calls anywhere within the WATS band spectrum that falls inside locally acceptable time periods.)

Government Regulation

Present restrictions on interviewing are limited. Chapter 2 talks about the Green River Ordinance and how this sometimes adds to the difficulties of house-to-house interviewing. These do not, of course, affect telephone interviewing.

But there are bills afoot, both nationally and within the states, that *would*, if passed, definitely affect the professional telephone survey.

On a national basis, Les Aspin introduced a Congressional bill on February 21, 1972, which would prohibit unsolicited telephone calls to persons who have indicated that they do not wish to receive such calls. Such telephone numbers would have an asterisk beside them in alphabetic listings, and those convicted of violating this law would be liable to a $1000 fine and/or thirty days in jail. Public opinion polling would be excluded, but who is to define the term?

State legislators in Maryland, Minnesota, Texas, and Wisconsin[20] are considering similar laws.

Either the national or statewide law, if passed, would presumably kill random-digit dialing, as well as the use of alphabetic selection of numbers. Net: these would spell the end of professional telephone surveys. It doesn't seem likely that such bills will be passed, but there is a possibility.

This possibility has already become fact in the case of listings (alphabetical or computer) in the case of collegiate student populations. Under the interpretations of the Bowling Green State University legal counsel[21], for instance, based on the Family Education Rights and Privacy Act, 1974, a student has the right to demand that the university not list him or her in any published directory and not provide his or her name or demographics on any computer printout. This is certainly not a major survey problem, for students represent only a small part of the total population. But it is a warning of what could happen in terms of the broader population.

REFERENCES

[1] "Favorable Findings Revealed by Walker Industry Image Study," *The Marketing Researcher*, Apr. 1975.

[2]Theodore R. Weiss, "Telephone Research: A Crisis in Privacy?" 17th Annual Conference, Market Research Association, May 31, 1975.

[3]"23-Cent Mail Rate Foreseen," *New York Times,* Jan. 18, 1976.

[4]"Field Service Hit for $85,000 as IRS Looks Hard at Employment Taxes," *Marketing News,* Aug. 1, 1975.

[5]Jack J. Honomichl, "IRS Back-Tax Moves Worrying Researchers," *Advertising Age,* Aug. 25, 1975.

[6]Gale D. Metzger, Letter of March 7, 1974, to the editor of *Advertising Age.*

[7]John D. Weber, "Completion Rates in Consumer Research: Problems and Proposed Solutions," Bowling Green, 1976, unpublished.

[8]Sanford L. Cooper, "Researchers' Complacency Would Be a Mistake Now on Issues Such as Consumer Privacy, Respondent Refusal," *Marketing News,* Mar. 14, 1975.

[9]Jack J. Honomichl, "Concerned Researchers Conduct Poll on Polls," *Advertising Age,* Apr. 21, 1975.

[10]Walker, op. cit.

[11]Richard Baxter, "The Harassed Respondent," in Leo Bogart (ed.), *Current Controversies in Marketing Research,* Chicago, Markham, 1969, chap. 3.

[12]Baxter, op. cit.

[13]"AMA, Researchers Told 'Improve on Public's Good Research Attitude,' " *Marketing News,* Dec. 1, 1974.

[14]R. O. Carlson, "The Issue of Privacy in Public Opinion Research, *Public Opinion Quarterly,* Spring 1967, vol. 31, pp. 1–8.

[15]Cooper, op. cit.

[16]Weiss, op. cit.

[16]M. N. Manfield, "The Status of Validation in Survey Research," in Leo Bogart (ed.), *Current Controversies in Marketing Research,* Chicago, Markham, 1969, chap. 7.

[17]Cooper, op. cit.

[18]"And now folks, what do you think?" *Changing Times,* June 1976.

[19]From discussion with Frank McHugh, president of The Data Group Incorporated, who was associated with MacMillan when they both were at Chilton.

[20]From J. T. Kenneym, supervisor, Yellow Pages sales planning, AT&T.

[21]"Guidelines Set for Student Record Review," *BG News,* Jan. 20, 1976.

BUYING A
PROFESSIONAL
TELEPHONE
SURVEY[1]

This chapter is chiefly for the potential buyer of a professional telephone survey who is not a professional market researcher. However, it should also be of some use even to the professional researcher, since it considers some subtle but important points concerning the quality of the professional telephone survey which the researcher may not have considered.

The buyer goes through a series of steps: defining the problem and information needed, obtaining names of appropriate firms, evaluating these firms with the aim of reducing the number of serious contenders, setting whatever specifications can be set, soliciting estimates and proposals and evaluating them. It's a formidable task if it is done thoroughly. Unless it is done thoroughly, buying a high quality professional telephone survey will be largely a matter of luck.

DEFINE THE PROBLEM AND
INFORMATION NEEDS[2]

Is It a Problem Which Can Be
Handled with a Telephone Survey?

It has been shown that while the telephone survey can handle most survey requirements, it will not do the job for all. One consideration is the length of the proposed questionnaire. While no arbitrary limit can be put on the telephone interview, the questionnaire must be relatively shorter than its personal counterpart, since it is easier for the respondent to break it off. The other chief constraint of the telephone survey is that visual materials cannot ordinarily be used.

Still another constraint is that the telephone questionnaire must be chiefly restricted to short-answer questions. The telephone is usually not considered a good device for handling depth studies.

Is It a National, Regional, or Local Study?

If it is a national or regional study, going to a firm with WATS lines may be a cost necessity. On the other hand, if it is only a local study, let's say in San Francisco, it may be wasteful to use a New York City professional telephone firm, because of the WATS or long-distance charges. A San Francisco firm may be able to perform less expensively.

Is It a Major Problem with a Large Budget
or a Minor Problem with a Small Budget?

The answer to this question will naturally help the buyer decide whether planning the study and going through all the steps in getting proposals is worth a large chunk of time.

LOCATING NAMES OF
APPROPRIATE RESEARCH FIRMS

There are two major ways of locating the names of apparently-appropriate research firms: using available lists of research firms or turning to informal sources. Both methods have their merits.

Available Lists

One available list is the Yellow Pages of the telephone book. Marketing research firms are listed under the heading *Market Research and Analy-*

sis. There is a problem, however. It is not always possible from the listing to identify whether the firm offers professional telephone surveys, or whether it even has WATS lines.

There's another problem, too. One may have to go through many directories in order to locate these firms. It is true that if New York, Philadelphia, and Chicago are looked into, many of these firms will be uncovered. But as has been pointed out earlier in this book, professional telephone survey firms do not tend to cluster in only the large cities. Many are located in smaller communities.

Perhaps a better source is the American Marketing Association Membership Roster, usually published annually. The front of this directory lists marketing research firms across the country and often provides some description of the specialties the firm offers. However, this listing is not complete; the International Directory of Research Houses, known as the Green Book, is published annually by the New York Chapter of the American Marketing Association and is a more complete list. It also tells the specialty of the firm.

With any of these list sources, however, buyers are entirely on their own. There is no evaluation of the firm provided.

Informal Sources

Going to an informal source—usually a person—can also provide a judgment of the firm. But the judgment may be a poor one, so the potential buyer must do lots of checking and not accept recommendations too readily.

One possible source is the advertising agency. But there are problems here, too. Only the larger advertising agencies today have real research departments. With rising agency costs and the tendency for the client to have a marketing research department, the advertising agency research department today is typically smaller (or nonexistent) and less specialized than it used to be. So the advertising agency may have no more information about professional telephone survey firms than the potential buyer.

Also there may be a risk in accepting such help. If it turns out that the research firm selected is one recommended by the agency, the research firm ends up in debt to both the agency and the buyer. There could be a conflict of interest on part of the research firm.

Another possible informal source is a marketing person in a noncompetitive company. If the buyer knows a marketing research person in such a firm, so much the better. A person active in the field of marketing research, even if not conversant in the field of professional telephone surveys, can readily, with a few telephone calls, locate sound sources of information.

Another possible informal source is a research firm. The buyer can tell the firm what is desired. If the firm is ethical, it will answer truthfully, providing the names of one or more appropriate firms. If it is unethical, the real tip will be that it attempts to sell the potential buyer away from the professional telephone survey onto some study where *it* has the needed facilities. So the purchaser will easily be able to evaluate the answer received.

If the potential buyer lives in an area where there is a college or university with a marketing department, this may be a good source. A potential buyer who is not in such a community may still have attended such a college or university, and can make a telephone call there to the person on the staff who is the specialist in marketing research. However, there is one big consideration: the professor must be active in marketing research, not merely a teacher of it. The professor should do consulting or be active in a professional association that stresses research. Otherwise he or she is not likely to have kept up with developments in the field which have not yet reached the literature, and there has been little written, up to this point, about professional telephone surveys.

EVALUATION OF THE FIRMS

The evaluation procedure outlined here is purely preliminary. It is a screening, to locate the few firms from which proposals will be requested. In making these evaluations, the potential buyer will depend in part on conversations with those in the research firms, but should not merely accept what is said. To do this job well, the buyer should examine policies, procedures, and records, to make sure that what has been said is correct.

Procedures and Policies

Procedures and policies of the particular research firm are pretty well fixed. When a study is purchased from a research house, these procedures and policies are applied to that study. The research firm is most unlikely to change any of them for a first-time buyer; it would probably take a major, repetitive customer to have that great an influence. The potential buyer can rate some of the outlined points only by making a value judgment. Others can be definitely measured, by their presence or absence or even by a numerical value.

Sampling. There are several important aspects of sampling that are typically a fixed portion of what is bought in the study. One is the *type of frame* (which applies in any case where the purchaser does not supply the frame, such as a list of physicians, account executives, etc.). It may be all listed telephone households, if the firm works from an alphabetical list. It may be some form of random digits, working from an alphabetical list. It may be computer-generated numbers from lists of working exchanges provided by the appropriate telephone companies. If it is some system of random-digit dialing, the firm should be scored some extra points.

The *recency of statistics on which sampling is based* is another important point. While it is impossible to make an absolutely black or white statement, in general the statistics should probably be no more than a year old; if they are, the data are likely to be out-of-date.

The *number of strata* used in stratifying the sample is yet another important aspect of sampling. In general the greater the number of strata used, the more desirable the sample, because this provides a greater possibility of getting a balanced sample within each cell of the strata. Finally, the *number of sampling points* should be determined. In general, the greater the number of points, the better the sample. No sample should be too greatly concentrated; dispersion is likely to provide a more representative sample.

Questionnaire Construction. The purchaser who does not have a research staff will probably have to rely on the research firm to build a questionnaire. (The purchaser who has a research staff will probably have them undertake this operation.) If this function is expected of the research firm, the potential buyer should ask to see some old questionnaires so as to judge their aptness. (The research firm may reply that all its questionnaires are proprietary, belonging to particular clients; if so, ask whether they have ever done a study for themselves, or whether it is possible to get permission to show some questionnaires prepared for clients.)

Interviewing. There are a number of points about interviewing that are significant in judging how well the professional telephone research firm performs. One is *interviewer selection.* Who are the interviewers? Through what procedures are they selected?

Pertinent, too, is *general training of the interviewers.* Is there a training manual? If so, the buyer should ask to see it. There should be no reticence on the part of a truly professional firm to allow a review. What training method is used? Who conducts the training? Over what period of time does it run?

Then there is the *training for a specific assignment.* Are written instructions prepared? Who conducts this session? Are there practice calls? How many? Is the client permitted to sit in?

There are questions about *supervision, monitoring, and editing.* How many interviewers are supervised per supervisor? In general, the fewer there are per supervisor, the higher the quality of interviewing. What proportion of interviews are monitored? Again, in general, the greater the proportion of calls monitored, the higher the quality of interviewing. In addition, does the supervisor edit recorded questionnaires? How soon after they are completed?

Finally, are *records* kept on the performance of each interviewer on each job? If so, are past records of individual interviewers available, so that the firm has a continuing method of knowing how well its staff is performing?

Editing and Coding. Is there a *written manual* for the general training of workers in these two functions? If so, it should be reviewed to determine how thorough it is. Will there be a *formal training session* for the particular assignment? Is the coding operation handled by a permanent, full-time staff?

Is all coding checked for accuracy, or is an accuracy check made on a sample of the work on a particular job, or only on the start of the work? In general, the greater the proportion of questionnaires checked, the greater the accuracy level that can be imputed. In coding, what error percentage is tolerated for the firm? Does the firm keep records of the coding accuracy achieved on each study? If so, these records should be examined. If not, how does the research firm know what level of accuracy it is obtaining?

What is the editing procedure? Who does the editing?

Data Processing. Is card punching done under supervision? In general, supervision means greater accuracy. How many punchers work under a supervisor? Does the supervisor oversee more than one job's punching simultaneously? If so, there is some risk that the punching is not getting the complete attention of the supervisor which it demands.

Is there verification of the punching? If so, is this done on every card, on just the beginning of the study, or on a continuing sample of the whole study? What proportion? What is the level of accuracy achieved and demanded in correct card punching?

Is there a computer program to determine when sufficient stability of results has been achieved? Such a program *could* mean a smaller sample size than anticipated, and therefore save the buyer money.

Speed, Promptness. This is difficult to estimate. However, it is important. Some firms are so busy that their facilities are overtaxed, and work has to be lined up for entry into the system. Some are slow in processing the data. The buyer should find out whether the firm typically delivers on the promised schedule.

Pricing. What is the firm's pricing policy relative to going rates? Does it price at what it believes is the market price, or does it have a policy deliberately of pricing above the market level, or perhaps below? Any policy the firm decides to have is up to the firm and can be defended, but the potential buyer, who is affected by the policy, should understand what it is.

Security. In most market research survey work the buyer wants to be sure that the work remains confidential. Marketing surveys are typically believed to provide a competitive advantage to the astute buyer. Therefore the risk of a security leak should be minimal. At one research firm, for instance, each visitor registers at the reception desk, recording the hour and the person he or she is there to see. The visitor is given an identification tag by the receptionist and signs out on departure. Care is taken to see that no unauthorized personnel are in the building, and that no visitors except those from the particular client are exposed to any part of the processing of that client's project. Finished materials, including questionnaires, are kept under lock and key. Questionnaires are carefully stored for a year; afterward if the client does not want them, they are shredded and buried.

All this may sound overzealous, but it makes the buyer realize that chances of a security leak are minimal.

Personnel

It is personnel which make the procedures and policies of the firm work; thus it is the personnel of the research firm that are really the heart of the operation, and who determine just how good or poor the end product will be. There are two people or groups of people in the firm that the prospective buyer should learn a great deal about: the account executive and the processing department heads.

Counseling. The account executive is the person—regardless of title—who handles relationships with the client and who typically acts as a project director of the particular study within the research firm, seeing that it goes through on schedule, seeing that the various department heads understand what is expected on their end of the work, designing the study (if that is a part of what is being bought), and preparing the report (if a report is desired). However, the prospective buyer should make sure that the person being dealt with *is* the project director, or should ask to meet the individual who will have that responsibility. Trust in the project director is an essential if the client and research firm are to be happy with one another.

Typically, the department heads that the prospective buyer will want to know include the head of the sampling department, the head of the interviewing department, and the head of the data processing department. The buyer must be convinced that these people can provide both the guidance needed and the proper kind of help in putting the job through their shop.

Integrity. The buyer will want to be sure about the integrity of the firm. Is it renowned for having high ethics and a generally good reputation for integrity? Most firms do, but this is so important a point that the potential buyer should check it out.

Here is a point that might *not* occur to a potential buyer: does the firm really keep the customer aware of what is happening on the study? There is no survey firm in existence that doesn't occasionally run into problems on a study. The survey firm cannot always be held responsible for the difficulties. But the real test is whether it makes a practice of informing the customer when things begin to go wrong, and what it is doing to remedy the situation.

Practicality. The buyer wants to make sure—in advance—that the particular firm and its handling of the assignment can be lived with. One test is whether the firm gets—and will provide the buyer with—a statement of daily progress on its projects. Almost all firms do, but the buyer will want to be absolutely sure.

Also, is the firm flexible? All firms have their own procedures, but the question is whether the firm will be willing to modify any of its procedures if this will help the particular study.

Finally there is the question of personal relations. The buyer doesn't have to live with the account executive, but on the other hand, if the account executive is not a person the buyer finds likable or has confidence in, there is a pretty great risk, down the road, of becoming unhappy with that professional telephone survey firm.

Creativity. Does the firm—its people—offer creativity? Creativity as an end in itself means little, but creativity applied to a research study, thereby improving it, can be an important ingredient. For a better study means possibly more reliable information, more pertinent information, a less expensive way to get information, and the like.

Sources of Information

Getting Material from the Firm Itself. This material is important to obtain and evaluate, but the potential buyer should remember one thing about all of it: it will, if anything, have bias in favor of the firm. About the only exceptions are manuals for internal use.

The manuals, or other internal procedural documents, are one of the most important guidelines for the potential buyer. There may be a sampling manual, an interviewer manual, and an editing and coding manual. There may be internal forms which tell a great deal about the operating methods. There may be a form for keeping a record of progress on a study. There almost surely will be one for keeping a record of interviewer performance on a project.

It is possible that the firm will not want to let any of these documents go out of its offices. That should present no great problem if they will allow examination on the premises.

Many firms put out newsletters. The content and tone of these may provide some insights into the thinking of the firm. The newsletter reflects what the company thinks is important.

Most professional telephone research firms have brochures. These typically describe the types of service provided, tell about the special facilities and strengths of the company, list the major personnel (and perhaps give a brief biography of each), and possibly mention some of the clients. But it should be remembered that the purpose of the brochure is to sell; this is definitely a promotion piece, so it can be expected to outline strengths, not weaknesses.

Ask about books and articles written by staff members. These don't really "prove" anything much about the firm except that the particular people have some recognized professional status. On articles, the buyer should differentiate those in trade journals and those in professional journals. The trade journals are looking for material. Professional journals are refereed; a small group of highly regarded professionals reads and criticizes any paper before it is accepted.

Visiting the Headquarters. This will generally be well worthwhile. The location and appearance of the physical facilities may be a tipoff. A crowded, low-rent district of the city might indicate a cash-poor firm that is sometimes forced to take shortcuts in its procedures, and could certainly mean that a firm would have difficulty in attracting the calibre of people it needed for interviewing. The typical professional telephone survey firm is, by necessity, doing a fair share of its telephone work at night, and a poor section of the city is not one to which many people of the type usually used on a survey would want to come. But the buyer should be careful in making judgments; a luxurious building and offices don't necessarily mean a topflight research firm. It *could* be a facade.

Talking with Customers. If the brochure doesn't contain a client list, the buyer should ask for one. Since the client list comes from the particular research house, however, there is going to be a bias. The firm will not list companies who have had unfavorable experiences with it and who no longer use it. The trick is for the buyer to construct a list of professional telephone survey users from the lists provided by the firms. Then the buyer can contact the users and ask whether they have worked with any firm on whose list their name does not appear. If so, the buyer can ask what the nature of the experience was, or if the firm has not been tried, why not. Naturally anonymity will have to be promised and maintained.

GETTING ESTIMATES AND PROPOSALS

An estimate is a statement of the costs a telephone research firm would incur in conducting a survey according to the specifications of the prospective client. It is parallel to a general contractor's giving a bid on a building where all specifications have been provided by an architect. A proposal, on the other hand, is a research plan that has been put together by the research firm after being given an idea of the prospect's problem and needs. In this case the telephone research company is providing all the specifications.

The estimate is desirable from the prospective client's viewpoint because it puts all the research firms approached on an equivalent basis, so that the buyer can determine the relative prices of each for the same package of merchandise. However, it assumes some research expertise on the part of the client, who otherwise could not have put together a list of the specifications. The buyer of research who lacks the research background can, and very likely should, retain a consultant to put together the specifications, for establishing the relative costs of each firm is an important part of the evaluation of research firms available to handle the assignment.

In addition to the cost estimate, it is of considerable importance to get a proposal for the study. The proposal, in this case, can be stated in terms of how the basic specifications might be altered to improve the study and what the cost of each recommended alteration would be. The proposal gives the buyer a fresh, outside interpretation of the research problem. It enables the research firm to apply imagination to the plan, and this will improve the value of the study to the client. It helps the buyer evaluate the capabilities of the research firm and the person who prepares the proposal. It shows the technical skill of the person preparing it.

Setting Up Specifications for the Estimate

For this first meeting, too, the buyer should have prepared, in advance and in a form to leave with the telephone research firm, a set of specifications. There are two kinds of specifications. One concerns obvious points, such as how many copies of the tables will be required. The other is much more subtle. It is a specification which sets up a ground rule of procedure or operation which would not be particularly obvious at the end of the study, but would have a distinct bearing upon costs. Take the number of call-backs, for instance. Most professional telephone research firms have set up their own standards for the number of call-backs. However, unless the buyer stipulates the number wanted, the firm that typically makes more effort to complete calls is unfairly penalized in the bidding. As another example, consider the research firm that has a national sample design from which it regularly pulls samples. The firm cannot readily change that. Thus some aspects which the buyer may wish to control cannot, in fact, be controlled without considerably adding to costs.

The specification areas to include cover the various processes outlined previously in this book: sampling, the questionnaire, interviewing, data processing, and the report.

Sampling. Sampling specifications should first define the universe. Total sample size should be indicated, and how the sample is to be spread in different geographic areas should be spelled out. The respondent selection method, assuming that it is necessary to select from within a sampling unit, should also be indicated.

The number of call-backs should also be stated. The research firm, in its estimate, should estimate the completion rate anticipated. But since different firms may calculate the completion rate in different manners, the completion rate formula the buyer wants used should be stipulated, including how *busy* signals are to be handled.

Questionnaire. Ideally, the questionnaire draft should be submitted as part of the specifications. If not, at least an outline of the specific information to be covered in the questionnaire should be listed. The buyer should also spell out the questionnaire-testing procedure that is desired. In the opinion of the author, no questionnaire should *ever* be used unless it has been tested; there is too great a risk that one or more of the questions will not work in the way anticipated. Thus the buyer should specify the minimum number of test calls to be made and the nature of the sample with whom they should be made. The buyer should also indicate plans to monitor during the test work and to be a participant in any decisions made to modify the questionnaire.

Interviewing. There is little to be specified in this phase of the study. However, the number of rings should be spelled out, so that all estimates are on the same basis. Evidence has already been presented to show that the proper number is probably four in home telephoning.

Data Processing. The nature and number of tables of data should be specified, and this specification should also show, for each question, what cross-tabulations are anticipated. If there are any statistical treatments required, these, too, should be outlined. Also, the number of copies of each table that will be needed should be stated.

Report. The specifications should also indicate whether a report is needed. If so, its nature should be indicated; is it to be merely a summary of findings, or is it also to provide a marketing interpretation of the findings?

Communication with the Research Firm

The buyer should give the telephone research firm some guidelines on the timing of the estimate.

A buyer who has had no previous contact with the professional telephone research firm can expect "sell" during these preliminary meetings. It is typically soft sell, with the seller describing the firm, its background and experience, the talents of its staff, and the areas of research in which the firm takes greatest pride. The buyer can learn a great deal during this process.

Contents of the Cost Estimate

What can the buyer expect in the cost estimate? A playback of all specifications should be expected because the seller's communication will almost become a contract if the estimate is accepted, and the buyer does not want to risk any misunderstanding of any of the specifications. The estimate will also include a dollar figure, with perhaps a range attached. If this is a study in which not every person qualifies as a respondent, the buyer may find that there are listed varying prices with varying incidences as obtained on the actual study. The buyer should also expect a statement of timing of the study, and ideally this should show the timing of each phase.

Preliminary Communications about the Proposal[3]

The buyer must first determine from how many firms to solicit proposals. There is no hard-and-fast rule. Research firms normally supply these without cost to the buyer; they consider it part of the cost of selling. But it is expensive to prepare a good proposal, demanding many hours of professional working time if the proposal is for an involved, important study. Therefore, a request to a telephone research firm to submit a proposal should not be made lightly.

However, there are advantages to the buyer in getting more than one proposal. One is that the thinking of more than one survey firm is obtained. The buyer who gets only a single proposal may end up with an unimaginative, mundane plan that doesn't do justice to the study. There is another advantage, too. Since the proposal becomes the property of the buyer, the best thinking and planning of several research firms can be combined into a single, final plan. However, research firms are well aware of such practices and often act accordingly. If a buyer approaches a telephone research firm too frequently without assigning it any studies, it may well decline to submit further proposals.

There is also a possible ethical issue here. While it may not be dishonest for the buyer to take the best ideas from each proposal and use them, is it fair to deal with research firms in this manner? It seems to be picking their brains if their material is constantly used but they are not assigned a fair share of the work.

One way to resolve the dilemma—if the study warrants it—is to pay a small fee to each research house for its plan. When this is done there cannot be a question of whether it is unethical to use ideas from the unaccepted proposal. The research firm has accepted a fee for the work, and the material therefore has been bought and paid for, rather than received as a gift. However, this is rarely done. In the author's experience he has participated in only two cases, once when he was a seller and once when he was a buyer of research. In each case, it must be admitted, the fee paid was so small that it did not cover the costs of preparing the plan, but it was nonetheless a fee. A second alternative is to let each survey firm know that competitive proposals are being solicited, giving the firm the option of declining to prepare a plan. Some research firms have a policy of refusing to propose against competition.

At least one, or perhaps more than one, meeting will have to be arranged with the research firm before it can prepare a cost estimate and proposal. For this first meeting the buyer should be prepared to state the problem and the background of the industry and the company. If the firms have been chosen well, the buyer need not be concerned about revealing the most confidential company facts and situations. Dependable telephone research firms never reveal such information, and by this time the buyer has presumably narrowed the choice down to firms which are ethical.

Contents of the Proposal

Style and format of the proposal will vary somewhat from one professional telephone research firm to another. But whatever the source, the proposal should cover the following topics, not necessarily in the order shown.

Background. The proposal typically includes a statement about the background of the problem. It describes the industry marketing situation pertinent to the study and the research firm's understanding of the environment within which the marketing problem or opportunity has arisen. This section, usually for the most part a playback of what the buyer has already told the research firm, is included simply to show that the telephone research firm does, indeed, understand the situation.

Problem. A clear statement of the marketing problem is also typically a part of the research proposal. The problem statement includes not only a statement of the *research* problem, but a statement of how the results can be applied to the marketing situation (in other words, showing an understanding of the marketing implications of the work).

Research Methods. This is the longest and most detailed section of the proposal, but how long and detailed it is depends on the sophistication of the buyer and the buyer's past relations with the research firm. If the buyer is thoroughly sophisticated about sampling, then the proposal does not have to outline all the detailed sampling. However, the proposal should clearly state—over and above what was in the specifications—material on the sample, on questionnaire content areas, and on data processing.

Nature of the Report. Presumably the proposal will follow the form requested by the buyer in earlier discussion unless the particular telephone research firm sees good reason to recommend some other form.

Timing and Costs. The proposal, as with the estimate, will provide a cost estimate and a time schedule. These will have to be given separately for each suggestion which was made in the proposal but was not included in the specifications.

Special Areas. If the proposal is the research company's first contact with the buyer and the company feels the need to make an impression using more than the content of the research plan, the proposal is likely to contain promotional material. Any bonuses the firm offers—special competencies or facilities in sampling, interviewing, data processing, etc.—will appear in the appropriate sections of the report. They may even be repeated for greater emphasis in a special section.

The firm may indicate major clients for whom it has worked over some time period, its size, age, and the like. Sometimes this and additional material are included by binding the company brochure into the proposal.

Many research firms, for the first proposal submitted to a prospect, will include a brief professional biography of several or all of their major executives.

Judging the Proposal

The Blankenship and Barker paper suggests five criteria for judging a proposal: soundness of the plan, content and organization, creativity, writing style, and timing and costs.

Soundness of the Plan. The proposal should be rejected if it is not basically sound. However, a buyer who is unsophisticated in research may not have the time or the patience to delve that deeply into research technology to make such a judgment. A consultant, of course, can be hired. But surprisingly, sometimes just use of ordinary common sense resolves the problem. Proposals were solicited from three nationally known research firms by an organization for whom the author serves as research consultant. Copies of the proposals were sent to the president and to the author. When the two got together to discuss the proposals, the president suggested, hesitantly, that he thought one proposal could be immediately discarded, that it just didn't seem very sound. He was right, even though he had had no previous experience in marketing research. Except for such technical aspects as sampling, a great deal of the planning in marketing research is a matter of common sense.

Content and Organization. The plan should be a concise statement of a course of action as well as an indication of the researcher's planning abilities and practical experience. Are all the study aspects that are pertinent to the problem and its solution included? A prospective client can ask for a revision of a plan that lacks these qualities, but is not likely to since a buyer will have misgivings about dealing with a research firm that displayed such oversights in the first place.

Creativity. The creative proposal will come up with new, fresh ideas that are a departure from the commonplace—ideas which improve the value of the planned research study. A creative research proposal will develop a research design to fit the problem rather than bend the problem to fit existing techniques.

Writing Style. If the buyer expects to get a written report from the research firm, then the writing style of the proposal becomes critically important. A writer who cannot communicate well in the proposal will not be able to do so in the report. The jargon of research should be minimized. Technical labels for specific sample or experimental designs may be necessary to avoid verbiage, but this is about the only justification for their use. Statements must be accurate and leave nothing to be interpreted (or misinterpreted) by the reader. From a proposal prepared by an unnamed research firm (to protect the guilty), here is an example of how not to express an idea:

> What is needed is a structural program to encompass all measures of the gestalt of the market's assessment of the contestants in the specific product field.

This means:

> We plan to have consumers rate all major brands in this product field.

Timing and Costs. If the proposal is to be accepted the timing and costs must be right. If either timing or cost is not acceptable, one or both may be negotiable with the telephone research firm. It is worth a try on the buyer's part.

This is not to suggest that the buyer should automatically bargain on price. Marketing research is a professional service, not an item to be bargained over in a street bazaar. Price should be questioned when the buyer finds it impossible to authorize the study at the quoted price or when the preferred proposal is priced substantially higher than its competitors. Recently three research firms were asked to submit proposals. One was both pedestrian and overpriced; it was rejected at once. The second was clearly superior to the third, but 30 percent more expensive. The circumstances were explained to the second firm. At its own choice, the firm sharpened the pencil, made a cost review, and came down in price.

Contractor Evaluation Scheme. Zaltman and Burger[4] review a Contractor Evaluation Scheme (CES) used by some agencies of the federal government. Figure 11-1 shows its elements.

In the plan, the maximum number of points any proposal can come up with is 100 (of course no proposal ever achieves that level). The CES is made up of six elements, and Figure 11-1 shows the maximum number of points allocable for each element. Those who evaluate the proposal indicate the number of points they believe each proposal should receive under each element. The most important elements are the proposal approach (25 points maximum), general experience in marketing research work (20 points), and grasp of the problem (20 points).

There are two questions to be raised about the possible use of this method. One concerns the elements in the list. Are they complete? They seem to be.

The second question is the use of the assigned weights. Who is to say whether each maximum potential score is right? This is a matter of judgment, and a particular buyer may decide that different weightings are superior for the purposes at hand.

But let's proceed with how the CES method is used. Once the total score has been calculated for each research firm submitting a proposal, the supplier with the highest score is generally chosen for further negotiation. However, there may be two firms with close scores, with a large price difference between them. If so, the lower price firm may well be the one that is selected.

FIGURE 11-1
Contractor Evaluation Scheme Used
by Some Government Agencies

	Weighted Score
1. General Experience in Marketing Research Work	20
What past jobs? How complex? How long has supplier been in the business? What is his reputation? Who are his past clients? Does his experience qualify him for this assignment?	
2. Experience in Marketing Research in Area of Concern	5
Does the company have relevant experience in the product area? Is the company aware of the formal and informal dynamics of the potential client?	
3. Overall Quality of the Proposal	15
How does the proposal appear as a whole? Is it well presented? Is it logical? Is it straightforward and easy to follow? Or is it complicated and difficult to follow? Is it complete?	
4. Grasp of the Problem	20
Does the supplier clearly understand the problem? Does the proposal state the problem as the potential client understands it? Is the research firm's understanding of the problem complete? Is the problem overstated?	
5. Proposal Approach	25
Exactly what does the research firm propose to do? How relevant is it to the problem? Is the approach imaginative? How realistic—from the potential client viewpoint—are the time and cost estimates? Is the approach overly complicated or simplistic?	
6. Experience and Qualification of Key Personnel	15
From biographical data supplied, how well qualified are those who will be chiefly working on the project?	
	100

Letter to Selected Firm (for
Either Estimate or Proposal)

Once a choice of firms has been made, the buyer should write a letter of acceptance, attaching either a copy of the specifications and the cost estimate, or the proposal.

In addition, should any elements in other research proposals seem attractive, the selected telephone survey house will have to provide an estimate of what each will cost. The buyer will have some idea of the reasonableness of each cost by comparing it with what the original proposer quoted as a cost.

REFERENCES

[1]While no specific reference is made, some important input in this chapter comes from Gale D. Metzger, "Be of Statistics a Little More Careful than of Anything," Presentation before the 21st Annual Midwest Conference on Statistics for Decision, Chicago, Mar. 27, 1974.

[2]The first part of this chapter closely parallels A. B. Blankenship and R. F. Barker, "Selecting Research Firms from Which to Get Proposals," *Journal of the Academy of Marketing Science*, Fall 1973, pp. 81–89.

[3]The proposal section of this chapter relies heavily on A. B. Blankenship and Raymond F. Barker, "The Buyer's Side of Marketing Research," *Business Horizons*, Aug. 1973, pp. 73–80.

[4]Gerald Zaltman and P. C. Burger, *Marketing Research*, Hinsdale, Ill., Dryden Press, 1975, pp. 665–667.

INDEX